Endangered Wildlife and Plants of the World

Volume 10
SHE–TAH

Marshall Cavendish
New York • London • Toronto • Sydney

Marshall Cavendish Corporation
99 White Plains Road
Tarrytown, NY 10591-9001

Created by Brown Partworks Ltd.
Editor: Anne Hildyard
Associate Editors: Paul Thompson, Amy Prior
Managing Editor: Tim Cooke
Design: Whitelight
Picture Research: Helen Simm
Index Editor: Kay Ollerenshaw
Production Editor: Matt Weyland
Illustrations: Barbara Emmons, Jackie Harland, Tracey Williamson

Library of Congress Cataloging-in-Publication Data

Endangered wildlife and plants of the world
p.cm.
Includes bibliographical references (p.).
ISBN 0-7614-7194-4 (set)
ISBN 0-7614-7204-5 (vol. 10)
1. Endangered species--Encyclopedias. I. Marshall Cavendish Corporation.

QH75.E68 2001
333.95'22'03--dc21
99-086194

Printed in Malaysia
Bound in the United States of America
07 06 05 04 03 02 01 00 7 6 5 4 3 2 1

Photo Credits
Cover: Birdlife International
Title page: Still Pictures, David McNew
Contents page: Mike Creel

American Fisheries Society: B. Cooke 1390; John N.
Rinne/U.S.F.W.S. 1307,1358, 1361, 1362, 1375; William N.
Roston 1308, 1428; Ardea London Ltd.: M. Watson 1335;
Peter Arnold Inc.: D. Halleux 1321; David Haring 1323; R.
Andrew Odum 1333; Ed Reschke 1339; Ray E. Ashton Jr.:
1334, 1346; Erwin & Peggy Bauer: 1391, 1436; Californian
Academy of Sciences: J. Game 1363; California Native Plant
Society: J. Fraser Minehead 1370; Bruce Coleman Inc.:
Delany 1355; Michael Freeman 1372; P.W. Sykes 1353;
U.S.F.N. 1381; Corbis: Rick Doyle 1368; Craig Lovell 1365;
Zandria Muench Beraldo 1429; Mike Creel (S.C. Dept of
Natural Resources): 1431; Ted Dingley: 1413; D.R.K. Photo:
1401; C. Kenneth Dodd Jr. 1334; M.P. Kahl 1398; Friends of
the Roanoke River: N.M. Burkhead 1411; Los Angeles Count
Museum of Natural History: Donald Meyer 1340, 1341,
1342, 1343; Robert & Linda Mitchell: 1345; James F. Parnell:
1328; B. "Moose" Peterson: 1337, 1357; Tom Stack &
Associates: Brian Parker 1377; Still Pictures: David McNew
1304; Hans Stuart: 1420; VIREO: M.P. Kahl 1395, 1397;
Doug Wechsler 1393; Warren D. Thomas 1315, 1348, 1402;
Wildlife Conservation Society (H.Q. at the Bronx Zoo): 1326,
1384; Zoological Society of San Diego: Ron Garrison 1317,
1387; Ken Kelly 1380; Bob Stiles 1310

Cover: Stork. Birdlife International
Title Page: Bighorn sheep. Still Pictures, David McNew
Contents page: Schweinitz's Sunflower. Mike Creel

TABLE OF CONTENTS/VOLUME 10

ESA and IUCN

In this set of endangered animals and plants, each species, where appropriate, is given an ESA status and an IUCN status. The sources consulted to determine the status of each species are the Endangered Species List maintained by the U.S. Fish and Wildlife Service and the Red Lists compiled by IUCN–The World Conservation Union, which is a worldwide organization based in Switzerland.

ENDANGERED SPECIES ACT

The Endangered Species Act (ESA) was initially passed by the U.S. Congress in 1973, and reauthorized in 1988. The aim of the ESA is to rescue species that are in danger of extinction due to human action and to conserve the species and their ecosystems. Endangered plants and animals are listed by the U.S. Fish and Wildlife Service (USFWS), which is part of the Department of Interior. Once a species is listed, the USFWS is required to develop recovery plans, and ensure that the threatened species is not further harmed by any actions of the U.S. government or U.S. citizens. The act specifically forbids the buying, selling, transporting, importing, or exporting of any listed species. It also bans the taking of any listed species in the U.S. and its territories, on both private and public lands. Violators can face heavy fines or imprisonment. However, the ESA requires that the protection of the species is balanced with economic factors.

The ESA recognizes two categories of risk for species:

Endangered: A species that is in danger of extinction throughout all or a significant part of its range.

Threatened: A species that is likely to become endangered in the foreseeable future.

RECOVERY

Recovery takes place when the decline of the endangered or threatened species is halted or reversed, and the circumstances that caused the threat have been removed. The ultimate aim is the recovery of the species to the point where it no longer requires protection under the act.

Recovery can take a long time. Because the decline of the species may have occurred over centuries, the loss cannot be reversed overnight. There are many factors involved: the number of individuals of the species that remain in the wild, how long it takes the species to mature and reproduce, how much habitat is remaining, and whether the reasons for the decline are clear cut and understood. Recovery plans employ a wide range of strategies that involve the following: reintroduction of species into formerly occupied habitat, land aquisition and management, captive breeding, habitat protection, research, population counts, public education projects, and assistance for private landowners.

SUCCESS STORIES

Despite the difficulties, recovery programs do work, and the joint efforts of the USFWS, other federal and state agencies, tribal governments, and private landowners have not been in vain. Only seven species, less than 1 percent of all the species listed between 1968 and 1993, are now known to be extinct. The other 99 percent of listed species have not been lost to extinction, and this confirms the success of the act.

There are some good examples of successful recovery plans. In 1999, the peregrine falcon, the bald eagle, and the Aleutian goose were removed from the endangered species list. The falcon's numbers have risen dramatically. In 1970, there were only 39 pairs of falcons in the United States. By 1999, the number had risen to 1,650 pairs. The credit for the recovery goes to the late Rachel

...arson, who highlighted the dangers of DDT, and ...lso to the Endangered Species Act, which enabled ...he federal government to breed falcons in ...aptivity, and took steps to protect their habitat.

Young bald eagles were also successfully ...anslocated into habitat that they formerly occu-...ied, and the Aleutian Canada goose has improved ...ue to restoration of its habitat and reintroduction ...nto former habitat.

IUCN–THE WORLD CONSERVATION UNION

...he IUCN (International Union for Conservation ...f Nature) was established in 1947. It is an alliance ...f governments, governmental agencies, and ...ongovernmental agencies. The aim of the IUCN ...s to help and encourage nations to conserve ...ildlife and natural resources. Organizations such ...s the Species Survival Commission is one of ...everal IUCN commissions that assesses the ...onservation status of species and subspecies glob-...lly. Taxa that are threatened with extinction are ...oted and steps are taken for their conservation by ...rograms designed to save, restore, and manage ...pecies and their habitats. The Survival ...Commission is committed to providing objective ...nformation on the status of globally threatened ...pecies, and produces two publications: the *IUCN Red List of Threatened Animals*, and the *IUCN Red List of Threatened Plants*. They are compiled from ...cientific data and provide the status of threatened ...pecies, depending on their existence in the wild ...nd threats that undermine that existence. The lists ...or plants and animals differ slightly.

The categories from the *IUCN Red List of Threatened Animals* used in *Endangered Wildlife and Plants of the World* are as follows:

...xtinct: A species is extinct when there is no reason-...ble doubt that the last individual has died.

Extinct in the wild: A species that is known only to ...urvive in captivity, well outside its natural range.

Critically endangered: A species that is facing an ...xtremely high risk of extinction in the wild in the immediate future.

Endangered: A species that is facing a very high risk of extinction in the wild in the near future.

Vulnerable: A species that is facing a high risk of extinction in the wild in the medium-term future.

Lower risk: A species that does not satisfy the criteria for designation as critically endangered, endangered, or vulnerable. Species included in the lower risk category can be separated into three subcategories:

Conservation dependent: A species that is part of a conservation program. Without the program, the species would qualify for one of the threatened categories within five years.

Near threatened: A species that does not qualify for conservation dependent, but is close to qualifying as vulnerable.

Least concern: A species that does not qualify for conservation dependent or near threatened.

Data deficient: A species on which there is inadequate information to make an asssessment of risk of extinction. Because there is a possibility that future research will show that the species is threatened, more information is required.

The categories from the *IUCN Red List of Threatened Plants*, used in *Endangered Wildlife and Plants of the World*, are as follows:

Extinct: A species that has not definitely been located in the wild during the last 50 years.

Endangered: A species whose survival is unlikely if the factors that threaten it continue. Included are species whose numbers have been reduced to a critical level, or whose habitats have been so drastically reduced that they are deemed to be in immediate danger of extinction. Also included in this category are species that may be extinct but have definitely been seen in the wild in the past 50 years.

Vulnerable: A species that is thought likely to move into the endangered category in the near future if the factors that threaten it remain.

Rare: A species with small world populations that are not at present endangered or vulnerable, but are at risk. These species are usually in restricted areas or are thinly spread over a larger range.

SHEEP

Class: Mammalia

Order: Artiodactyla

Family: Bovidae

Wild sheep are the ancestors of modern-day domestic sheep. They originated in central Asia, but now they are spread across Asia, Africa, Europe, and North America. They generally inhabit high mountain ranges, but some species are adapted to live in the desert. Sheep can range in harsh environments that cattle cannot tolerate.

There are approximately eight species of sheep, with numerous subspecies, of which many types, such as the Barbary sheep or Bighorn sheep, are considered to be vulnerable or endangered.

Sheep eat grasses, leaves, and shrubs. They can feed low to the ground, enabling them to find vegetation that cattle cannot find.

Wild sheep are susceptible to diseases from domestic sheep. They are vulnerable to extinction in the wild because they are often found in small populations that are genetically isolated and have low rates of reproduction. They are also susceptible to attack by predators such as leopards. Habitats are also being degraded by human development and encroachment from domestic livestock. Wild sheep are killed for their horns, which are prized as hunting trophies. Humans also hunt them for their meat, hides, and hair.

Some animals are protected in zoos, and others by a variety of conservation programs.

Barbary Sheep (Aoudad)
(Ammotragus lervia)

IUCN: Vulnerable

Class: Mammalia
Order: Artiodactyla
Family: Bovidae
Subfamily: Caprinae
Tribe: Caprini
Weight: 220–320 lb. (100–145 kg)
Shoulder height: 35-45 in. (89–115 cm)
Diet: Grasses, leaves, and shoots
Gestation period: 150–165 days
Longevity: 20 years
Habitat: Mountainous desert
Range: North Africa

SHEEP AND GOATS are among the hardiest of all the bovines (the cattle family). Even though people think that sheep are timid animals, they are able to survive under harsh conditions. Sheep can range where cattle cannot; for example, they can exist in mountainous terrain where vegetation is often scarce and low to the ground. Sheep have a split upper lip that enables them to feed lower to the ground, reaching blades and shoots that cattle leave behind.

Sheep are also more adaptable than their bigger bovine cousins because they can survive longer periods of drought. They are also more tolerant of extreme heat and cold temperatures. Such extremes are not uncommon in

The Barbary sheep prefers the high desert, where mountainous terrain receives low rainfall and offers sparse-to-medium vegetation.

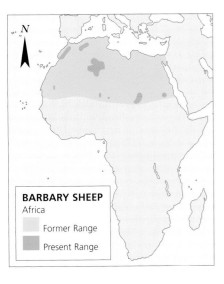

BARBARY SHEEP
Africa

Former Range

Present Range

North Africa, the historic range of the Barbary sheep.

The Barbary sheep, or aoudad, once was found over much of North Africa, from the Atlantic Ocean to the Red Sea. It is now extinct in Egypt and it is reduced to small pockets in northern Mauritania, Algeria, Morocco, Libya, northern Chad, and northwestern Sudan. Three living subspecies still remain.

The Barbary sheep eats grasses, leaves, and shrubs. It is extremely hardy and is affected only by the most severe droughts. It lives on its own or in small family groups.

Old males have massive, curving horns and long hair that grows on their dewlap (chest area) and between their upper legs. The horns can grow up to 3 feet (1 meter) in length, sweeping backward and then down. When two aoudad males fight over females, they run at each other with heads lowered, forcefully butting their horns together.

The dewlap hair and big, sweeping horns combine to give these sheep a goatlike appearance. In fact, this species is the only member of its genus and is considered by experts to be a cross between a goat and a sheep.

Barbary sheep are extremely prolific breeders, which means that under normal circumstances they have a high survival rate. In the wild they are preyed upon by leopards and other felids. Their present status, however, is not normal. They are considered a threatened species in the wild, mainly because they are hunted by local people for their hide, hair, and meat.

Captive growth

Barbary sheep were common in European zoos toward the end of the last century and were introduced into U.S. zoos around 1900. Most of the early records of these relocations are no longer available, but it appears that several different subspecies were imported. They were apparently interbred with other species, and became so hybridized that the wild subspecies and captive population are now quite distinct from each other. One difference with the captive-bred aoudads is that they have a slightly larger stature than the wild populations of Africa.

Large population

At least there is a huge, healthy, captive population. In addition to the existing zoo populations, Barbary sheep have been introduced into the wild in New Mexico, Texas, and California, where they have been so successful that they have damaged the local environment, and displaced indigenous animals. Barbary sheep are so successful in these transplantations that they may begin displacing Rocky Mountain bighorn sheep, if introduced into their range.

Peninsular Bighorn sheep
(Ovis canadensis cremnobates)

IUCN: Endangered

Weems Desert Bighorn Sheep
(Ovis canadensis weemsi)

IUCN: Critically endangered

Weight: 154–264 lb. (70–120 kg)
Shoulder height: 36–42 in. (95–105 cm)
Diet: Grasses, leaves, and shoots
Gestation period: 175–180 days
Longevity: 14–17 years
Habitat: Mountainous desert
Range: Baja California, Mexico

WILD SHEEP PROBABLY originated in central Asia and spread over Eurasia and North America in what is popularly known as the "great arc of wild sheep." This distribution pattern and radiation of the wild sheep stretches from Europe, across Asia, over the Bering Straits, and down through Alaska and the Rockies as far south as Mexico.

Distribution

The southern terminus of this distribution arc in North America is in the desert southwest of the United States and in Mexico, and is occupied by several different forms of bighorn sheep that we group together with the term desert bighorns.

The two bighorns considered here both occur in the state of Baja California, Mexico. The peninsular bighorn (O. *canadensis cremnobates*) occupies the northern two-thirds of the peninsula of Baja California. The other form, Weems bighorn (O. *canadensis weemsi*) occupies the southern one-third of the peninsula.

Different or the same?

There is some confusion over the taxonomy of these two forms. Some scientists believe that the Weems bighorn is a valid subspecies and should be kept separate. However most people believe that they are synonyms of each other and should not be listed separately. This view is supported by cranial measurements that suggest the two forms are indistinguishable. However, in physical appearance, the Weems bighorn is darker in color and slightly larger.

The early chronicles recorded by Jesuit missionaries of southern California in 1697 are so carefully written that we can identify today where observations were made. Some of the first wild sheep observed by the western missionaries were these Peninsular bighorn.

Harsh environment

The peninsula of Baja California is a rugged, dry and generally hostile environment. The highest peak is Cerro de la Giganta, which is about 5,500 feet (1,675 meters). The vegetation and rainfall are sparse at best. Yet in this harsh environment the desert bighorn flourishes.

The curved horns of a bighorn sheep are very long, occasionally measuring up to 31 inches (80 centimeters).

Of all the desert bighorn, those of Baja California are the largest and darkest in color. Females have surprisingly long horns, while males have horns with a spectacular length and girth. Older males have been recorded with horns that are more than 31 inches (80 centimeters) long, with a medium curl.

Similar to other bighorns, their territory is dictated by the vegetation and water available. They show strong territorial tendencies, with males battling over territory and domination of females. Spectacular battles can take place during the breeding season, with the dominant males monopolizing the available females.

One or two offspring are born after a gestation period of 175 to 180 days. The females are very protective of their young, so if they come into contact with the diseases and parasites of domestic sheep, there is a reasonably good survival rate. They are preyed upon by mountain lions, bobcats, and coyotes. The females are sexually mature at around one and one-half to two years old. Male bighorn mature a little later.

Bighorn were probably never very numerous. Their decline in

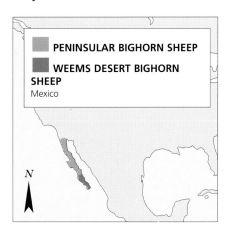

PENINSULAR BIGHORN SHEEP

WEEMS DESERT BIGHORN SHEEP
Mexico

N

Baja California mirrors what has happened to the rest of the desert bighorn population. The numbers have dropped due to the loss of habitat; intrusions by humans; and contact with domestic sheep. The problem with domestic sheep contact is that they carry diseases and parasites to which the desert bighorn is susceptible. One example is a parasite that causes a condition called lungworm. In domestic sheep, the parasite is quite common and well tolerated. Bighorn sheep, however, have little defense against this parasite and it can quickly be fatal.

Captive breeding

They are protected over much of their range. However, they are subject to a fair amount of poaching, so private ranchers in Sonora and Baja California have started up a captive breeding program. This began with around 40 sheep and is still progressing. Six hunting permits were issued for private land owners in 1995. Each permit sold for around $40,000.

There has also been a private conservation effort for the Weems bighorn. A number of wild-caught specimens were introduced to Carmen Island, with the idea that surpluses would be taken off the island if the animals thrived. They would then be reintroduced to the mainland.

Possible future

All of the bighorn subspecies found in Mexico are in jeopardy. If Weems is a valid subspecies, it is the most endangered. With the present conservation programs, it may yet have a future.

Warren D. Thomas

SHINERS

Class: Actinopterygii

Order: Cypriniformes

Family: Cyprinidae

Shiners represent one of the largest groups of fish found in North America. These are the fish that most people know by the name *minnow*. However, many other members of the family Cyprinidae do not resemble minnows. For example, while most minnows are on the small size, the grass carp (*Ctenopharyngodon idella*) and the Colorado squawfish (*Ptychocheilus lucius*) can reach 3 feet (1 meter) in length.

Shiners are found everywhere in North America, from Mexico to northern Canada and Alaska. They live in a wide variety of aquatic habitats: ponds, lakes, creeks, and large or small rivers. Some shiners can only tolerate clear, cold-water habitat, while others prefer to live in muddy, warm water.

The stomach of a shiner is really just an enlargement of the intestine, although there are some variations depending on the type of food each species eats. They have teeth in the back of the throat, called pharyngeal teeth, but none in the mouth. Shiners only have one dorsal fin and no fleshy adipose fin behind the dorsal fin as do salmon and trout. They also lack hardened spines in any of their fins.

Shiners have relatively large scales on the body but none on the head. Although these scales are round, they appear diamond-shaped because of a criss-cross pattern of color on the skin.

Although shiners are usually small, they are extremely important to the ecosystem. By eating smaller organisms, they convert energy that would normally be unavailable to larger animals, such as turtles, snakes, birds, larger fish, and certain mammals. These larger animals, in turn, eat shiners.

All shiners are known to spawn in the spring, but some reproduce twice in one year. The male shiners are usually much more colorful than the females, especially during mating season. Their splendid colors give this group its name. In addition to spectacular coloration, the males also develop nuptial tubercles: numerous tiny bumps extending from the top of the head toward the dorsal fin on the back.

When preparing to spawn, some shiners like to build nests and deposit their eggs in carefully prepared places. Some require clear, clean flowing water over gravel, while others prefer to lay eggs around vegetation. Other shiners scatter their eggs randomly. These different approaches to reproduction demonstrate one of the reasons why shiners have been so successful throughout North America.

Beautiful Shiner

(Cyprinella formosa)

ESA: Threatened

IUCN: Vulnerable

Length: 2¾ in. (7 cm)
Reproduction: Egg layer
Habitat: Desert rivers, streams, and temporary ponds
Range: Arizona, northern Mexico

THE BEAUTIFUL shiner is found throughout the Guzman region of Chihuahua, Mexico, particularly in the Rio Casas Grandes, Rio Santa Maria, Rio Del Carmin, Rio Yaqui, and the Bavicora and Sauz basins. It is also found in Cochise County in Arizona and was reintroduced into the San Bernardino National Wildlife Refuge in Arizona in 1990. Surprisingly, the beautiful shiner was not formally described as a species until 1982. Minor variations in the beautiful shiner from one river to the next in its native range has prompted some biologists to consider the possibility that the fish is comprised of three or four subspecies. Given the somewhat subjective nature of the science of classification, unclear distinctions between species and subspecies can cause disagreement between equally qualified biologists with slightly different strategies for classifying fish.

Although it is much more common than its cousin, the sardinita bocagrande (*Cyprinella bocagrande*), the beautiful shiner is a victim of some of the same environmental problems. The major culprit is the high demand for water in a desert region where water is naturally scarce. When water is diverted from the streams and rivers of the beautiful shiner's historic range, the species' population is bound to be affected. In this particular area, irrigation and livestock affect water quality, as runoff containing pesticides, animal waste, and dirt clog these waters.

Appearance

This shiner's colors are yellow to yellow orange on the sides, blending to a steel blue or greenish blue on the back. The lateral band along the midline of the

Male shiners, including the beautiful shiner, develop nuptial tubercles, or tiny bumps, that extend from the top of the head toward the dorsal fin on the back. These become more prominent during the mating season, hence the name *nuptial*.

minnow's side is dark violet. One unique feature of the beautiful shiner is the low number of pores in the lateral-line (the sensory system located on the side of the fish used to detect motion or disturbance of nearby water). It is robust from top to bottom and slender in width. The lateral stripe is much less pronounced than in other closely related shiners and is somewhat higher on the side of the body. The cheek and gill cover have a bright silver patch on the bottom half. One of the most distinguishing characteristics of this species is the extremely rounded anal fin on the underside.

Like many southwestern minnows, the beautiful shiner has adapted to extreme aquatic habitats: its native streams, often situated in the hot, dusty deserts, occasionally dry up completely. This minnow may often be forced to survive in small pools or pockets of water during dry seasons, waiting for rains to restore the flow of water. The beautiful shiner has been observed in small, muddy pools that appear to be unlikely places to find fish; they have, no doubt, adapted to this type of habitat over many years of evolution.

Blackmouth Shiner

(Notropis melanostomus)

IUCN: Vulnerable

Length: 1¼ in. (3 cm)
Reproduction: Egg layer
Habitat: Quiet backwaters of small streams and rivers
Range: Northwest Florida

THIS SHY, RARE little minnow is found only in a few rivers and creeks in the Blackwater-Yellow River drainage of northwestern Florida. It was first collected in 1939 from Pond Creek, a tributary of the Blackwater River. Since that first collection, it has also been observed in the Shoal River and Blackwater River. It has never been very abundant and is presently threatened by the encroachment of people into its native habitat. While the Blackwater River and many of its associated tributaries are considered relatively pristine, commercial and domestic development of adjacent lands are likely to spread to the narrow home range of this shiner.

Black stripe

Very little is known about the blackmouth shiner, and it was not even given a formal scientific name until 1989. As the name suggests, the fish has a band of dark black pigment around the mouth. This is actually a continuation of the black lateral stripe that extends from the tail to the snout. The minnow is similar in appearance to many of the shiners, and only an expert could correctly identify it. Counting the number of rays in its anal fin is one identification method.

To accent the silvery coloration and black stripe along the side of its body, the back and sides are speckled with bright green flecks of pigment. Unlike most shiners, the blackmouth shiner male does not develop tubercles (small bumps) on the back and head when it is in spawning condition. All the fins are darkly pigmented and strongly pointed, with darkened highlights on all of the fin rays.

Both government agencies and private organizations have taken measures to protect this small minnow, and attempts have been made to purchase parts of the lower Blackwater River system. This effort is being coordinated through Florida's

1307

Conservation and Recreational Lands Program, an organization designed to protect Florida's vast aquatic resources.

There have been few efforts to observe the behavior of the blackmouth minnow. It is generally found close to the stream banks in the quiet, shallow backwaters, where cypress and juniper provide cover and shade. Staying in depths of up to 3 feet (1 meter) where the water is calm and clear (but darkly colored due to the bottom conditions), these small minnows swim in groups or schools. In addition, these waters are often rather acidic (pH 5.4 to 6.2), more so than is usually suitable for freshwater fish.

Because of the rarity of this shiner, the Florida Game and Freshwater Fish Commission

The blue shiner is a member of the large group of closely related minnows in the genus *Cyprinella*.

began a study in 1990 to learn more about it. Hopefully, efforts to conserve parts of the Blackwater River will be successful, and this rare shiner will survive in the rivers of northwest Florida.

Blue Shiner
(Cyprinella caerulea)

ESA: Threatened

IUCN: Vulnerable

Length: 2¾ in. (7 cm)
Reproduction: Egg layer
Habitat: Clearwater streams and rivers
Range: Northern Alabama and Georgia, southern Tennessee

THE BLUE SHINER was historically known from the Cahaba and Coose Rivers in Alabama. It was

last collected from the Cahaba River in 1971 and is no longer found in this river. The current range in Alabama is the Weogufka and Choccolocco Creeks and the Little River. In Tennessee the range includes the Conasauga River, while in Georgia, the blue shiner is found in the Conasauga River and the Coosawattee River.

The blue shiner was added to the list of threatened fish of North America in 1989. The reasons for concern are similar to those on behalf of many small fish in North America. It is threatened by the ongoing development around its native habitat, and the reduction in water quality due to human activities. The situation is aggravated because this shiner has a limited distribution to begin with. Even under ideal, pristine conditions, the blue shiner was relatively scarce; today it is no longer found in most of its former range.

The blue shiner was discovered in 1877 by the famous ichthyologist David Starr Jordan. As the name suggests, the fish is a vibrant blue color, which becomes extremely intense during spawning periods. The prominent diamond-shaped scales are highlighted by a dark horizontal stripe along the side of the fish (known as the lateral line area). A snout overhangs its small mouth. There is a distinct dark patch on the cheek, called an opercle, and a characteristic blue-black vertical band of pigment just behind the cheek.

Bumpy males

When the blue shiner is ready to begin spawning in early May, the males develop numerous small bumps on the head and back. These tubercles are common to the minnow family and are thought to be important in the mating ritual. The females generally lay their eggs over some sort of small cavity in the stream bottom or amid submerged aquatic vegetation. Males tend to occupy the area around the deposited eggs and usually guard this territory against intrusion.

The blue shiner prefers medium to large streams that are cool and clear. It is usually observed in waters that have gravel, rubble, or small boulders on the stream bottom. Although no detailed studies of its habits have been published, it is likely that this shiner prefers these streams because it is adapted to feeding on the small aquatic insects that thrive in these water environments.

Like many other minnows, the blue shiners can be found in groups or schools, especially when the spawning period has passed. Their preferred habitat is the quiet, still backwaters of the headwater reaches of the Coosa and Cahaba rivers. With appropriate conservation measures, these vibrant blue minnows may continue to swim the streams of the American South.

Cahaba Shiner
(Notropis cahabae)

ESA: Endangered

IUCN: Critically endangered

Length: 2⅓ in. (6 cm)
Reproduction: Egg layer
Habitat: Stream pools and slow-moving water
Range: Cahaba River, Alabama

THE CAHABA RIVER shiner is a rare minnow that is endemic to the Cahaba River drainage in the Mobile Bay Basin of central Alabama. This shiner is so scarce in the Cahaba River that it was only recently given a formal scientific name. As soon as it was described in 1989, it was included in a list of species considered to be in danger of extinction by the U.S. Fish and Wildlife Service. The Cahaba shiner not only has a relatively narrow distribution, but is also not very abundant within its native range.

The Cahaba shiner is now limited to about 20 percent of the former range, approximately 15 miles (24 kilometers) of river.

Recent developments in this central Alabama drainage basin have served to reduce significant amounts of available habitat for this minnow. Construction of dams and alteration of historic flows have also modified conditions in the Cahaba River. In addition, a deterioration in water quality as a direct result of agricultural and domestic water usage has placed further stress on the native fish of this upper portion of the Mobile Bay drainage basin. Consequently, the Cahaba shiner is becoming more difficult to collect in the Cahaba River.

Siltation

The Cahaba shiner has evolved to inhabit clear, cool streams that have gravel, rubble, and small boulders on the stream bottom. Their specialized reproductive and feeding behavior is dependent on the presence of these specific habitat areas (known as substrate). Any major changes, such as increased siltation, have a dramatic effect on many organisms because they can no longer function in ways that have been ingrained over long periods of evolutionary time. Pollution from sewage effluent, mining, and quarrying have also been a major cause in their decline. Changes in the composition of small aquatic plants and insects can also have a dramatic effect on animals that are higher up the food chain, such as this minnow. Thus, the disappearance of a fish from a particular stream or river may only be the "tip of the iceberg" in terms of the amount of actual damage to an ecosystem.

The Cahaba shiner is very similar in shape and size to other members of the genus *Notropis*. It is long and slender, with a lateral band of dark gray pigment that extends from behind the cheek to the base of the caudal (tail) fin. Subtle accents of yellow are found at the base of each fin. The fins are primarily blue, with dark black streaks along the fin-rays. Males are generally more colorful than females, and this is especially true when they are reproductively active.

Very little is actually known about the biology of the Cahaba shiner, but it is likely that they begin spawning in May and continue to reproduce, intermittently, throughout most of the summer.

Cape Fear Shiner
(Notropis mekistocholas)

ESA: Endangered

IUCN: Critically endangered

Length: 2⅓ in. (6 cm)
Reproduction: Egg layer
Habitat: Small to moderately large streams
Range: Cape Fear drainage, North Carolina

THE CAPE FEAR shiner is endemic to the Cape Fear drainage of east-central North Carolina, and is found only in a limited area of that drainage. It is confined to two streams: Neals Creek and Rocky River. These waters are characterized by moderate changes in the bottom levels, causing alternating riffles (flowing water) and long, deep pools. The water is generally clear, but is subject to occasional

high rainfall, which results in high flows that produce turbid or rough water conditions.

The most serious threat to this species has been the dam construction in the Cape Fear system. Its narrow native range has been dramatically reduced in recent years, causing the tiny minnow to be considered endangered by several conservation organizations (including the U.S. Fish and Wildlife Service and the American Fisheries Society). It has the smallest native range of any minnow in North Carolina, which makes it even more susceptible to decline. It is believed that its distribution is strongly limited because of closely related minnows in the genus *Notropis* that are much more abundant in the Cape Fear drainage basin. They can outcompete the Cape Fear shiner for food and reproductive habitat.

The Cape Fear shiner is a silvery minnow with a dark olive back and head. A prominent dark lateral stripe about as wide as the eye extends from the snout to the base of the tail fin. The pronounced diamondlike scales are

The natural history and biology of the Cahaba shiner remain very much a mystery, and because so little is known about the species, a precise recovery plan is impossible to conceive.

strongly highlighted by a black cross-hatch pattern. The cheek is bright silver on the lower half and black on top. Its pointed snout overhangs a rather small mouth that is on the underside of the head. The fins of this shiner are curved at the margins (or falcate) and the tail is deeply forked.

Long intestine
Perhaps the most unique features of the Cape Fear shiner are its unique dietary habits and the anatomy of its internal organs, particularly the gut and intestine. Studies have shown that the diet is almost exclusively algae, diatoms, and various other small aquatic plants. The intestine is extremely long and coils back upon itself several times. In fact, this shiner's scientific name (*mekistocholas*) literally means "longest gut."

It is believed that the food habits of the Cape Fear shiner are a direct result of competition with the various other minnows that cohabit with it. Over time the Cape Fear shiner learned to use a different type of food than the typically more carnivorous minnows that rely on aquatic insects. By dividing up the available resources, it was able to coexist and survive with these other very similar fish. Unfortunately, it will be more difficult for this fish to learn how to live in degraded rivers in which the flows have been altered along with the water chemistry.

Conchos Shiner

(Cyprinella panarcys)

IUCN: Endangered

Length: 2 in. (5 cm)
Reproduction: Egg layer
Habitat: Desert streams and rivers
Range: Rio Conchos of northern Mexico

THE CONCHOS SHINER is found only in the Rio Conchos and its tributaries. The Conchos headwaters begin on the eastern slope of the Sierra Madre Occidental in the Chihuahuan desert of north central Mexico. It enters the Rio Grande in the so-called boot heel region of Texas above the confluence with the Pecos River. It is the only river of this dry, arid region of Mexico with an external outlet, surrounded by closed basins to the west, south, and east. This geographic isolation is considered to be a major factor in the creation of unique species of plants and animals, and this is one of many species of fish that can be found only in the Conchos Basin.

In this dry region of Mexico, demand for limited water resources is high. Small fish are very low on the list of priorities when it comes to obtaining water in the Chihuahuan desert. Much of the Rio Conchos is diverted into irrigation channels for agricultural use. When water does return to the Rio Conchos, either from limited annual rainfall or from irrigation runoff, it is often quite polluted. To compound the problem, poorly treated or untreated sewage also finds its way into the Rio Conchos. The relatively narrow native range of the Conchos shiner makes it vulnerable to begin with. Add these changes to decreases in water quality and quantity, and the result is yet another fish in immediate danger of extinction.

The Conchos shiner is quite typical of the large group of closely related minnows from the genus *Cyprinella*, especially in its bright colors. The upper third of the body is a murky shade of blue, becoming lighter toward the stomach. The cheek region is pale orange with golden glints. The fins on the stomach are pinkish orange to bright orange, with a margin of white at the outer edge. Colors become very intense in spawning males, and the bumps on the top of head and back of the nape (nuptial tubercles) appear at breeding time as well.

Diamond scales

Females are similarly colored but to a lesser degree, as is true with most minnows. Both males and females have scales that appear to be diamond-shaped due to the strongly outlined black borders. This creates a netlike appearance to the back and sides.

The habitat of the Conchos shiner varies greatly with the season. Water generally remains clear through the dry season (November to March), but becomes turbid for much of the summer and fall. The river bottoms vary from clear gravel bottoms in the headwaters to silt and mud in the lower sections of the Rio Conchos Basin. Scientists believe these shiners require the gravel-bottom streams that are free of silt in order to successfully reproduce. This fact adds to their dilemma in northern Mexico because livestock grazed in areas near the Rio Conchos often have the effect of increasing the amount of silt in the river. Silt chokes off the oxygen-rich gravel bottoms.

Conchos shiners begin to spawn in the early spring and continue to reproduce intermittently throughout the summer. Males are much more territorial during the spawning period and usually find a small area of the river to claim as their own.

Most of the Rio Conchos contains a variety of endemic fish consisting of several other minnows, some suckers (*Catostomidae*) and a catfish (*Ictaluridae*), as well as one mosquitofish (*Gambusia*). However, in the tributary Rio San Pedro, five non-native fish have been documented. One of these, the largemouth bass (*Micropterus salmoides*), is a serious potential threat to the Conchos shiner. If it spreads in the basin, it may provide a fatal blow to the Conchos shiner and other native minnows of the Rio Conchos.

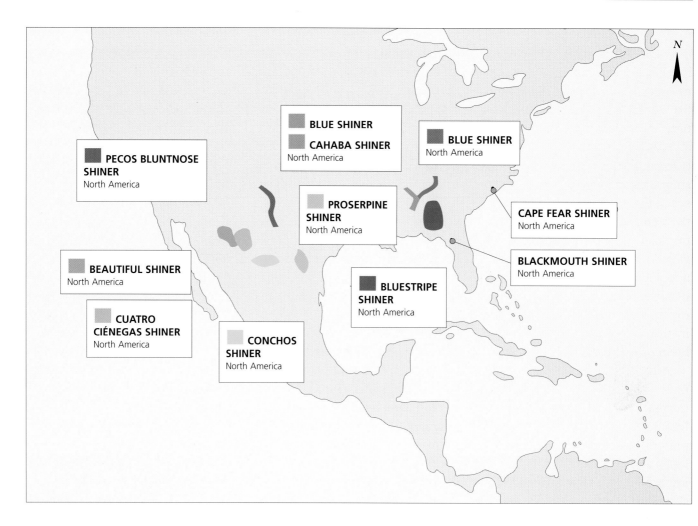

North America labels on map:
- BLUE SHINER — North America
- CAHABA SHINER
- PECOS BLUNTNOSE SHINER — North America
- BLUE SHINER — North America
- PROSERPINE SHINER — North America
- CAPE FEAR SHINER — North America
- BLACKMOUTH SHINER — North America
- BEAUTIFUL SHINER — North America
- BLUESTRIPE SHINER — North America
- CUATRO CIÉNEGAS SHINER — North America
- CONCHOS SHINER — North America

Cuatro Ciénegas Shiner

(Cyprinella xanthicara)

IUCN: Endangered

Length: 2 in. (5 cm)
Reproduction: Egg layer
Habitat: Small desert streams and rivers
Range: Cuatro Ciénegas basin, Coahuila, Mexico

IN THE MEXICAN state of Coahuila, south of the Texas Border and the Rio Grande, is a small closed basin approximately 25 miles wide and 20 miles long (40 kilometers by 32 kilometers). Surrounded by mountains on all sides except the south, this is the Bolsón de Cuatro Ciénegas (or the basin of four marshes). It is nourished by a number of small desert springs that support a unique group of aquatic organisms found nowhere else. Isolated for many thousands of years—perhaps even a million years—the aquatic habitats of the Cuatro Ciénegas Basin provide a clear picture of evolution at work. Over this long period of time, gradual changes have produced a host of endemic fish species. Among these is the Cuatro Ciénegas shiner.

Water problems

Demand for water in this parched desert climate has threatened this shiner and many of the other species isolated in this basin. Much of the limited flow of the Cuatro Ciénegas springs has been diverted for irrigation and human or animal consumption. To compound the problem, agricultural run-off and pollution from sewage have caused further deterioration in the water quality. Reduced flows have caused the water temperature to rise, in some cases to dangerous levels for most freshwater fish.

When human demands for water conflict with the needs of seemingly small and insignificant fish, there is rarely any doubt about the ultimate outcome. The Cuatro Ciénegas shiner is in extreme danger of extinction, and unless dramatic changes are instituted, it may join the ever-increasing number of extinct species in the 21st century.

This shiner's scientific name (*xanthicara*) literally means "yellow head." The name refers to the dramatic yellow color of the breeding males. The fins and back, as well as the head, take on a brilliant yellow hue. A dark black stripe along the side of the small shiner is highlighted by a spectacular pinkish orange, while the pelvic fins (on the stomach in front of the anus) develop a vibrant blue. The tail fin, which is also yellow, is highlighted by jet-black stripes on the fin rays. The result is a sparkling gem of a fish in the scarce waters of this Chihuahuan desert basin.

Although this attractive minnow was once fairly abundant throughout the basin, it is now limited to just a few locations. It prefers the open waters of larger lakes and deeper marshes, which are rapidly diminishing. It is also sometimes observed in quiet backwaters or slow-flowing areas in the small desert streams. At times, this shiner has been seen to travel in small schools. This changes during spawning periods when the colorful male becomes protective and doggedly guards its territory.

Nocturnal or diurnal?

Close observation has also revealed clues about the feeding habits of the Cuatro Ciénegas shiner. While it can be seen near the surface actively feeding during the day, nighttime finds it clinging to the bottom of the stream, spring, or lake.

There has been some effort to make a portion of the Cuatro Ciénegas Basin a nature preserve or a Mexican National Park, but these efforts have met with little or no success. Unfortunately, if more water projects such as irrigation canals are built, the future of this shiner looks bleak.

Pecos Bluntnose Shiner

(Notropis simus pecosensis)

ESA: Threatened

Length: 2¾ in. (7 cm)
Reproduction: Egg layer
Habitat: Small streams and rivers
Range: Pecos River in New Mexico

THE PECOS BLUNTNOSE shiner is one of two described subspecies of the bluntnose shiner. These two closely related shiners are found in the Rio Grande Basin in New Mexico. As the name implies, the Pecos bluntnose shiner is isolated in the Pecos River, a major tributary of the Rio Grande. Historic collections indicate that the Pecos subspecies was abundant throughout the entire drainage from the headwaters in north-central New Mexico to the merging of the two rivers below the boot heel of Texas.

Today this fish is extremely rare in the Pecos River Basin and has been considered in danger of extinction by several conservation organizations for two decades. There are two main factors that have caused the serious decline of this shiner. First, dramatic alteration of the historic flow of the Pecos River (by irrigation withdrawals and major dam construction) has changed the basic form and relative abundance of the native aquatic habitat. Second, there have been a number of non-native species of fish introduced to the Pecos River in the last 100 years. Some of these fish are closely related shiners, such as the red shiner (*Cyprinella lutrensis*). These fish compete directly with the bluntnose shiner for the ever-decreasing resources.

Some of the non-native or exotic fish are deadly to the smaller minnows, and directly reduce their numbers by consuming them whenever possible. The combination of habitat degradation and heavy predation may prove to be fatal to the Pecos bluntnose shiner.

The Pecos variety of bluntnose shiner is a slender silvery minnow that is gray on the back, blending to silver-white on the belly. Its relatively large mouth is accentuated by a flattened snout. It lacks the distinct cross-hatching pattern that emphasizes the diamond-shaped scales often observed in other members of the genus *Notropis*. The fins are silvery tan and rounded, especially the dorsal fin (on the back) and the anal fin (between the anus and tail).

Specific habitat

Limited information on the biology of the Pecos bluntnose shiner indicates that spawning begins between mid-June and mid-July and is associated with an increase in water temperature. The temperature is changed by the annual spring runoff from snow pack that melts and then drains into the Pecos Basin.

These small shiners enjoy a wide range of aquatic foods, including small fly larvae, adult beetles, and other aquatic insects, as well as a limited amount of algae. The broader the diet, the better chance a species has to survive when some of its food sources are hard to find. This may be one fact in this shiner's favor.

Water structure

Another beneficial factor is the structure of the Pecos River, which has many spring seeps along its course and a limited amount of tributary input to supplement its flows. Furthermore, much of the irrigation demands are downstream, and often a good portion of water is left in the river channel to meet such needs. This provides a limited amount of habitat for the Pecos bluntnose shiner. Still, conditions are by no means constant or sufficiently stable.

Proserpine Shiner

(Cyprinella proserpina)

IUCN: Vulnerable

Length: 2 in. (5 cm)
Reproduction: Egg layer
Habitat: Desert streams and rivers
Range: Southern Texas and northern Mexico

THE PROSERPINE shiner is native to three adjacent tributaries of the Rio Grande: the Pecos and Devils Rivers and Los Moras Creek in Texas, and the Rio San Carlos in Mexico. This small minnow is known as the hardhead in southern Texas. It was given the name in response to the prominent bumps (nuptial tubercles) on the head and back of breeding males. These tubercles are quite large compared with the tubercles on other, closely related shiners in the genus *Cyprinella*. The tissue on and around the head develops a distinctly calloused look when males are reproductively active.

The proserpine shiner was first discovered in 1857 in the Dirty Devil River, Utah, where it was quite abundant.

Specific habitat

This vibrant little fish is found only in clear tributaries of the Rio Grande and has not been collected in the main stem of the Rio Grande itself. This evidence supports the assumption that relatively clear, flowing water is an important requirement. The main cause of their recent reduction in numbers and range is the degraded water quality in the streams and rivers of southern Texas and northern Mexico. Much of the historic flows in this region have been dramatically reduced as well, a result of heavy irrigation and other agricultural usage. The Pecos and Dirty Devil Rivers have also seen the emergence of a number of non-native fish, and competition and predation from them has meant a decline in native fish such as the proserpine shiner.

The colors of this shiner are extremely brilliant. The upper sides of the body are brassy green, with a spattering of iridescent blue spots along the midline. The stomach is shiny yellow to white, with the fins on the underside (the pelvic and anal fins) developing yellow highlights along the fin rays. The side of the head is a brassy-rose color, becoming a watery violet under the chin. There is a distinct indigo bar behind the cheek that intensifies when these fish spawn, making the proserpine shiner really live up to its name. Females have the same essential coloration, but are much less brilliant, being olive on the back, blue on the sides, and silvery white on the belly.

Behavior

The proserpine shiner usually feeds near the bottom of its favorite rivers or streams. Its diet consists of small aquatic insects and some algae. The fish has also been observed spawning, starting in May and continuing throughout most of the summer. For some reason, reproduction becomes more rapid and prolific immediately after severe flooding. This behavior probably evolved to take advantage of harsh desert conditions where flash floods are common. The species learned to take advantage of available abundant water.

Environmental plasticity

The ability to use a variety of habitats, particularly in response to environmental disturbance such as a flood, is quite typical of fish found in harsh climates such as desert. Scientists call this feature environmental plasticity. The proserpine shiner is among the species that possess this quality. A large portion of the Texas range of this species was inundated by the creation of the Amistad reservoir, though the effect this has had on the proserpine shiner is unknown.

Donald S. Proebstel

Shou

(Cervus elaphus wallichi)

Class: Mammalia
Order: Artiodactyla
Family: Cervidae
Subfamily: Cervinae
Shoulder height:
Approximately 47–55 in.
(120–140 cm)
Diet: Leaves, shoots, and grass
Gestation period: 230–240 days
Longevity: 16–20 years
Habitat: Open forest
Range: Southern Tibet, Bhutan

Red deer are among the largest and most numerous of all the deer groups, yet many subspecies, such as the shou, remain little known.

DEER OF THE GENUS and species *Cervus elephus*, which includes the shou, are a group commonly referred to as red deer. These are found not only in Eurasia, but also in North America. Experts disagree on just how many subspecies there are: some say five, others claim as many as 20 or more.

Classification

Regardless of what classification is used, this debate does not change the natural history of this deer. In Europe and Asia the red deer genus ranges from Great Britain all the way to China. In southeastern Tibet and Bhutan there is a red deer subspecies known locally as the shou or Tibetan red deer (or sometimes Wallich's deer).

The shou stands about 4½ feet (1.4 meters) at the shoulder. The hair on its neck grows in a pattern that resembles a mane. In the spring its coat is a uniform yellowish or sandy brown that changes into a summer coat of dark grayish brown. The shou's antlers are large and generally have five tines or points. The third and fifth tines angle toward each other, giving the shou's antlers an unusual and distinctive appearance.

Much to learn

No definitive study has ever been made of this deer, so little is known of its particular habits. However, it is probably much like the other members of the red deer genus. The mating behavior of red deer (the rut) is perhaps their most distinctive behavior. In order to attract female attention, males (stags) will put on many displays: they vocalize loudly, use their antlers to shred vegetation, spray urine around, and generally cause a disturbance.

Mating combat

If another male wants to challenge for the right to mate with a female, the two males strike poses and walk closely together until they lock antlers and duel. If one of the combatants is thrown off balance to the ground, the other male has a chance to stab an exposed area of his opponent with his antlers. Fights like these are not lethal in most cases, but many deer display a variety of battle scars.

Hunting pressure

As with many of the hooved mammals of Eurasia, the shou has been subjected to habitat degradation and severe hunting pressures. It was thought to be totally eliminated from Bhutan until a small group was rediscovered in 1982.

The status and numbers of this subspecies are unknown, but its prospects are probably not good, simply because its range has been an area of military dispute between China and India for years. Many troops are sta-

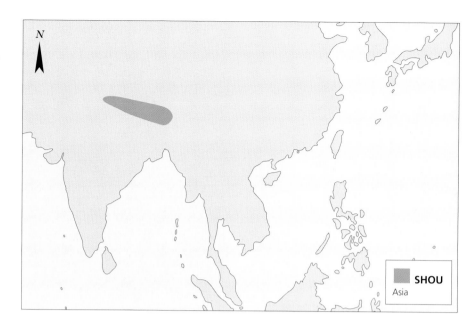

tioned in the region, and the presence of military forces often leads on to an increase in hunting, not to mention the accidental killing of animals that are caught in fighting between opposing forces.

There are currently no shou known to be in captivity, except for a group based in the summer palace, the former home of the Dalai Lama (Tibet's religious leader) in the city of Lhasa.

Warren D. Thomas

San Clemente Loggerhead Shrike

(Lanius ludovicianus mearnsi)

ESA: Endangered

Class: Aves
Order: Passeriformes
Family: Laniidae
Length: 9 in. (23 cm)
Weight: Probably 1¼–1¾ oz. (40–50 g)
Clutch size: 4–5 eggs
Incubation: 14 days
Diet: Large insects, small birds, small mammals, and lizards
Habitat: Woodlands, shrublands
Range: San Clemente Island, United States

THE LOGGERHEAD shrike is an attractive bird. Unpatterned, neutral gray upperparts cleanly contrast with white underparts faintly barred with gray, and black bars accent its plumage on the wing, tail, and mask. Nothing about the loggerhead shrike's appearance shows it to be a killer.

Shrikes survive by preying on other small birds, small rodents, lizards, large insects, and various other animals. Their food preferences and feeding habits are not unlike those of hawks (*Falconiformes*), but shrikes are actually songbirds (*Passeriformes*). They have stout beaks, strongly hooked at the tip. Their legs and feet are surprisingly short, and their toes are not equipped with talons. To secure their prey when perching, shrikes use thorns. They impale their food so it will not drop or

escape, even though they nearly always kill the victim before impaling it. Barbed wire has proved useful to the shrike. A mouse, skink, or grasshopper stuck to a barb advertises the presence of a shrike.

Endangered subspecies

The loggerhead shrike lives across North America from coast to coast. It ranges far north into Alberta, Canada, and south to Oaxaca and Veracruz in Mexico. The loggerhead population has dwindled steadily in the northeast, but a subspecies in the southwest of the United States has almost become extinct.

San Clemente Island lies 62½ miles (100 kilometers) west of San Diego, California, in the Pacific Ocean. Shrublands and woodlands once covered the island's 87 square miles (226 square kilometers). Historically, San Clemente was visited by whalers, sealers, explorers, fishers, and privateers, and some of these people left goats (*Capra hircus*) on the island. Stocking goats on islands was a common practice worldwide in the early centuries of maritime exploration. Ships would anchor at an island, and the crew would go ashore to resupply the ship with firewood and drinking water. Several goats would be left behind so they could breed and populate the island. On return trips or subsequent voyages, sailors could restock wood and water, and shoot a few goats to supply fresh meat.

The goat problem

Goats have radically changed the character of the island. They eat a broad variety of plants and plant parts, including flowers, fruits, stems, leaves, bark, and roots, and will eat both woody and non-woody plants. Left unattended and uncontrolled, goats will eat their favorite plants until nothing is left. They then forage other species more heavily. Because San Clemente Island harbored no population of wolves, coyotes, lions, or bobcats, the goats were not restrained by any predation. Their population grew unchecked into the thousands. With 5,000 individuals in the 1980s, the goats averaged about 58 animals per square mile (1.6 square kilometers).

Plant threat

Botanists found the goat situation on San Clemente intolerable. Three species of plants unique to San Clemente Island

were directly threatened with extinction because of the introduced goats.

Controversy

Pushing for the immediate eradication of goats on San Clemente, botanists soon found out that the issue was embroiled in great controversy. Resource management on the island is handled by the Fish and Wildlife Service. Their plans to shoot the goats were unacceptable to animal rights activists, who won a court injunction that prevented any shooting. A judge awarded the activist group an opportunity to trap the goats alive and remove them from San Clemente Island so that the animals would not have to be exterminated.

Live traps

As it turned out, the island's extremely rugged terrain did not favor live-trapping efforts, and the large expense of trapping and transporting the goats soon exceeded the group's financial resources. Despite trapping many goats, the activists could not trap

If the San Clemente loggerhead shrike continues singing from the island shrubbery, it will do so because people have aggressively worked to correct the mistakes of previous generations.

them faster than they could reproduce. The effort ultimately failed. The court action against the shooting was lifted, and all but a few goats were eliminated. Although goats on San Clemente were not completely eradicated, the population was reduced enough to satisfy the botanists that the plants were protected from overgrazing.

A quiet decline

During the goat controversy, the San Clemente loggerhead shrike drifted toward extinction. The goats so heavily grazed the tree and shrub communities on San Clemente that the shrike lost nesting habitat. The goat-altered plant communities also affected populations of the shrike's prey species. Feral house cats (*Felis sylvestris*) complicated the shrike's struggle because nestling and fledgling shrikes are particularly vulnerable to cats. Those few shrikes that continued nesting seldom raised their offspring to adulthood.

The San Clemente loggerhead shrike lived abundantly on the island early in the 20th century, but by 1991 less than two dozen survived. In April and May of 1991, four eggs and six young shrikes were removed from San Clemente Island and flown by helicopter directly to the San Diego Zoo where they were carefully raised in captivity. Additional recovery efforts are still underway.

Native vegetation

The U.S. Fish and Wildlife Service plans to replant the island with appropriate native shrubs. Also, the American kestrel (*Falco sparverius*) has attracted some attention. Kestrels have become much more abundant on San

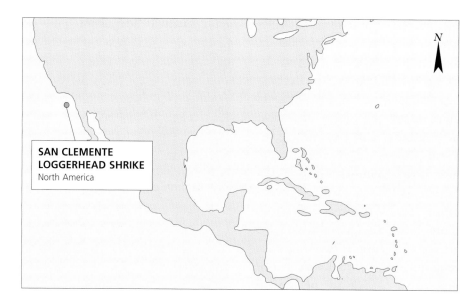

SAN CLEMENTE
LOGGERHEAD SHRIKE
North America

Clemente island as shrikes have become increasingly scarce. Some ornithologists suspect that the American kestrel may be competing with the shrike for food. Both species hunt large invertebrates and small vertebrates, but on the mainland they occupy slightly different habitats.

The increase of kestrels on San Clemente further indicates that the plant community has changed. Specific research will be needed to evaluate any competition between the shrike and the kestrel before corrective action can be recommended.

Kevin Cook

FRESHWATER SHRIMP

Class: Crustacea

The animal phylum *Arthropoda* contains about 80 percent of all known animal species. Although insects are the dominant class of arthropods on land, the class *Crustacea* dominates in the water.

One of the reasons that crustaceans are popular with humans is because they include favorite sources of food, such as lobster, crab, and shrimp.

Crustaceans have been known to people since ancient times and because of this they are also a source of legend. Cancer, one of two invertebrates in the astrological zodiac, is a crab.

Even though more than 75,000 species of crustaceans have been described, scientists who study

crustaceans (known as carcinologists) estimate that more than 100,000 species remain to be discovered and described. Crustaceans exhibit an incredible diversity of form and habit, ranging in size from tiny planktonic forms that are less than a millimeter in length to giant crabs with leg spans of 13 feet (4 meters) and lobsters that weigh up to 44 pounds (20 kilograms).

Crustaceans have been found living at all aquatic depths in marine, brackish, and freshwater environments. They are the most widespread and diverse group of invertebrates inhabiting the world's oceans.

A few groups of crustaceans, notably the sow bugs or pill bugs, have successfully evolved to live

in terrestrial habitats. The incredible diversity of this animal class has often led to them being referred to as the *insects of the sea*.

Freshwater shrimp include members of two subclasses: Branchiopoda and Malacostraca. Endangered branchiopods come in two orders: Anostraca (fairy and brine shrimp) and Notostraca (tadpole shrimps).

Branchiopods are among the most characteristic inhabitants of temporary ponds and pools of water, especially vernal pools that form in the spring after winter rains. They are absent from running water and, unlike all other groups of crustaceans, there are no true marine species. However, brine shrimp are adapted to live in saline habitats.

All species of branchiopods have developed life cycles specialized for living this way. This is because they have to survive in temporary bodies of water. One obvious survival mechanism is the long periods that eggs can remain dormant until conditions permit hatching. Females carry eggs externally in an egg or brood sac for a few days and then drop them in mud. In some species and individuals, the egg sac remains attached until the female dies and sinks to the bottom of the pool. Thin-walled so-called summer eggs hatch almost immediately, but thick-shelled winter eggs can withstand heat, cold, and long periods of drought. Viable eggs have been kept in dried pond mud on laboratory shelves for as long as 15 years.

Hatching

Eggs hatch within a few days after the pools are re-flooded with water. The immatures (known as *nauplii*) molt about 12 to 20 times, growing until they become sexually mature. With each successive molt they increase in size, add more segments and appendages, and their appendages become well developed. The number of instars (the period between molts) varies with each species, the water temperature, and available food supply. Fairy shrimp have been known to complete their entire life cycle in just 16 days. Their quick life cycle enables them to reproduce successfully in temporary bodies of water and in longer-lasting water habitats where predators such as aquatic insects often colonize and decimate the shrimp population.

Fairy and brine shrimp

In North America, mostly in the southwestern and western United States, there are fairy shrimp and brine shrimp. Approximately 200 species have been described. All these species have delicate, elongated bodies with 20 trunk segments, including 11 segments that bear pairs of legs; 2 genital segments; and 7 posterior segments. Fairy shrimp have compound eyes that are mounted on the ends of stalks. Most species are about ½ inch (1 centimeter) in length when fully grown, although some are known to grow as long as 4 inches (10 centimeters).

Fairy shrimp swim on their backs by beating their legs in a wavelike motion from front to back (not unlike paddling in a canoe). This not only propels them through their water habitat but also allows them to obtain food. Most species feed on algae, phytoplankton, bacteria, protozoans, rotifers, and other microscopic material that is suspended in the water. This is why they are known as suspension feeders.

Fairy shrimp have few natural predators. They are unlikely to be heavily preyed upon by other vernal pool inhabitants because they use the pool before most of the carnivorous insects have colonized it. In addition, the frogs and salamanders breeding in the pools have not regained their regular appetite after winter hibernation and so are not major predators. However, these amphibians, caddis fly larvae, dytiscid larvae, and other insects, as well as waterfowl, sometimes prey on the fairy shrimp. Because fairy shrimp inhabit temporary wetlands there are no predatory fish. The abundance of food is less of a factor affecting the population of fairy shrimp than it is for other organisms. The need for one part per million oxygen dissolved in water is the real limiting factor in the size of fairy shrimp populations.

Tadpole shrimps

Tadpole shrimps have a thorax made up of 11 segments (each with a pair of legs), and a ringed abdomen formed by the fusion of several segments. A broad, shieldlike or paddle-shaped carapace is fused with the head, but extends to cover the thorax and a portion of the abdomen. Because of their broad carapace and narrow trunk, these shrimps have the appearance of the immature tadpole stage of amphibians such as frogs. Their compound eyes are not mounted on stalks, as with fairy or brine shrimp. Just nine species have been described, and all are in a single family, the Triopsidae. Mature individuals range in size from ¾ to 4 inches (2 to 10 centimeters).

Tadpole shrimps move about mainly by crawling, but they are also capable of swimming, at least for brief periods, by beating together their legs. Most species apparently feed on organic matter stirred up from the sediments of their aquatic habitats; however, some species are known to scavenge or prey on other aquatic animals including mollusks, other crustaceans, frog eggs, and small tadpoles. Because they feed on a variety of items, they are probably best classified as omnivores.

As stated above, most fairy and brine shrimp are found in

the American Southwest and West. California is part of this region, and because California is also the most populous state, it follows that more problems have been created for the habitats of certain freshwater shrimp. Urban development, water and flood control projects, as well as agricultural production, have resulted in the loss of many vernal pools throughout California. It has been estimated that six million acres (243 million hectares) of vernal pool habitat existed in the Central Valley during the time of the first American colonies. By 1970 approximately 90 percent of these pools were gone. It is this huge loss of vernal pool habitat that has led to the endangerment of several fairy and tadpole shrimp species.

One example is the conservancy fairy shrimp (*Branchinecta conservatio*), found in widely separate counties of California, from Solano in the north to Ventura in the south. This shrimp is found in lake-sized bodies of water that have turbid (cloudy) water.

Other examples include the longhorn fairy shrimp (*Branchinecta longiantenna*) in central California, which occurs in around 15 grass-bottomed, clearwater pools formed by sandstone depressions. The vernal pool fairy shrimp (*Branchinecta lynchi*) is found in the same area, as far south as California's Riverside County. These pools have grassy bottoms, and the water in them is clear to tea-colored. The California linderiella (*Linderiella occidentalis*) is also commonly found in these pools.

The Riverside fairy shrimp (*Streptocephalus woottoni*) is found in a few locations in Riverside and San Diego counties. At maturity this species measures about ¾ inch (2 centimeters) in length.

The vernal pool tadpole shrimp (*Lepidurus packardi*) can reach a length of 2 inches (5 centimeters) when fully grown. This species occurs in wet, marshy ground pools with either clear or highly turbid water. It is only found in some 15 locations around the Sacramento Valley.

Mono Lake

The lake known as Mono Lake is an eerie sight. This pool is highly saline; that is, the water has a high salt content. Mono Lake is located in the Great Basin desert of California beneath the eastern slopes of the Sierra Nevada Mountains. Years ago the city of Los Angeles bought water rights to this lake (even though Los Angeles is hundreds of miles away) and began to drain it. As the lake level has dropped, the salt concentration in the water has doubled. Eventually the lake's salt level will be more than the Mono brine shrimp (*Artemia monica*) can tolerate.

One stream-dwelling species, the California freshwater shrimp (*Syncaris pacifica*), lives in tree-lined portions of small streams in Northern California. Local agricultural activities (such as grazing livestock) create erosion, which can clog streams with more silt than local species can tolerate. The streams in Marin, Napa, and Sonoma Counties are no exception to this form of water pollution. Besides the usual assaults on its habitat, the California freshwater shrimp is also threatened by exotic predators such as the sunfish.

In order to protect endangered freshwater shrimp, their habitats need to be protected, but modern civilization makes that task difficult. Every new construction, such as a dam or flood control channels, affects the flow, temperature, and turbidity of a stream or river, and this affects the species living in the river. Many of these species, from freshwater shrimps to the largest fish and amphibians, can only tolerate a narrow variation in their environment before their breeding and feeding habits are harmed. When particular species begin to decline and disappear, other species that rely on them for their food become threatened as well.

Three species of cave shrimp are recognized as threatened or endangered in the southern United States. These shrimps are cave dwellers that live in subterranean, aquatic habitats. All are characterized by extremely limited geographic ranges. The Alabama Cave shrimp (*Palaemonias alabamea*) is known from only two caves in Madison County, Alabama; the Kentucky cave shrimp (*P. ganteri*) is known only from Mammoth Cave in Kentucky; and the Squirrel Chimney Cave shrimp (*Palaemonetes cummingi*) is restricted to only one site in Alachua County, Florida. Potential development and groundwater contamination pose major threats to these particular species.

More study of these tiny freshwater creatures would help conservationists to decide how specific habitats should be carefully managed in order to save these species.

Richard Arnold

SIFAKAS

Class: Mammalia

Order: Primates

Family: Indriidae

Sifakas are the second largest members of the lemur family, second in size only to the indrii. The name *sifaka* (pronounced she-FAHK or see-FAHK) imitates the cry these animals make when alarmed.

Madagascar is the home of the lemur, a spectacular and unusual family of primates, of which the most remarkable are surely the sifakas. These animals stand over 3 feet (1 meter) tall, nearly the size of a grown chimpanzee. Most of them are covered with a coat of silky brown, gold, and black hair. They are found in a surprising variety of forested areas from the hot, humid rain forest of eastern Madagascar to the dry, arid prickly forests of western Madagascar.

Social life among sifakas is not well understood. They are found in small groups of 2 to 12 animals, but these do not appear to be stable family units. Instead, individuals appear to form temporary foraging parties, and the composition of these groups changes as animals come and go.

Sifakas spend most of their time in the trees and other vegetation, where they are capable of making incredible leaps of over 20 feet (6 meters). Like other members of the family Indriidae, sifakas are vertical climbers and leapers. They have long, robust legs and elongated, hooklike hands. They make spectacular leaps by using their hind legs to push off from one vertical support to another. In fact, they can easily leap forward or backward at least 20 feet (6 meters).

Even at rest, sifakas maintain a vertical posture. They sit upright with their long legs bent up at the hips and down at the knees, grasping the tree trunk with their feet.

When sifakas move on the ground, they are equally fascinating to watch; they run on two feet (bipedal) in a peculiar, sideways manner quite unlike any other animal except a crab. While running they also jump or bound up to a height of 10 to 15 feet (3 to 4.5 meters).

Sifakas suffer due to habitat destruction. Their historic range has been cleared for farming, charcoal production, and other human uses. They are sometimes hunted for food, which further compromises their situation.

Diademed (Crowned) Sifaka

(Propithecus diadema)

ESA: Endangered

IUCN: Endangered

Weight: 12 lb. (5.45 kg)

Head-body length: 21 in. (53 cm)

Tail length: 20 in. (51 cm)

Diet: Leaves, fruit, buds, flowers

Gestation period: Approximately 150 days

Longevity: 12–14 years

Habitat: Primary rain forest

Range: Eastern Madagascar

DIADEMED SIFAKAS live in the eastern rain forest of Madagascar. There are at least four subspecies, and all are faced with extinction. They are diurnal in their habits and usually peak in

Sifakas, including the diademed sifaka, are primarily diurnal, with their highest level of activity occuring toward the middle of the day.

activity at midday. Diademed sifakas are spectacular-looking, normally having sable brown-to-black silky hair and large buff or golden patches over the back. However, coloration can vary from nearly all white to black, depending on the subspecies. This fur is punctuated by a pair of orange-yellow eyes.

These primates eat mostly leaves, fruit, and flowers. They spend most of their time in the trees but will come to the ground to forage as well. They sleep in trees at night. Little else is known about their behavior or ecology. They appear to live in small groups of from two to eight animals, but these may just be temporary foraging parties made up of animals that are familiar to each other.

The population size of one subspecies, *Propithecus diadema perrieri*, was estimated to consist of a maximum of 2,000 individuals in the late 1980s.

Since they are primarily a rain forest animal, the diademed sifakas have suffered severely due to the extensive logging and destruction of the eastern Madagascar rain forest. In addition, some researchers have reported that these sifakas are hunted by humans for food, much more so than other lemurs. Even though they have been afforded government protection, law enforcement is lacking. The sifakas' plight is still severe and their future is precarious.

A national park is being set up at Ranomafana which will contain a study site run by Duke University, North Carolina. It is hoped that this will offer the lemurs better protection. There is also one sifaka in captivity at Duke University. However, with the lessons learned by the Duke University Primate Center, there is no reason why a captive population could not be established and maintained.

Golden Crowned Sifaka
(Propithecus tattersalli)

ESA: Endangered

IUCN: Critically endangered

Weight: 7¼ lb. (3.3 kg)
Diet: Probably leaves, fruit, buds, and flowers
Habitat: Dry gallery forest
Range: Northeastern Madagascar

THE GOLDEN CROWNED sifaka is the most recently described of these lemurs. It was discovered in 1974, but was not thoroughly studied until 1987, when investigators from Duke University, Carolina, found that it was a new species. The golden crowned sifaka was ultimately described in 1988 by Dr. Elwyn Simons.

Habitat loss
This sifaka is similar to the diademed sifaka, but is considerably smaller. It has white silky fur with a golden crown, as well as a buff golden patch on its chest and inner arms. The muzzle is blackish, and the eyes are orange. It is limited to a tiny area in northeast Madagascar near a place known as Daraina. The total population of this sifaka is no more than a few hundred.

The golden crowned sifaka has been observed in small groups of from three to six and makes its home in gallery forests. Not much is known of its habits and ecology. It is thought to have a diet similar to other sifakas, but it has only been observed eating in the wild a few times. The golden crowned sifaka may be active day and night, but this is not known with certainty.

The main threats to this sifaka's survival are the destruction of its habitat due to logging and the seemingly unending problem of hunting. Even though local customs forbid the eating of a lemur, this does not prevent outsiders coming in and destroying it.

Captive population
There is a small captive population (a pair caught in the wild that has since reproduced) at the Duke Primate Center and it is believed that this species can be successfully maintained in even larger groups in captivity.

The golden crowned sifaka is considered to be one of the most endangered lemurs. Unfortunately, its range is not within any protected area. Biologists have suggested that a well-guarded national park be set up near Daraina to provide this lemur with better protection. If a successful captive breeding program were established, then this species might also be released back into the wild. Without such active intervention, however, this sifaka is almost certain to become extinct.

Verreaux's sifakas, similar to other species in the Indriidae family, have a series of glands on their bodies, which they use to mark territory.

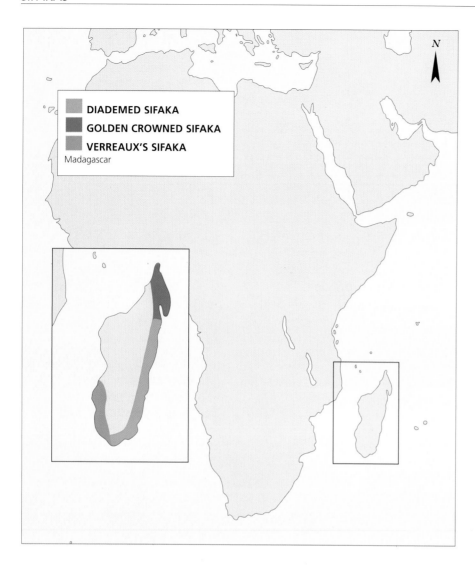

DIADEMED SIFAKA
GOLDEN CROWNED SIFAKA
VERREAUX'S SIFAKA
Madagascar

Verreaux's Sifaka

(Propithecus verreauxi)

ESA: Endangered

IUCN: Vulnerable

Weight: 11 lb. (5 kg)
Head-body length: 20 in. (51 cm)
Diet: Leaves, fruit, flowers, buds, bark
Habitat: Dry forest
Range: Southwestern Madagascar

OF ALL THE SIFAKAS, the Verreaux's sifaka is the most numerous. Nonetheless, its actual population size is unknown and certainly declining. This sifaka has been more thoroughly studied than the others. There are at least three known subspecies distributed in the dry, deciduous forests of the west and riparian forests of the south.

It is found in small groups, usually from two to twelve individuals, but these are thought to be temporary foraging parties rather than stable family units. Its diet consists mainly of fruit, leaves, and flowers.

Color mixing

Variation in color depends on the subspecies, but the coat is mainly buff colored to almost white, with some dark markings on the head, chest, or legs. The hair is fine and silky.

This sifaka usually occupies from 5 to 25 acres (2 to 10 hectares) of territory. In some areas Verreaux's sifaka marks its range with scent glands and engages in territorial battles. Breeding occurs between January and March. Like other sifakas, it is very agile, and is capable of incredible vertical leaps.

The plant material in the south (the spiny *Didiereaceae*) is usually armed with long spikes, but this does not deter the Verreaux's sifaka making 30-foot (9-meter) leaps between spiky branches with no apparent injury.

Hunted lemur

This sifaka is threatened over much of its range because of the extensive destruction to its habitat, through forest clearing for crop farming and destruction by charcoal production. Most investigators report that the local Malagasy people do not normally hunt this animal for food, but that non-Malagasy residents, who control much of the commerce, do. Hunting has cleared many areas of the Verreaux's sifaka.

Captive groups

Verreaux's sifaka has been successfully maintained in captivity and has reproduced at the Duke Primate Center, North Carolina. A breeding pair of *P. verreauxi verreauxi* is kept by the Los Angeles Zoo in California, and there is a small group of *P. verreauxi coronatus* living at the Paris Zoo.

Warren D. Thomas

See also Lemurs.

Sikas

(Cervus nippon)

ESA: Endangered

IUCN: Data deficient to Critically endangered

Class: Mammalia
Order: Artiodactyla
Family: Cervinae
Weight: 100–220 lb. (45–100 kg)
Shoulder height: 25–44 in. (63.5–112 cm)
Diet: Leaves, bark, shoots, and grass
Gestation period: 217 days
Longevity: 15–20 years
Habitat: Open and dense forest
Range: Eastern Asia, offshore islands

THE SIKAS ARE A LARGE group of 13 different races or subspecies of deer, all of which are found in eastern Asia. Their range extends from northern China and the Japanese island of Hokkaido to Vietnam in Southeast Asia. They are a tough and hardy deer.

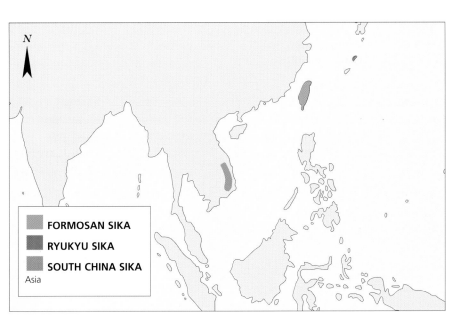

FORMOSAN SIKA
RYUKYU SIKA
SOUTH CHINA SIKA
Asia

Although there is a fairly broad range of sizes, they are, on average, medium-sized.

The antlers of the adult male usually have eight tines or points, four on each side (rarely five). Most sikas show a color change between summer and winter, their coats changing from a bright chestnut red with white spots to a dusty brown with virtually no spots. There are dark stripes along the neck and back, leading down to the tail.

Breeding usually occurs in the fall, with fawns born in midspring. Sikas are known as intermediate feeders, meaning they are both browsers and grazers, eating vegetation off the ground as well from low-hanging tree branches and tall bushes. Their diet consists of leaves, shoots, bark, and grass.

Sikas have been introduced into a number of countries where they are not indigenous, and they have usually done well. There are currently large populations of the more common subspecies in Europe, New Zealand, North America, Morocco, and Madagascar. One Japanese subspecies, *Cervus nippon pulchellus*, is classified as data deficient. However, a number of the subspecies of sika are in danger of extinction. The following three subspecies are all listed as critically endangered by IUCN.

Formosan sika

The Formosan sika *(Cervus nippon taiouanus)* originates from the island of Taiwan, once known as Formosa. The male can stand nearly 40 inches (102 centimeters) at the shoulder. The summer coat of the Formosan sika is a bright copper color with large white spots. In winter its coat becomes a drab brown with much smaller spots. There is a black line that borders the white rump patch and runs down the center of the tail.

The Formosan sika once ranged over the mountainous and forested interior of the island and, during the Japanese occupation of World War II, was actually a protected species. However, after the war there was uncontrolled hunting and extensive destruction of the sika's habitat for agriculture, to the point that the animal is now critically endangered. Fortunately, there are large captive populations in North America and Europe. There are also large captive populations in Taiwan and some adjacent islands, where the Formosan sika is kept mainly for the commercial harvesting of its antlers, which are a popular ingredient of folk remedies.

Ryukyu sika

The Ryukyu or Kerama sika *(Cervus nippon keramae)* comes from the Ryukyu Islands, an archipelago just south of the

For an island deer, the Formosan sika is unusually large. The other mainland forms of sika are generally smaller.

major Japanese islands. The Ryukyu variety resembles the common Japanese sika deer in most respects. There are some differences, however. It is much smaller than the common Japanese sika. Its coat tends to be darker and almost totally without spots. Instead, it has a dark stripe that extends down the back to the tail. There is a high percentage of melanistic, or black, forms of the Ryukyu sika.

Comeback

In 1964 it was estimated that there were just 30 animals remaining in the wild. It has been given great protection, and the Ryukyu has made a limited comeback. All existing specimens, however, are on one small,

uninhabited island called Yakabi, which has an area of a mere 304 acres (123 hectares). This habitat severely limits the maximum population size.

To be more accurate, the South China sika (*Cervus nippon pseudaxis*) should really be known as the Vietnamese sika because its historic range is in Vietnam. It is one of the more attractive sika subspecies. Like some of the northern races, this deer is well-built, with a bright copper spotted coat. Despite originating from northern stock and having spread south, the South China sika is not a tropical deer. It has retained the habits and biology of the other sika. For example, the annual cycle of growing, shedding, and regrowing antlers is not typical for tropical deer. The South China sika continues this cycle, however, despite living in tropical surroundings.

The South China sika is considered by the IUCN to be critically endangered due to severe habitat destruction.

Sadly, decades of warfare from the 1950s through the 1980s have devastated much of Southeast Asia and has badly affected all indigenous wildlife, not just the sika. Fortunately there is a small captive population in European and North American zoos, numbering perhaps 100. These may be hybrids, but another 40 purebred specimens live in Cuc Phnong National Park in Vietnam.

Recently a breeding program was undertaken by the Vietnamese government and some European zoos. Some ten South China sika arrived in Warsaw in December 1991 and were being prepared for shipment to other breeding destinations.

Warren D. Thomas

SILVERSIDES

Class: Actinopterygii

Order: Atheriniformes

Family: Atherinidae

Silversides are small to medium-sized fishes that represent about 160 different species within 30 genera. They are best known for their schooling behavior and silvery appearance, which help to confuse predators and increase an individual's chances of survival.

This is an example of the old adage that there is safety in numbers.

Silversides are found in tropical and some temperate environments, including both freshwater and saltwater. Most can be found in tropical coastal areas, but quite significant numbers of species have adapted to inland freshwater areas in the Mississippi River Basin of the United States, northern and eastern Australia, and eastern South America, primarily in Brazil.

Individual silverside species are important members of the food chain of many aquatic communities. Because of their small size, they are a very important food source for a great number of larger fish, aquatic birds, reptiles, amphibians, and mammals. The loss of these species through human activities severely disrupts a natural food chain that has existed for millennia. The alteration of habitat is particularly destructive to these very sensitive aquatic creatures.

Key Silverside

(Menidia conchorum)

IUCN: Lower risk

Length: 4⅓ in. (11 cm)
Reproduction: Egg layer
Habitat: Near-shore saltwater areas
Range: Lower Florida Keys, Florida

BEFORE THE FLORIDA KEYS (at the southern tip of Florida) were intensively developed, the key silverside fish inhabited environments that were relatively undisturbed by humans. Most human activity occurred either on land or in boats above the coral-lined bottom of near-shore areas. Large groups of these silvery, schooling fish could often be seen throughout the key system. As more people heard about the Florida Keys, the area grew in popularity as a tourist resort and along with the people came development. The number of piers, boat landings, marinas, and onshore support facilities very rapidly increased. The result was disturbance and destruction of the key silverside's habitat.

Along with physical destruction came chemical pollution from domestic waste water that was minimally treated before being dumped into the ocean. All these factors led to falling numbers of key silverside and other fish sensitive to degradation of their habitat.

A highway death sentence

The final blow for this fish was the construction of U.S. Highway 1 from the Florida mainland to Key West. This major construction project eradicated the last key silverside from the upper keys—from Key Largo to Long Key—and further reduced its total numbers in the lower keys. Construction projects such as this destroyed the stands of mangrove trees along the shoreline that the key silverside used for cover and for food.

The survival of this species in its natural range will require clear understanding of the sensitivity of the key silverside to poor habitat and water quality and a commitment to maintain an appropriate environment.

This relatively small fish is not difficult to identify, due to its unique shape, silver coloration, and schooling behavior. This species has an upturned mouth and chin, large eyes for detecting and capturing its prey, two triangular dorsal fins on its back (the forward fin is a somewhat smaller size), large pectoral fins just behind the gills, paired pelvic fins on the belly, a long anal fin, and a deeply forked tail fin. The distinctive dark horizontal stripe located on each side helps to aid identification.

Consumption

This fish consumes primarily planktonic animals and other aquatic invertebrates. Its species name, *conchorum*, is derived from the most famous underwater resident of the Florida Keys, the queen conch (*Strombus gigas*).

The key silverside is a short-lived fish with a life span of a year or less. It reproduces throughout the year, with a peak during February to March. The eggs have tendrils that aid in their dispersal, as the tendrils wrap around objects such as plants and even bird's legs.

Waccamaw Silverside
(Menidia extensa)

ESA: Threatened

IUCN: Vulnerable

Length: 2¾ in. (7 cm)
Reproduction: Egg layer
Habitat: Open shallow water over darkened bottom
Range: Lake Waccamaw, North Carolina, and upper Waccamaw River

THE COASTAL REGION of the United States from Virginia to Georgia has long been an area of interest for geologists and biologists. Within this region is a series of lakes known as the Carolina Bays; most are concentrated in the southeastern region of North Carolina. Some scientists speculate that they were formed during one event many thousands of years ago: a meteorite shower cratered the earth's surface along the mid-Atlantic coast, and over time the depressions filled with water. Other experts theorize that underground artesian wells and the forces of wind and water hollowed these basins out over an extended period of time.

Whatever the answer, the shallow coastal Carolina Bays (Lake Waccamaw in particular) have played a key role in the history of North Carolina and in our understanding of the evolutionary process. Lake Waccamaw is, literally, a hotbed of evolutionary activity and the Waccamaw silverside, a native species of the lake, is an important piece of the puzzle. Most fish within the same family as the Waccamaw silverside (*Atherinidae*) are saltwater inhabitants. This means that the Waccamaw silverside probably moved into this lake from the Atlantic Ocean during a time when the sea level was slightly higher.

Appearance

As the name suggests, the Waccamaw silverside is silver in color, with some darkening on the top of its head and back. Other pigmentation includes a dark stripe down each side from the base of the head to the base of the tail. This species has an upturned mouth and chin, large eyes for seeing and capturing its prey, two triangular dorsal fins on its back, large pectoral fins just behind the gills, paired pelvic fins on the belly, a long anal fin, and a deeply forked tail fin.

Spawning takes place from March to July in shallow shoreline areas of the lake. An average female lays about 150 eggs. Waccamaw silverside eggs are unique in that they each have a small adhesive strip that secures them to the bottom. This keeps the eggs in place and away from deeper, less nutrient-rich water. After hatching, the fry form large schools in order to protect themselves from birds and larger fish, and they feed on free-floating plankton and other small plants and animals. The adults have similar tastes in food.

The Waccamaw silverside has a very short life cycle of approximately one year. The fish spawn and then most of them die, therefore a year with failed reproduction could prove to be disastrous for the species because no new fish would be added to the population.

Food source

In addition to its importance as a native fish, predatory fish in Lake Waccamaw depend on the Waccamaw silverside as a source of food. Local fishermen use this species as a reliable source of bait because it has a tendency to school in shallow shoreline areas. Happily, neither this fish's natural predators nor fishermen seeking bait are responsible for

The small size and exceedingly narrow shape of the Waccamaw silverside make the fish difficult to see.

WACCAMAW SILVERSIDE
North America

KEY SILVERSIDE
North America

the decline in the Waccamaw population. However, the presence of people does play a role in this situation. As human development and agriculture encroach around the lake, the amount of sediment and nutrients that flow into the lake have increased. These smother eggs and food and degrade water quality.

If the Waccamaw silverside is allowed to perish, a vital member of the lake's ecosystem will be lost forever. As a result of federal listing of the Waccamaw silverside and other Waccamaw fish as threatened and endangered, the lake is being given some protection. In addition, some protection against development of the surrounding areas is provided by the nearby Lake Waccamaw State Park.

William Manci

Sinarapan

(Mistichthys luzonensis)

IUCN: Lower risk

Class: Actinopterygii
Order: Perciformes
Family: Gobiidae
Length: ½ in. (1 cm)
Reproduction: Egg layer
Habitat: Large lakes and tributaries
Range: Camarines Sur Province, Luzon, Philippines

POSSIBLY ONE OF the most unusual freshwater fish found anywhere on Earth, the sinarapan is native to Lake Buhi and Lake Bato in the Camarines Sur Province, on the Philippine island of Luzon. When it was first discovered in 1902, an ichthyologist at the National Museum described it as the smallest known vertebrate. At the time it was thought that the smallest vertebrate was a killifish (*Heterandria formosa*) found in waters from South Carolina to Florida. The largest of these killifish was 22 millimeters long. Extensive collecting of the sinarapan revealed that the biggest specimen was a diminutive 15 millimeters.

Food source

Historically, the native peoples of the Philippines prized the tiny sinarapan as a food. Caught in large quantities, these fish were then dried in the sun to make a meal called *badi*. At the turn of the century in Manila, these fish were favored above all else in the little native restaurants where they were served.

Today *badi* is no longer served in the native restaurants. Years of exploration have taken a serious toll on these fish, which are found nowhere else on the planet. Furthermore, the introduction of various non-native fish has also been a factor in depleting the numbers of sinarapans to at times critically low levels.

Exotic pets

The tiny sinarapan is unique among the fish of the world. It is the only species of goby known to exist solely in freshwater. It is also extremely unique because the adults retain many characteristics of the larval (immature) form. This unusual strategy to cope with the rigors of aquatic life may be of great

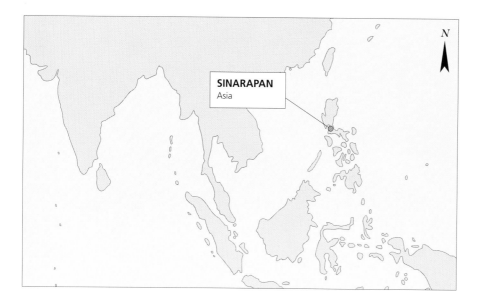

SINARAPAN
Asia

N

now family (*Cyprinidae*) in terms of its total number of species. Sinarapan are found throughout the world, both in freshwater and saltwater. There are two dorsal fins on its back, one of which has hardened spines. The tail, or caudal fin, is rounded. The remaining fins do not develop as fully as in other gobies, particularly the pectoral fin located just behind the cheek, or opercle. This species has a large head dominated by prominent eyes, and a mouth that is relatively large.

The small size of the sinarapan allows it to inhabit places that larger fish cannot occupy. It is this ability to use what scientists call microhabitats that has made the family successful, and the fish is now at lower risk.

Donald Proebstel

interest to science. The mechanisms by which this small fish develops and, even more importantly, the evolutionary significance of maintaining larval characteristics throughout the adult life of the sinarapan, could offer a new understanding about

the interaction of development and evolution.

The sinarapan, aside from its diminutive size and retention of some larval traits throughout adulthood, is not unlike other gobies (family *Gobiidae*). This family is second only to the min-

Red Siskin

(*Carduelis cucullata*)

ESA: Endangered

IUCN: Endangered

Class: Aves
Order: Passeriformes
Family: Fringillidae
Subfamily: Carduelinae
Length: 4–4½ in. (10–11.5 cm)
Weight: ⅓–½ oz. (8–11 g)
Diet: Seeds and insects
Range: Northeastern Colombia, northern Venezuela, and coastal islands

PEOPLE HAVE LITERALLY loved the red siskin to death. A beautiful yet tiny songbird, the red siskin appeals to those who keep

birds in cages. More than a century of trapping has left the red siskin just a memory in most of its former haunts. Continued trapping, which is illegal but profitable, may ultimately cause this bird to become extinct.

The male red siskin looks hooded, with an entirely black head, chin, throat, and nape that contrast sharply against a bright red back and breast. The shoulder and tail are also black. The outer half of the wing's flight feathers are also black, but the inner half of each feather is a dull red. The edges of the inner flight feathers are whitish, so the folded wing looks a bit striped. The female has a more subdued, brownish plumage washed with faint red on the crown and back. Her underparts, from chin to undertail, are gray, darker toward

the throat and lighter toward the tail. A patch of orangish red colors the breast. A little orangish red also shows in the wing.

At first the red siskins were trapped and sold just for their own appeal. Captive breeding soon proved that the siskins could be successfully crossed with canaries (*Serinus* sp.). The red siskin belongs to the same genus as the pine siskin (*Carduelis pinus*) and the American goldfinch (*Carduelis tristis*), both familiar songbirds in the United States. The canaries are closely related, but in a different genus of the same subfamily (*Carduelinae*). By mating red siskins with canaries, which are mostly yellow, breeders could produce red birds with the singing ability of canaries. The cross proved to be extremely valuable because

bird fanciers paid large prices for such birds. Also, male siskins mated to female canaries yielded fertile males that could be used for other breeding purposes.

Exotic pets

The global interest in cage birds really began in the early centuries of world exploration. Previously unknown animals were brought back by almost every expedition. The reception for new birds was especially great. The closing decades of the 1800s brought an unparalleled appetite for bird feathers that were suitably fancy for hats, and for live birds suited to parlor cages. In such a cultural atmosphere, the trapping and selling of red siskins progressed so quickly that the birds disappeared before they could be studied in the wild.

Vanishing

Collectors knew where to go to pay the local citizens to trap the birds, but they had neither the time nor the interest to study birds that they traded. The consequence was that the red siskin vanished before ornithologists

Brightly colored, active, and cheerful singers, red siskins have been desirable cage birds since the late 1800s.

could learn what it eats; when, where, and how often it nests; the average number of eggs laid; the survival rate of nestlings and fledglings; and so on. So rapid was the bird's decline that ornithologists were not even sure of its original habitat.

RED SISKIN
South America

Recent sightings of red siskins have been in mostly dry shrub lands or prairies with scattered shrubs. Ornithologists suspect that many, if not all, of these areas were formerly forests and woodlands. What cannot be determined is whether the trees were cut down before or after the red siskins disappeared. Although the red siskin has not been found in Colombia since 1947, the species has been introduced to several islands of the West Indies, including Puerto Rico.

Red siskins have been legally protected in Venezuela for many years. Because the species occurs in Puerto Rico, it is also covered by the U.S. Endangered Species Act. Internationally, it is covered in the Convention on International Trade in Endangered Species of Wild Fauna and Flora (CITES), which has a membership of 150 countries.

Caged trading

Despite this, some red siskins are still smuggled into foreign countries. In addition, not all cage bird fanciers live far away: many local people keep birds in cages. Even small-scale local trading could doom the red siskin. In 1990, ornithologists estimated that less than 1,000 red siskins survived in the wild.

The act of buying threatens the species' survival and drives up the price, which further inflates their appeal for collectors. This unethical behavior affects many more species than the red siskin, but none of the other cases matter for the siskin. If the collecting does not cease, the red siskin will eventually disappear from the wild.

Kevin Cook

SKINKS

Class: Reptilia

Order: Squamata

Suborder: Sauria

Family: Scincidae

Skinks are generally rather small, insectivorous lizards with cylindrical bodies and long, tapered tails. Their limbs are often small, and in some species they are missing completely. Some skinks live in trees, others live near water sources and are known to readily enter the water. As a rule, however, these reptiles are ground-dwellers or burrowers. Some skinks give birth to fully formed young, while others lay eggs.

The tail is perhaps the most interesting feature of the skink, as well as other lizards. It is useful to this reptile as a limb and helps to balance the body.

The tail has a more unusual characteristic, however. When skinks and many other lizards go on the defensive, they have the ability to lose part of their tail when attacked by a predator.

Usually the break in the skink's tail occurs at a fracture where it has been attacked. The severed tail may continue to move, and the predator is often distracted, allowing the skink to escape. The skink will regenerate a new tail, though this will probably be shorter, but it, too, can be used for escape.

Skinks are the most abundant lizards in Australia and New Guinea. Asia, Africa, and the western Pacific islands also have their share of skink species, which are found throughout the world. Worldwide, there are about 600 species. These reptiles are rather poorly represented in the Americas, and two New World skinks are now considered to be threatened.

Blue-tailed Mole Skink

(Eumeces egregius lividus)

ESA: Threatened

Length: 3½–5 in. (9–13 cm)

Clutch size: 3–7 eggs

Diet: Insects

Habitat: Pine scrub

Range: Central Florida

THE BLUE-TAILED mole skink has the short, stubby legs typical of skinks, as well as the cylindrical body common to its family, *Scincidae*. The tail is long, making up more than half of the total body length. Little is known of this skink's behavior, but mole skinks are known to eat insects such as cockroaches, spiders, or crickets.

Although this species may occasionally dig into the soil in search of food, it will most often forage on the surface.

Habitat

The blue-tailed mole skink lives in sand pine scrub areas where the most prolific vegetation includes pine trees, rosemary, and turkey oak. Skinks live in areas where there is an abundance of leaf litter, which provides food and nesting sites. A moist environment is needed for this species as well, because moisture plays an important role in the regulation of skink body heat.

Florida is one of the most rapidly developing regions in the United States. This has placed its wildlife, from alligators and panthers to skinks and deers, in a precarious situation. The blue-tailed mole skink is among these imperiled species. This species is found in Polk and Highland counties in central Florida. Since 1965 about 65 percent of this habitat has been lost because of large-scale conversion of land to agriculture or residential development. At least 14 species of birds and plants endemic to this area are threatened or endangered.

Natural fires

There are probably 20 population sites where the blue-tailed skink can still be found. Much of its range is privately owned, and has been converted to other uses such as citrus groves or rezoned for residential development. The remaining areas, where sand and long-leaf pines are prevalent, have recently been faced with another human-made dilemma. Many species of pine depend on naturally occurring fires for renewal; without these, hardwoods or other plants can take over and eventually overpower the pine scrub. People suppress these natural fires, and the encroaching vegetation eventually replaces scrub, changing the natural habitat of the blue-tailed mole skink.

The blue-tailed mole skink is found in a few protected sites within Florida, including Archbold Biological Station and Lake Kissimmee State Park.

The Florida government is trying to acquire pine scrub habitat in the central portion of the state to create a wildlife refuge. A recent acquisition of 1,000 acres (405 hectares) of habitat may help to protect some of Florida's native animals and plants from extinction.

Sand Skink

(Neoseps reynoldsi)

ESA: Threatened

IUCN: Vulnerable

Length: 4–5 in. (10–13 cm)
Clutch size: 2 eggs
Diet: Insects and other invertebrates
Habitat: Areas with loose, well-drained sand
Range: Central Florida

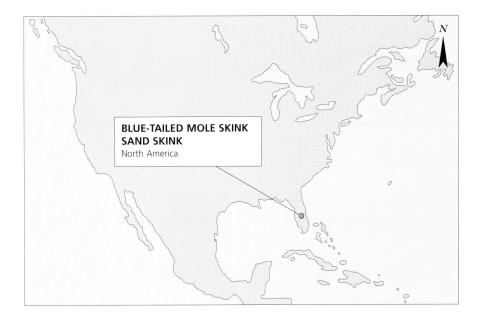

BLUE-TAILED MOLE SKINK
SAND SKINK
North America

THE SAND SKINK spends most of its time beneath the ground, burrowing up to 4 inches (10 centimeters) into the sand. It is specially adapted to move beneath the surface of the loose sands found in its habitat, pushing with its rear legs. Many of its physical traits are adaptations for this activity. For example, the tiny forelegs have one toe and can be retracted into body grooves, reducing the drag as the skink dives into the sand. A wedge-shaped head is another body feature that allows the skink to move in sand. Like other burrowing skinks, the sand skink has transparent patches that replace the usual lower eyelid, allowing it to see while burrowing, but which also protect its eyes.

Underground eater

Not surprisingly, this skink does most of its foraging underground. It eats a variety of small arthropods, but the diet consists principally of beetle larvae, termites, and spiders.

The sand skink's mating season is from March to May, and it is at this time that the animal is most active. The female deposits her eggs in early summer beneath some sort of cover, often a log or leaf debris, and remains close to the eggs to protect them.

Loose sands are an important part of the sand skink's environment. Its preferred habitat is in

The blue-tailed mole skink probably mates during the winter, with females laying the eggs underground.

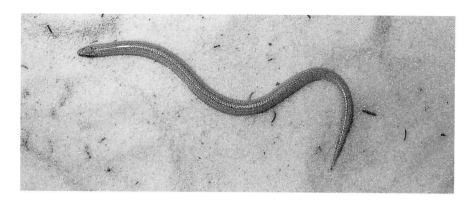

The sand skink is one of the many animals benefiting from Florida's commitment to saving its endangered wildlife.

areas of sand pine scrub, much like its close neighbor, the blue-tailed mole skink. Moisture is retained in the sand beneath the surface, generally by a covering of leaf litter. As with all skinks, the moisture in the sand helps to maintain body temperature. Leaf litter also provides the proper conditions for egg incubation. The sand skink's preferred habitat—sand pine scrub and pine scrub—depends on naturally occurring fires at intervals of about 20 years for renewal. Without these fires, hardwoods take over, which changes the natural habitat of the skink. In addition, because sand pine scrub and sand hills are suitable for conversion to orange groves, suitable habitat for the sand skink has recently been greatly reduced.

The sand skink was once found throughout the Lake Wales region of central Florida. Today, it occurs in isolated populations of Marion, Orange, Lake, Polk, and Highlands counties, where the habitat remains less disturbed. Census takers have recorded 31 sand skink populations. Fortunately, many of these occur on public land that offers some degree of protection for endangered species. The Nature Conservancy organization is actively involved in protecting the pine scrub habitat of central Florida. Their actions may help to preserve many types of the region's flora and fauna.

Elizabeth Sirimarco

See also Lizards.

Maned Sloth

(Bradypus torquatus)

ESA: Endangered

IUCN: Endangered

Class: Mammalia
Order: Xenarthra
Family: Bradypodidae
Weight: 8–10 lb. (3.5–4.5 kg)
Head-body length: 22–27 in. (55–69 cm)
Diet: Vegetation, twigs, buds
Habitat: Dense jungles, often near river banks
Range: Coastal forests of eastern Brazil

SLOTHFUL MEANS IDLE, lazy, and lethargic. As a consequence, humans have named a slow-moving, tree-dwelling mammal, the sloth. The maned sloth is not the most active of creatures and is rarely seen to exert itself, but this is partly due to the humid jungles where it lives, which are known to slow the pace of even the most active living creatures. A particularly sluggish circulatory system slows the sloth down even further, as does the weight of its heavy coat of body hair. The sloth is a sluggish eater as well and, even with the help of a stomach divided into several subchambers, it digests only the smallest percentage of the leaves, twigs, buds, and fruit it eats.

Lazy life

It is probably correct to say that the maned sloth moves just about as much as it needs to and no more. One of three species of three-toed sloths, the maned sloth hangs upside down from tree branches and sleeps 15 to 20 hours a day. Its diet consists almost entirely of buds, tender shoots, leaves, and small branches. This means that it almost never has to travel to meet its basic need for food.

Nocturnal at heart

Only at dusk does this small animal begin to move, shifting its position slightly on a branch, chewing on selected leaves, and sometimes moving in studied slow motion to a sitting position at the base of a tree branch.

The maned sloth has a small, round, flat face and small, round, inexpressive eyes to match. The ears are tiny and entirely hidden by long hairs. A short, stubby tail appears to serve no real purpose. It has a small mouth with thick, horny lips, which are used to break twigs and branches. The sloth lacks incisor teeth that might normally do such tearing work. Inside the mouth it has 18 enamel-free molars that grow throughout the animal's life, even as they are worn down by continuous chewing.

The maned sloth has a long, gray-blond coat that parts in the ventral region on the front of the animal's body instead of along the animal's spine, enabling rain and moisture to run off more easily. Most mammals have seven neck vertebrae (bones that make up the spinal column of an animal's skeleton), though a few have eight. The maned sloth has no fewer than nine. These extra vertebrae enable it to tuck its head onto its chest while sleeping and rotate it a full 270 degrees without moving the rest of its sluggish body. Once again, the sloth only moves as much as it needs.

Green camouflage

Some experts have speculated that the animal's preference for hanging with its head tucked onto its chest is a survival strategy intended to fool predators into thinking that the immobile sloth is not an animal at all. Whether or not this is true, it is certain that the sloth derives another type of protection from its coloring: one or two forms of algae grow in the long, grooved hairs of the animal's fur. In a perfect example of what biologists call a symbiotic relationship, the sloth provides the algae with a home and, in return, it is granted the benefits of a greenish camouflage. The sloth's greenish cast makes the animal look like a

naturally occurring pod or nest, particularly when seen from below in direct sunlight.

More than one naturalist has joked that the sloth is the only mammal that grows on trees. Indeed, in more than one sense, the sloth does grow on a tree. It eats, sleeps, mates, gives birth, nurses, and even dies—usually while hanging upside down—on a tree. The maned sloth is able to spend most of its life hanging upside down, thanks to its three long, hooked claws that resemble meat hooks. So securely do its claws fasten onto tree limbs that, under normal circumstances, it cannot be shaken off a tree limb. Even in death the sloth clings to its perch. The maned sloth

The maned sloth is highly arboreal, spending most of its time in trees. This animal eats leaves, shoots, and small branches almost exclusively, so it seldom has to move from its tree home to find food.

descends to the ground perhaps twice a week in order to urinate and defecate. Otherwise, it will only descend in order to move to another tree that is inaccessible from the one it is currently in.

Movement

As slow as it is under normal circumstances, the sloth can move in a hurry when it has to, provided it is in a tree. Yet, if given the choice, the maned sloth would probably choose to swim a wide river rather than climb down a tree and move overland to the next desirable tree. For while the maned sloth is an excellent swimmer, it is almost helpless on the ground.

Nocturnal at heart

Unfortunately, the razor sharp, nonretractable claws that allow the sloth to hang upside down indefinitely also help to prevent it from walking. Unable to balance itself on its claws, the sloth is compelled to drag itself over the ground. If cornered, a sloth will fight for its life and use its claws to inflict wounds in an overconfident jaguar or ocelot. It will also use its claws to defend a particular tree branch from fellow sloths. Other than those exceptions, the sloth is not a fighter. Its survival depends on its ability to go unnoticed.

MANED SLOTH
Brazil

Breeding mostly takes place in March or April, although sloths have been observed mating during other times. Females rarely give birth more than once every two years. Single sloth babies are born after a gestation period of around 17 to 26 weeks.

The baby attaches itself to its mother's fur and stays attached, whether nursing or resting, until it becomes independent.

The maned sloth population has been reduced by human hunting: natives have long had a taste for its lean meat, and its shaggy coat is used to cover saddles by horse riders who prize its water-repellent qualities. Even jewelry is made from sloth claws.

Recently the sloth has felt the pressure of deforestation. Although there have been efforts to introduce the sloth to other areas, the animal has been unresponsive to forced habitat changes. Unlike two-toed sloths, three-toed sloths do not thrive in captivity, often dying within a week after being removed from their original environment.

Renardo Barden

Delta Smelt

(Hypomesus transpacificus transpacificus)

ESA: Threatened

IUCN: Endangered

Class: Actinopterygii
Order: Salmoniformes
Family: Osmeridae
Length: 4⅓ in. (11 cm)
Reproduction: Egg layer
Habitat: Stream channels and bays in fresh or brackish water
Range: Sacramento-San Joaquin River Delta, California

THE DELTA SMELT has long been a familiar species to fishermen in Suisun Bay and the delta region of central California. Named for

the region where the Sacramento and San Joaquin Rivers meet and finish their journey to San Francisco Bay, until recently this fish has been present in large numbers. It was only relatively recently that has the delta smelt been the subject of concern, with a reduction in total numbers of at least 90 percent since 1970.

Many people are aware that the state of California is renowned as one of the top agricultural regions in the world. What many people are unaware of is that water from the Sacramento and San Joaquin Rivers makes much of this agricultural success possible. Each year it seems that more and more water is demanded by the growing agriculture industry. Compounding this demand is an increasing human population, which

requires more river water for rapidly growing cities and towns. As more water is diverted from both these rivers and pumped from underground sources, changes in the physical, chemical, and biological makeup of the delta region are inevitable.

Short life span

For the delta smelt the stakes are high; the delta is its only home. As river water flows diminish, the ability of the delta smelt to adapt and cope with the situation diminishes.

Biologists are concerned about the short one- to two-year life span of the fish. As a result, reproductive failure during any single year can have a devastating effect on the species as a whole (fish species with longer breeding lives can better withstand a bad breeding year). Data collected in the field indicate that these failures have occurred.

Adding insult to injury is a small potential threat by a non-native relative that was introduced to the state in 1959. The Japanese variety of the delta smelt, the wakasagi (*Hypomesus nipponensis*), has been stocked into reservoirs as forage for other, larger predators. The opportunity exists for this non-native species to escape from these reservoirs and move downstream to the delta region. If this migration occurs, competition for scarce and precious spawning and nursery habitat could occur.

Appearance

The delta smelt is slender in shape and streamlined to reduce drag, a typical characteristic of river fish. The mouth is upturned, and the lower jaw juts forward prominently. The dorsal fin on the back, the pectoral fins just behind the gills, and the pelvic fins on the belly are triangular in shape. The tail fin is

deeply forked, a sign of a strong swimmer. A fleshy adipose fin is located on the back between the dorsal and tail fins. This feature is common to many fishes in the order *Salmoniformes*. The anal fin is long and is deepest at it leading edge. This fish is uniformly light metallic blue in color, with a luster that makes it appear almost transparent.

This fish spawns from February to May, with a peak from March to May when a female can produce about 2,000 eggs. Both

The tiny range of the delta smelt is a key problem in its struggle to survive. Found only in the Sacramento-San Joaquin River Delta, any damage to its habitat leaves this fish with nowhere to go.

sexes spend most of the year in the lower end of the delta and move upstream before spawning begins. Most individuals reach sexual maturity after their first year, but some wait until their second to reproduce; usually adults do not survive to spawn a second time. This fish's favorite food includes the planktonic animals that live near the surface and in the water column, as well as bottom-dwelling invertebrates.

Securing the future of this species will depend on the priorities of decision makers who allocate water from the Sacramento and San Joaquin Rivers. Recent events indicate that the tide may be turning in favor of the delta smelt and other fish that use these rivers. However, these efforts will be wasted if non-native fish compete with the delta smelt. Unfortunately, this problem is as difficult to cope with as habitat degradation.

William Manci

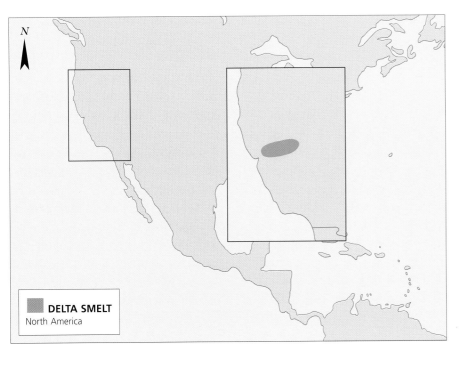

DELTA SMELT
North America

SNAILS

Class: Gastropoda

So much of the current predicament of endangered species is related to the loss of habitats that some animals need to survive. One animal that is very affected by the continuing human destruction of valuable land is the snail. Because of its size, is is often overlooked in the debate surrounding progress versus wildlife protection.

There are three major groups of snails. The first are from the subclass called Prosobranchia. These have gills, a shell, and an operculum (an opening that the snail can use to seal itself inside its shell). They occupy mostly marine and freshwater habitats, although some have also adapted to terrestrial habitats.

The second major group of snails are the sea slugs, all inhabitants of marine habitat and part of the subclass Opisthobranchia. Nearly all of these snails have no shell or only a remnant of a shell. There are no known species of the Opisthobranchia that are believed to be endangered at this time.

The third major group of snails are the air-breathing snails of the subclass Pulmonata. These snails—called pulmonates—have primitive lungs. Pulmonates can be found in all three major habits: terrestrial, freshwater, and marine.

The marine varieties live only in the intertidal zone where, with their air-breathing capabilities, they have the ability to survive in a habitat that is exposed at low tide. The advantages to snails that can live in this zone include the richer available food resources and a greater chance of avoiding predators.

Freshwater pulmonate snails have developed the ability to attach themselves to the surface of the water, floating in order to utilize oxygen at the very place where the air and water layers join up.

Some freshwater snails live on the stems of aquatic plants that grow above the water's surface, so that they are able to climb up the stem and out of the water whenever they need a breath of fresh air.

Others snail species live just beneath the water's surface at the shoreline, enabling these snails to crawl easily out of the water for fresh air.

Most pulmonates are land snails, and they can only manage to obtain water through taking advantage of rainfall or a heavy morning dew.

As with the sea slugs, none of the known marine snails are considered endangered. In fact, many species of marine snails are so widespread that they can be found from Hawaii to the east coast of Africa and from Finland to Argentina. All known examples of endangered snail species occur either in fresh water or on land. The reason these snail species are endangered is that their habitats are threatened with pollution or affected by the damming of rivers that alter water flows and create artificial lakes, and the snails themselves are often devastated by harvesting.

Freshwater species

The problems faced by freshwater snails are not unlike those faced by freshwater fish. One snail that illustrates this is the tulotoma (*Tulotoma magnifica*). This snail lives in cool, clean, oxygen-rich water in free-flowing rivers. For the past 150 years the tulotoma was known to be widely distributed in the Alabama and Coosa River systems. However, today it is extinct in the Alabama River and occurs in only a few tributary streams of the Coosa River. The creation of artificial lakes by the building of dams stopped the free flow of the rivers, and without the constant renewal of fresh water into the tulotoma's habitat it will not thrive. The tulotoma is close to extinction today.

Mexican snails

In Mexico there are 12 species of freshwater snails that are endemic to the intermontane desert basin known as Cuatro Ciénegas in the state of Coahuila, Mexico. Cuatro Ciénegas (which literally means *four marshes*) is a region fed by small desert springs and is home to many aquatic species not found anywhere else. The evolutionary uniqueness of these species is due to the isolation of the Cuatro Ciénegas from the ocean. The aquatic habitats of this basin have been isolated for perhaps one million years. The snails native to this region are listed by the Convention on International Trade in Endangered Species of Wild Fauna and Flora (CITES), meaning that their exportation is prohibited.

A number of snails known as the Mexipyrgus (*Mexipyrgus* sp.) are found in isolated locations within the Cuatro Ciénegas. Species of the genus *Mexipyrgus* live buried in the very top of the soft ooze and mud that covers the bottom of each laguna (the Spanish word for lake). Each snail is named after its specific location, for example, Mexipyrgus de

Oeste Laguna El Mojarral (*Mexipyrgus mojarralis*) or Mexipyrgus de Lugo (*Mexipyrgus lugoi*). The Mexithauma de Ciénegas snail (*Mexithauma quadripaludium*) is found in several lagunas within the Cuatro Ciénegas, where it lives on hard surfaces such as stone and shell. The Nymphophilus de Minckley snail (*Nymphophilus minckleyi*) lives on water lily leaves in several rivers and lagunas within the Cuatro Ciénegas.

There are other endangered snails in Mexico. Miller's pebblesnail (*Cochliopina milleri*) is known only from the Rio Mesquites, where it occurs in the soft mud of backwaters away from the main current. Coahuilix de Hubbs snail (*Coahuilix hubbsi*) is known only from one pool of Boso de la Becerra, where it lives in a groundwater spring. Durangonella de Coahuila (*Durangonella coahuilae*) is known from Laguna Grande close to the mouth of the Rio Churince, where it lives on the soft bottom mud of the laguna. The beautiful Paludiscala de oro snail (*Paludiscala caramba*) lives in subterranean groundwater of a spring in the area of El Mojarral. Until recently, this snail was known only from its elegantly ornamented shell, which resembles the marine snail genus *Epitonium*, or Wentletrap. Because of its subterranean existence, this snail is blind.

Cumberland and Tennessee

The Cumberland and Tennessee River systems in the eastern United States make up a vast, six-state region that came to prominence during the Great Depression. As a way to revitalize these states' economy, the Tennessee Valley Authority was created to build dams and other flood control mechanisms in order to generate hydroelectric power and help agriculture. A flurry of construction greatly altered these river systems in the decades since that time. Needless to say, many freshwater fish species suffered as a direct consequence.

Snails are not immune to these changes in their habitat. The muddy rocksnail (*Lithasia salebrosa*) was recovered from numerous localities in the Cumberland and Tennessee River systems of Alabama, Tennessee, and Kentucky between 1834 and 1940. Since then, however, it has only been found at two very localized areas of the lower Tennessee River in Alabama and Tennessee, and in the Duck River in Tennessee. The warty rocksnail (*Lithasia lima*) once inhabited the Tennessee River system in Alabama and one of its large tributaries, the Elk River, in Alabama and Tennessee. Today it is found only in the Elk River. At one time the rugose rocksnail (*Lithasia*

The rare *Liguus* tree snail is found in hardwood hammocks. There may be as many as 50 varieties of this rare gastropod.

jayana) lived in the Cumberland and Tennessee River systems of Tennessee and Kentucky. However, recent studies have found this snail living only in the Duck River of Tennessee, where it inhabits algae-covered rocks in riffle and shoal areas.

The spiny riversnail (*Io fluvialis*) formerly inhabited the entire middle and upper portions of the Tennessee River system above Muscle Shoals, Alabama. Numerous snail species were described at different times from specimens of the spiny riversnail, before biologists realized that they were all one species. What fooled the scientists was the size and number of spines on the snail's shell. It is not unusual for the same species of snail to generate shells with different numbers of spines.

Recent studies prove that naturally occurring populations of this snail are restricted to small portions of the Clinch and Nolichucky rivers in Virginia and Tennessee. However, a successful population transplant recently took place into the north fork of the Holston River in Virginia and Tennessee. This species appears to be thriving in a habitat where chemical waste had once driven it to local extinction.

American land species

Historically confined to Stock Island in the southern Florida Keys, the Stock Island treesnail (*Ortholicus reses*) has recently been introduced into Key Largo as well as mainland Florida. The species has been extensively studied by Jane Deisler, curator of natural history at the Corpus Christi Museum. During the early 1980s she observed two

More than half of the 41 described species of Oahu *Achatinella* are now believed to be extinct. These tree snails from the island of Oahu are victims of a predatory snail introduced by humans to Hawaii.

populations of this species on Stock Island. One of these two remaining populations has apparently been eradicated by renovations made to a golf course, while the other population has been seriously reduced by the construction of a parking lot. Seemingly small changes in our environment can represent huge, life-threatening changes to other species.

Distinctive name

The painted snake coiled forest snail (*Anguispira picta*) is listed as a threatened species by the U.S. Fish and Wildlife Service. It is known only from Buck Creek Cove southwest of Sherwood, in Franklin County, Tennessee. There it lives between elevations of 750 to 800 feet (229 to 244 meters), feeding on lichen that grows on limestone outcrops. This snail is considered to be threatened because its population is restricted to a small

area. Unregulated timber cutting, a chance forest fire, or ambitious quarrying could easily destroy what is left of this beautiful snail's entire habitat.

The Iowa Pleistocene snail (*Discus macclintocki*) is listed as endangered by the U.S. Fish and Wildlife Service. Based on fossil evidence, this medium-sized snail was widely distributed in the Midwest during the Pleistocene epoch (hence the name). However, by 1984 the Iowa Pleistocene snail had become restricted to about 18 small sites in the region of Clayton and Dubuque Counties in Iowa and Jo Davies County in Illinois.

The tiny Virginia fringed mountain snail (*Polygyriscus virginianus*) is a geographically restricted species known from only a 1½-mile (2.5-kilometer) strip along the north bank of the New River in Pulaski County, Virginia. One of the rarest and most unusual land snails in North America, the Virginia fringed mountain snail is apparently a blind burrower, living in lower layers of leaf litter. It is listed by the U.S. Fish and Wildlife Service as an endangered species.

Protective coating

The Santa Barbara shelledslug (*Binneya notabilis*) was known only from a single locality: the head of a ravine about 250 feet (76 meters) from the sea on Santa Barbara Island, one of the California Channel Islands. There it thrived for a few months each year during the rainy season. During the dry season it would burrow itself down into a mat of plant roots and cover itself with mucus that would dry to

form a tough, leathery coating. As early as 1948 this species was feared to be extinct, but more recent surveys suggest that it may still exist.

Farming on the island apparently destroyed much of the habitat necessary for the survival of this species.

Another Channel Islands species, the Santa Barbara island snail (*Micrarionta facta*), was abundant during the Pleistocene epoch, three million years ago, as shown by the fossil record. Today it is considered rare. Farming, again, was the apparent culprit.

The Chittenango ovate amber snail (*Succinea chittenangoensis*) is a threatened species. It occurs only in an area that includes the Chittenango Falls in Madison County, New York. There it lives on rock ledges covered by seepage or spray from the falls. It prefers cool, sunlit areas of lush, herbaceous growth, areas made possible by the spray zone of the falls. It apparently feeds on microflora growing on the limestone rocks. The Chittenango ovate amber snail is threatened by its very limited geographic range and by pollution.

Cliff dweller

The noonday snail (*Mesodon clarki nantahala*) is known only from high cliffs that rise from 1,900 to 3,100 feet (579.5 to 945.5 meters) above sea level along a small southeast bank of the Nantahala River in Swain County, North Carolina. This snail is threatened due to the extremely restricted range of its habitat and by increased human activity from canoe users and campers trampling its natural habitat. The threat of forest fire could do serious damage to the noon day snail population as well.

The flat-spired three-toothed snail (*Triodopsis platysayoides*) is another threatened species because of its geographically restricted range adjacent to the Cheat River in Monongahela County, West Virginia. Most of the species' known range is within Coopers Rock State Forest. The population, estimated to contain only a few hundred individuals, lives in leaf litter among sandstone boulders. The snails feed on lichen that grow on the sandstone. Tourism, which can narrow the region inhabited by the snail, is one of the biggest problems for a species with such an initially tiny range.

Lichen eater

The Trinity bristlesnail (*Monadenia setosa*) mainly occurs along stream margins with dense deciduous underbrush in Trinity County, California. The Trinity bristlesnail feeds on one or more species of encrusting lichens in leaf litter and on tree trunks.

The costate mountainsnail (*Oreohelix idahoensis idahoensis*) covers the soft limestone of the east bank of the Salmon River in Idaho. The limited distribution of this species makes it highly vulnerable to extinction because of the potential destruction of its natural habitat. Another Idaho species, the boulder pile mountainsnail (*Oreohelix jugalis jugalis*), is nearby. As with the costate mountainsnail, the boulder pile mountainsnail is highly vulnerable to extinction as a result of its limited distribution and the potential for destruction of its natural habitat.

Pacific terrestrial species

Snails that live exclusively on land have their share of habitat problems. The swarthy cyclophorus (*Cyclophorus aquilus*) is one of many unique terrestrial snails from the tropics that breathe using gills rather than lungs and have an operculum, or door, with which to seal themselves inside their shells when they are threatened. The swarthy cyclophorus is able to breathe with gills due to the high humidity of the tropical rain forests it inhabits (located in the Singapore region of the Malay Peninsula). Recently it has been reported that this snail has probably become extinct.

On the island of Oahu are snails that belong to the genus *Achatinella*. As of 1979, 22 of the 41 described species from this genus were believed to be extinct, and the remaining 19 are all endangered. These beautiful tree snails live in the forests of the Koolau and Waianae mountain ranges. There are less than 50 individuals remaining of certain *Achatinella* species, and only three species are believed to have populations of 1,000 individuals.

Habitat destruction caused by the clearing of native forests for farming is one major factor in these snails' decline. Another is the introduction of feral goats, pigs, and rodents. Ironically, one of the worst culprits is another snail. A predatory, carnivorous snail (*Euglandina rosea*) was introduced by humans to control populations of the giant African snail (*Achatina fulica*). Unfortunately, *E. rosea* is so efficient that it has probably made a number of *Achatinella* species extinct and reduced the numbers of the remaining species.

A genus of Hawaiian snails, the Kauai carelia (*Carelia* spp.), had a total of 31 species or subspecies on the island of Kauai. All known species of this genus are now believed to be extinct, and this has been attributed to the introduction of the same carnivorous snail, *E. rosea*.

In another part of the Pacific, the snail genus *Partula*, once endemic to the island of Moorea near Tahiti in French Polynesia, is now critically endangered. Some of these species were relocated to laboratories where they could be raised. The same carnivorous snail, *Euglandina rosea*, had almost destroyed the remaining wild populations of *Partula* by 1988. Species of the genus *Samoana* are also in danger from *E. rosea*.

Austalasian snails

Further south and west in New Zealand, Busby's paryphanta (*Paryphanta busbyi*) is reported to be near extinction in the forests of Northland Peninsula. The total range of this species occupies only a small area, and its decline is a result of clearing lowland forests for the purpose of

Busby's paryphanta (*Paryphanta busbyi*), a species from New Zealand, is on the edge of extinction.

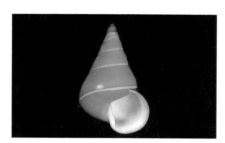

From left to right, the snails pictured above are as follows: Kauai Carelia (*Carelia* spp.), family Amastridae; Hong's Placostyle (*Placostylus hongii*), family Bulimulidae; Stock Island treesnail (*Ortholicus reses*), family Bulimulidae; Cambodian Bertia (*Bertia cambodjiensis*), family Trochomorphidae; Manus Green Papuina (*Papuina pulcherrima*), family Camaenidae; Daphne Helicostyla (*Helicostyla daphnis*), family Bradybaenidae.

agriculture. In addition, the introduction of rats and mice to New Zealand has added increased pressure from predation toward this species.

The flax snail (*Placostylus hongii*) is now restricted to the Poor Knights Islands. These are two small islands off the east coast of the Northland Peninsula. This species used to be endemic to mainland New Zealand, but agriculture and urbanization have eradicated this species entirely.

South of Australia is the large island of Tasmania. There, in the temperate rain forest of the northeast, lives the granulated Tasmanian snail (*Anoglypta launcestonensis*). A moderately large, beautiful land snail, the

granulated Tasmanian lives in deep leaf litter and fern gullies. The clearing of the rain forest for agricultural purposes has affected the few thousand remaining individuals. Perhaps the only way to guarantee the survival of this species would be to establish a natural reserve. This species is not listed as vulnerable by IUCN–The World Conservation Union.

Beautiful green snail

The Manus green tree snail (*Papuina pulcherrima*) is endemic to the rain forest of Manus Island in northern Papua, New Guinea. Unfortunately, it lives closely with trees that are highly desirable to the timber industry. Its brilliant green makes it highly attractive to collectors. While shell collectors have had some impact on this species, it is the local timber industry's desire to remove this snail's natural habitat that will certainly result in extinction if something is not done to prevent it. The Manus green tree snail is listed by the U.S. Fish and Wildlife Service as an endangered species, so none may be

legally be brought into the United States. However, there are reports that specimens are being illegally brought in for the shell trade.

Freshwater species abroad

Of the freshwater pulmonate family Lymnaeidae, the glutinous snail (*Myxas glutinosa*) is found in many countries in Europe but is known only from two sites in Britain. It is listed under the U.K. Wildlife and Countryside Act of 1981.

The Tasmanian freshwater limpet (*Ancylastrum cumingianus*) is found only in a few lakes and streams of the mountainous region of central Tasmania. This species is an important source of food for trout that have recently been introduced into some Tasmanian lakes for sport fishing. Unfortunately, because of the introduced trout, this Tasmanian species is nearly extinct.

Several species of the genus *Vertigo*, such as the Des Moulins snail, the *Vertigo moulinsiana*, the narrow-mouthed whorlsnail, the *Vertigo angustior*, and the round-mouthed whorlsnail are known to occur in small, localized populations in some European marshes. As the habitat of *Vertigo* species becomes decimated through the actions of people, these species will increasingly be in danger of extinction.

The Madeiran land snail (*Leiostyla abbreviata*), known only from the island of Madeira in the eastern Atlantic Ocean west of Morocco, is a small but attractive snail that was reported to be rare as early as 1878. Threats to its survival include overgrazing by domestic animals and tourism development. It is now listed as critically endangered by the IUCN.

Plant's Gulella snail (*Gulella plantii*) is a medium-sized, carnivorous land snail living in coastal brush in the area of Durban, South Africa. This rare

These are costate mountain snails, found only in one place: the Salmon River of Idaho.

species is threatened by habitat loss due to increased urbanization and brush clearance.

Extinct Asian species

The Cambodian bertia (*Bertia cambodjiensis*) is a large member of a family of land snails that typically has small to medium sized, top-shaped shells. An unusual feature of the Cambodian bertia is the fact that the aperture, or opening of the shell, is sinistral (meaning left handed), rather than the more typical dextral or right handed opening.

A former inhabitant of the steamy tropical jungles of Cambodia, the Cambodian bertia is now believed to be extinct.

The daphne helicostyla (*Helicostyla daphnis*) was known only from the rain forests near Barili, a town on Cebu Island in the Philippine Islands. Destruction of the rain forests by agriculture and the logging industry have had a serious impact on this large, beautiful tree snail. The daphne helicostyla is also believed to be extinct.

C. Clifton Coney

SNAKES

Class: Reptilia

Order: Squamata

Suborder: Serpentes

Snakes are limbless, scaly reptiles with long, flexible bodies. They are closely related to lizards, making up the order Squamata. The two reptile groups differ only in that snakes lack forelimbs, as well as movable eyelids and external ears. Certain adaptations also differ in the skull and jaw.

Like other reptiles, snakes are poikilothermic, meaning that their body temperature varies with the environment, so snake populations are often damaged by slight habitat changes.

Snakes can be found all over the world, from the Arctic Circle in Europe to the southernmost tip of South America. Snakes

occupy important ecological niches wherever they occur, but they are particularly important in agricultural regions, where they prey on rodents and other pests. Nonetheless, people have traditionally feared snakes, and this has led to the disappearance of certain types of species.

All the following snakes are members of the large snake family Colubridae. The Atlantic salt marsh snake, the Concho water snake, the Eastern indigo snake, and the San Francisco garter snake have not been studied extensively, so recovery plans are hard to devise. The first three were previously listed by IUCN–The World Conservation Union as threatened and the latter as endangered, but they were not evaluated by the time the Red List was compiled. Until more data is available, the species are included with other endangered taxa, because they may still be at risk.

Atlantic Salt Marsh Snake

(Nerodia fasciata taeniata)

ESA: Threatened

Length: 2 ft. (0.6 m)
Reproduction: Oviparous, 2 to 4 young born live
Diet: Small fish
Habitat: Tidal wetlands
Range: Florida

THE ATLANTIC SALT marsh snake is also known as the East Coast striped water snake because it has a pattern of dark stripes down either side of its pale olive body. The stripes fragment and turn to blotches as they approach

The Atlantic salt marsh snake is found in coastal salt marshes and mangrove swamps along the Atlantic coast of central Florida.

the tail. A single pale stripe extends down the center of the spine, and the belly is black with a row of yellowish spots.

Watery habitat

Salt marsh snakes are the only group of North American snakes restricted to salt water. The Atlantic salt marsh snake is generally active at night during low tides. It preys upon small fish trapped in shallow tide pools of the wetlands where it lives. The action of the tides greatly influences the activities of the snakes. A shy reptile, the snake will seek shelter when disturbed, often in fiddler crab burrows, which are commonly present in its habitat.

Reduced habitat

As with much of Florida's flora and fauna, this snake has declined in numbers largely because of the state's increasing agricultural and residential development. As the coastal wetlands are drained or filled to develop properties along the waterfront, the available habitat of the Atlantic salt marsh snake and its range are significantly reduced.

Interbreeding

Habitat disturbances are also suspected to encourage the interbreeding of this subspecies with the more common freshwater snake species, *Nerodia fasciata pictiventris*. If this hybridization continues, the Atlantic salt marsh snake could disappear as a distinct subspecies. An additional threat comes from reptile collectors, although the number of snakes that are collected remains unknown.

The U.S. Fish and Wildlife Service, as well as Florida biologists, are now conducting research on the species. These studies may assist in future conservation efforts. Prohibitions on collecting the snake are being strictly enforced.

Concho Water Snake
(Nerodia harteri paucimaculata)

ESA: Threatened

Length: 3 ft. (0.9 m)
Reproduction: Egg laying
Diet: Minnows, amphibians, crustaceans
Habitat: Flowing streams
Range: Texas

THE CONCHO WATER snake makes its home in deep, flowing waters or in shallow areas where rocks and boulders provide cover. This snake uses the woody vegetation along banks for basking, and seeks protected pools or rock piles for its nesting sites. It eats minnows, frogs and toads, as well as small crustaceans.

The Concho water snake once occupied a range of more than 280 miles (450 kilometers) along the Colorado and Concho rivers in western Texas, but this habitat has been divided by the construction of dams and reservoirs. Tributaries of these two rivers have also been affected by smaller water diversion projects. These dams and reservoirs are used primarily for irrigation.

Dams create a problem for aquatic animals by taking over habitat in upstream areas and altering the water flow downstream, leaving only small portions of the river unaltered. Water level and flow is often reduced, which can lead to increased sedimentation. In addition, populations are separated by these dams and reservoirs, which further limit an endangered creature's chance for survival. Water pollution increases at the same time, caused by the surface runoff of fertilizers, herbicides, and pesticides used for agriculture in the region.

Today, this water snake can be found in fragmented areas along some 200 miles (320 kilometers) of the Colorado and Concho Rivers.

The Concho water snake is grayish on its upperparts, with four rows of sporadic, dark brown blotches along the top and sides.

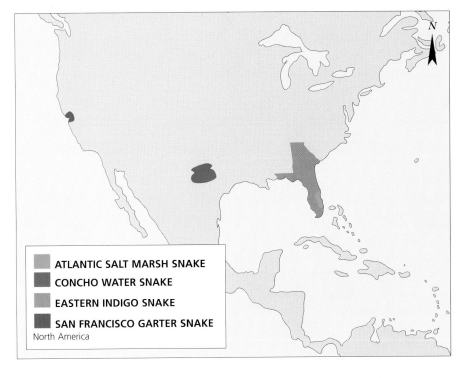

ATLANTIC SALT MARSH SNAKE
CONCHO WATER SNAKE
EASTERN INDIGO SNAKE
SAN FRANCISCO GARTER SNAKE
North America

In an area where agriculture is important, preserving native flora and fauna is often a low priority. The human population is growing in the western Texas habitat of the Concho water snake, increasing water demand. This almost certainly means additional water diversion projects will be developed for residential, industrial, and agricultural use. A number of such projects can be expected in the future.

Eastern Indigo Snake
(Drymarchon corais couperi)

ESA: Threatened

Length: 8½ ft. (2.5 m)
Reproduction: Oviparous
Diet: Small animals
Habitat: Mature pine forests, gopher burrows
Range: Alabama, Florida, Georgia, Mississippi, South Carolina

THE EASTERN INDIGO snake is a member of the family Colubridae. It is one of the largest and stoutest of the North American colubrids, reaching a length of more than 8 feet (2.5 meters). The body color is a uniform blue-black, from which it gets the name *indigo*. The chin, throat, and cheeks are a faint red or cream color.

This snake can feed on a variety of animals, including other snakes, small tortoises, mammals, and amphibians. It is often found in burrows excavated by the gopher tortoise (*Gopherus polyphemus*), another endangered species. In these burrows, it seeks refuge, particularly during harsh winter months. The gopher tortoise plays an important role in the survival of the eastern indigo snake, as well as of other species within its range.

Distribution

Indigo snakes can be found from the coastal plains of southeastern United States to northern Argentina. There are several subspecies, but only the eastern indigo and the Texas indigo are found in the United States. Today the eastern indigo snake is found primarily in Florida and Georgia. It was once found from South Carolina through Georgia and Florida into the Keys, and westward to southern Alabama. It may have also occurred in Mississippi. In Florida, mature pine forests are its favorite habitat. It is also found in flat woods, dry glades, farmland fields, and along canal banks, where it uses crab holes for its den. In Georgia, it inhabits sandhill regions in communities where periodic fires renew the plant life. When these naturally occurring fires are suppressed by people, hardwoods can overtake the longleaf pines, turkey oaks, and wiregrass of the sandhills, making the habitat unsuitable for the indigo snake.

As the mature longleaf pine forests of the South have declined, so too has the eastern indigo snake. Agricultural and residential development have deforested millions of acres throughout the region and the remaining lands have been degraded or affected by fire suppression. Many acres have been logged, then replaced with pine species that will grow more quickly than hardwood trees. Such forests cannot support the eastern indigo snake.

Value

Indigos have commercial value because they are attractive, docile, and nonpoisonous. These snakes are known to sell for as much as $225 through mail order. Public education is necessary to stop the persecution of snakes. If people are made aware that the eastern indigo snake does not pose a threat, it is less likely that the species will be killed on sight. Collectors must realize that the indigo snake is threatened; existing laws about the trade of the reptile must be enforced. The U.S. Fish and Wildlife Service has suggested that a program be initiated to monitor sales in trade catalogs in order to stop illegal dealers.

Survival

For the eastern indigo snake to survive, steps must be taken to save its habitat. The survival of a large number of Florida's other unique animal and plant species depends on the preservation of mature forests. Controlled burning should be implemented to prevent overgrowth of hardwoods. In addition, portions of the forests must be maintained as wilderness areas where development is prohibited. In 1989, a new refuge was created in south

Because the eastern indigo snake is a large, conspicuous, and slow species, it is easily persecuted by people who kill snakes. Loss of suitable habitat has only worsened this problem.

Florida to protect the Florida panther and other endangered species. Many other animals will benefit from this refuge, including the eastern indigo snake and the gopher tortoise on which it depends. Birds such as the bald eagle (*Haliaeetus leucocephalus*) and the peregrine falcon (*Falco peregrinus anatum*) are other species protected within the Florida Panther National Wildlife Refuge. The eastern indigo snake reproduces well in captivity, and its re-introduction to the wild may be attempted once its habitat has been protected.

Giant Garter Snake

(Thamnophis gigas)

ESA: Threatened

IUCN: Vulnerable

Class: Reptilia
Order: Serpentes
Family: Colubridae
Diet: Amphibians and fish
Reproduction: 10–45 young
Habitat: Wetlands, ponds, and streams
Range: California

THAMNOPHIS, A new world genus, is related to the more cosmopolitan water snakes. Due to their wide distribution, which ranges across from British Columbia through Mexico and into South America, and due to numerous species, they could be regarded as possibly the most successful of all species of new world snake. Garter snakes are generally asso-

ciated with wetlands or wooded, moist habitats where their preferred prey, frogs and earthworms, are abundant. These snakes can also be found in large, urban areas.

The giant garter snake once occupied the Central Valley of California, including the Sacramento and San Joaquin Valleys from Butte County to Kern County. Waterways pollution, loss and fragmentation of wetland habitat through agricultural and flood control, along with the introduction of predators such as the bullfrog, largemouth bass and feral cat, have reduced its numbers, leading to species decline.

The giant garter snake was listed as threatened by the State of California in 1971 and by the United States Fish and Wildlife Service in 1993. This species is more aquatic than most other species of garter snake and occupies small lakes, open marshland, and shallow streams. They are known to inhabit irrigation and drainage channels.

As its name implies, the giant garter snake is the largest species in the genus, though females are much larger than males. A female giant garter snake was recorded measuring 5½ feet (1.7 meters) long and weighing 12 pounds (68 grams). The dorsal color varies from brownish to olive with three yellow stripes. Some younger specimens have a checkered pattern of black spots between the stripes.

These snakes are inactive during winter, although some individuals may be observed basking in the sun. Giant garter snakes are most active from early spring to late fall. They begin to emerge from their winter retreats in early

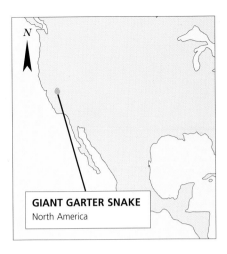

GIANT GARTER SNAKE
North America

April; by mid-April they are actively searching for food, and by early May, all the snakes will have emerged. As early as October, the giant garter snake has begun to seek winter retreats, and by early November all of these snakes will have retreated into winter seclusion.

Natural predators include several species of hawk, egret, and blue heron, as well as raccoon, opossum, and striped skunk.

Giant garter snakes feed on aquatic prey such as fish and amphibians. They are known to feed on both larval and adult frogs and newts. They also feed on native fish species, as well as introduced species of carp and mosquito fish. The giant garter snake seems to fill the ecological niche of the water snakes. It has been recorded stalking and ambushing certain fish species under water, using a similar technique to water snakes.

The breeding season begins soon after snakes emerge from overwintering. Females brood internally (ovoviviparity) and give birth to 10–45 young with an average of 23 per litter. Average birth length is 8 inches (20 centimeters). Females give birth from late July to early September.

Edward Maruska

Kikuzato's Brook Snake

(Opisthotropis kikuzatoi)

IUCN: Critically endangered

Class: Reptilia
Order: Squamata
Suborder: Serpentes (Ophidia)
Family: Colubridae
Length: About 22 in. (55 cm)
Number of young: 11 developing eggs found in one specimen, but other details are as yet unknown
Diet: Freshwater crabs and possibly other aquatic animals
Habitat: Mountain streams
Range: Kumejima Island, Ryukyu Archipelago, Japan

THIS SMALL, non-venomous, aquatic snake has smooth, shiny scales and is gray-brown to dark gray in color, with no obvious pattern. It has a narrow head and its tail is short, accounting for less than 20 percent of its total length. It was not discovered until 1958 and, even by 1985, only four specimens had been collected. It lives in small, clear, rocky streams, where it hides among boulders and rocks on the bottom, occasionally raising its head to the surface to breathe. It appears to be most active early in the morning, and may then move onto the land for short periods, but it usually stays in the water during the afternoon and night. This contrasts with the other members of its genus, which

The San Francisco garter snake is found in 20 locations on the San Francisco Peninsula.

appear to be active by night, and could be an adaptation to cool conditions in its hilly environment. Snakes and other reptiles are dependent on external heat sources, and their ability to move decreases as they become colder.

Eating diets

In captivity the Kikuzato's brook snake has been observed eating only once. Although it shares its habitat with a variety of fish and frog species, the snake was observed eating a freshwater crab, a food that is eaten by only a handful of other snakes.

All its closest relatives (there are 13 other species in the genus *Opisthotropis*) live on the mainland of East Asia, in the Philippines, or on Taiwan. The Kikuzato's brook snake is thought to have become stranded on its tiny Japanese island when it became surrounded by the sea at about the time of the Miocene Period. A large part of the East Asian landmass subsided, leaving only a few of the higher mountaintops above sea level. These now form the Ryukyu Archipelago, a chain of islands to which Kumejima belongs. Despite a number of villages on the island, the extent to which it is cultivated is limited by its rocky terrain, and

KIKUZATO'S BROOK SNAKE
Japan

N

so a significant proportion of natural vegetation is still intact. Some land clearance has taken place in recent times, and the snakes' habitat is shrinking.

Conservation

Due to the snake's rarity and the fact that its entire population is limited to such a small island, the Okinawa Prefectural Government designated it as a National Monument in 1985, thus giving it the highest category of protection. There are even legal restrictions in place on handling the snake.

A conservation program has been devised to gather basic species data, such as its activity patterns, and feeding and reproductive behavior, so that the snake can be protected effectively. There have been no attempts to breed it in captivity.

Chris Mattison

San Francisco Garter Snake

(Thamnophis sirtalis tetrataenia)

ESA: Endangered

Length: 4 ft. (1.3 m)
Reproduction: Oviparous
Diet: Amphibians and fish
Habitat: Wetlands near standing water
Range: Northern California in the San Francisco Bay Area

THE SAN FRANCISCO garter snake has a wide, greenish yellow stripe edged in black running down its back. This is bordered on either side by a broad red stripe that may be broken or divided. A third black stripe runs parallel to this. The belly is a greenish-blue color, and the top of the head is red. This snake is harmless and rather wary; if it is disturbed it will often flee into water or undergrowth. As with most garter snakes, the San Francisco garter snake is oviparous, meaning that its eggs hatch within the body. The average litter sizes of related species are from 12 to 24. Mating begins in March, and birth occurs in July or August. These snakes feed on frogs, newts, toads, and fish. Small mammals may also occasionally be taken.

This water snake can be found near ponds, lakes, marshes, and sloughs. For cover, the San Francisco garter snake uses bankside vegetation and sometimes rodent burrows; it often basks on floating algae or rush mats.

Alteration of habitat is the primary reason for this snake's decline. The human population of the San Francisco Bay Area is huge and continues to grow. Wetlands have been filled in or developed for residential sites to meet the increasing need for housing. Water diversion projects have greatly changed the region. Together with increased recreational use of the waters, these factors have driven the remaining snakes into the ever-smaller protected areas within its range.

The snake occurs in four areas that are protected and managed for other endangered species. The garter snake benefits from these refuges as well.

Sardinian Grass Snake

(Natrix natrix cetti)

IUCN: Critically endangered

Length: 2–4 ft. (0.6–1.2 m)
Reproduction: Egg laying
Diet: Fish and amphibians
Habitat: Areas near water
Range: Sardinia

THIS SUBSPECIES of the genus *Natrix* is confined to the island of Sardinia, off the western coast of Italy. It is a light gray or steel blue, with about 40 vertical dark bars on the upper parts. There is a distinctive black band across the rear of the head behind the eyes, which fades as the snake grows older. It also has a moderately stout body.

The Sardinian grass snake is another member of the family Colubridae. It is semi-aquatic, feeding primarily on fish or amphibians. This snake seizes

SARDINIAN GRASS SNAKE
Europe

prey in its jaws, in or out of water, then swallows the victim alive. Like other members of its genus, this snake is an excellent swimmer and diver. It also has a protective mechanism, discharging an acrid-smelling fluid from an anal gland when seized or handled.

As with many plant or animal species that are confined to islands, this snake is gravely affected by any changes to its isolated environment. When its habitat is altered, it has nowhere to go. Sardinia has changed a great deal over the past decades. Parts of this ruggedly beautiful land have been developed into vacation resorts and more of the island is sure to follow.

Another threatened European colubrid, *Coluber cypriensis*, is found only on the island of Cyprus. Both these colubrids are suffering from water pollution and development that are altering their aquatic habitats. Persecution of snakes, common around the world, is another reason for the threatened status of these colubrids.

Protection of habitat and intensive field studies are necessary if these snakes are to survive within their island habitats.

Elizabeth Sirimarco

See also Boas, New Mexico Ridgenose Rattlesnake, Indian Python, and Vipers.

SOLENODONS

Class: Mammalia

Order: Insectivora

Family: Solenodontidae

The solenodon is one of the most mysterious mammals on earth. Little is known of this animal's evolution or of its current natural history. It is a mammal with only one genus (*Solenodon*) and two species: Cuban (*Solenodon cubanus*) and Haitian (*Solenodon paradoxus*). These two species of solenodon were first discovered by Europeans in 1833 on the islands of Hispaniola and Cuba.

The solenodon is prized by the scientific community as a sort of living fossil. Except for its size, this creature appears to have changed relatively little since its ancestor, the giant solenodon, roamed the New World during the Tertiary Period. Fossils of this animal have been dated as being 30 million years old.

The solenodon is a type of large shrew and a member of the same order as hedgehogs, tenrecs, shrews, and moles. It is a stout animal with a lengthy, pointed snout. In most animals the snout forms a cushion of flesh just in front of the tips of the nasal bones. The feet and tail are relatively bare. A solenodon has excellent claws, which it uses to help tear into vegetation. It uses its snout to root about the ground for its food. Together, these features make the solenodon an efficient hunter.

In addition to its curious and ancient history, the solenodon uses many of the survival mechanisms normally found in other animals, even those outside of the mammalian order. For example, it produces a poisonous venom like a snake. It also has odor-producing glands like a skunk (the aroma is said to smell like a goat). One species of solenodon even has an echolocation ability similar to that found in bats.

Although the solenodon is an insectivore, it will also eat small animals, such as birds and reptiles, and some fruit (chiefly bananas and oranges). In other words, this animal appears to eat just about anything it can find, with the exception of plants.

The solenodon is a social animal that usually lives with eight or more individuals in small hollows in the midst of dense, wet forests. Like most mammals, it appears to be protective of its young and will defend its home against intruders, including other solenodons. A solenodon female is limited to one or two young a year. Little else is known about its social or reproductive habits, except that mating appears to be irregular and occurs in different seasons.

The solenodon appears to be somewhat intelligent. A specimen raised in captivity can recognize its name, come when called, follow its human host around like a pet, and even allow itself to be held. Scientists took a long time to discover the solenodon because these animals are nocturnal and not very numerous.

Today the solenodon is confined to just two islands, both in the Caribbean: Cuba and Hispaniola (the island containing the nations of Haiti and the Dominican Republic). This animal has no known natural enemy native to its habitat. However, humans brought dogs and cats that preyed upon the solenodon. In addition, mongeese were imported in the 1700s to control the snake population. Human expansion into its range and the introduction of non-native species has brought both species of solenodon to the brink of extinction.

Cuban Solenodon
(Solenodon cubanus)

ESA: Endangered

IUCN: Endangered

Weight: 1½ lb. (0.68 kg)

Head-body length: 10–12 in. (25.4–30.5 cm)

Tail length: 10–12 in. (25.4–30.5 cm)

Diet: Insects, small rodents, birds, lizards, fruit

Longevity: 6 years in captivity

Habitat: Dense, wet mountain forests

Range: Oriente Province, Cuba

IN THE EARLY part of the 20th century the Cuban solenodon was believed to be extinct. Of the two species of solenodon, the Cuban is not only the smaller of the two but also the least well known.

The coat of this solenodon is blackish brown, mixed with a buff or white color. Some specimens have been described as mousy gray.

Today there is no Cuban solenodon in captivity, and its population in the wild is unknown. Occasional sightings from locals appear to confirm its continued existence, but none of these sightings has ever been verified by a scientific source.

Many endangered species are victims of the political condition of countries through which they range. One reason for this is that political turmoil often creates obstacles to continued scientific observation as well as to the protection of the population.

For the Cubans, the end of the Soviet Union as a nation also marked the end of financial aid to its poverty-stricken people. These conditions will no doubt cause new difficulties, thereby greatly limiting what help is extended to wildlife. Despite these problems, the solenodon is currently protected by Cuban law, and areas that seem favorable to the solenodon have been labeled off-limits to hunters. This effort was undertaken by the Cuban Academy of Sciences in cooperation with the IUCN and the World Wildlife Federation.

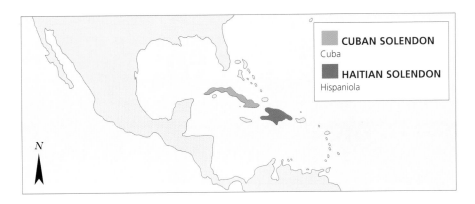

Haitian Solenodon
(Solenodon paradoxus)

ESA: Endangered

IUCN: Endangered

Weight: 1⅓–2¼ lb. (0.6–1 kg)
Head-body length: 11–13 in. (28–33 cm)
Tail length: 7–10½ in. (17.5–26 cm)
Diet: Insects, small rodents, birds, lizards, fruit
Habitat: Dense, wet mountain forests
Range: Mountains of Haiti and Dominican Republic

THE HAITIAN solenodon is larger than its Cuban cousin by about ¾ pound (0.4 kilogram) and 1–2 inches in length (up to 5 centimeters). It also has fur of relatively the same color: blackish brown and white or buff, mixed with a little reddish brown. This solenodon is most readily recognized by the presence of a unique white, square-shaped tuft of fur on the nape of its neck. This patch of white fur is found only on the Haitian variety of solenodon.

Special abilities
The Haitian solenodon has a unique ability not shared with its Cuban cousin: it possesses echolocation abilities similar to the bat, which allow it to orient itself while hunting. During this process, the animal generates a high frequency clicking sound.

Although the adaptable solenodon is willing to eat almost anything and has no natural enemies, it is still close to extinction. Humans have altered the destiny of an animal that has survived for more than 30 million years.

Currently data is limited, and it is unknown how this ability is used by the solenodon or why its Cuban relative does not have the same ability.

The population of this solenodon is also unknown. As of June 1969, at least ten of these animals were held in captivity in zoos around the world.

No protection
The conditions of poverty in Haiti and the Dominican Republic are similar to those in Cuba, contributing to the lack of funding directed toward saving this animal.

Today, there are no known conservation measures used to protect this animal.

George Jenkins

Solo Goodeido

(Xenoophorus captivus)

IUCN: Endangered

Class: Actinopterygii
Order: Atheriniformes
Family: Goodeidae
Length: 3 in. (8 cm)
Reproduction: Live bearer
Habitat: Montane streams and spring isolates
Range: Rio Pánuco, Central Mexico

THIS UNIQUE fish of central Mexico is a representative of the interesting family Goodeidae. Perhaps the most distinct group of fish found in central Mexico, these fish give birth to live young, as opposed to the typical egg-laying reproductive habits of most fish species.

One of these goodeids is the solo goodeido, found in the Rio Pánuco and its tributaries. This relatively short river drains the eastern slope of the Sierra Madre Oriental mountains and enters the Atlantic ocean at the city of Tampico. This region, known as the San Luis Potosí, has a diversity of fish fauna that includes many of the familiar fish found in North America, such as catfish, minnows, and suckers. It also includes a number of fish that are typical of the neotropical region of Central and South America. Thus, San Luis Potosí is located in what might be considered to be a transitional zone between two major geographic groups of fish.

The major causes for concern over the solo goodeido result from reduction of its habitat as a direct result of human activity. A rapidly expanding population in central Mexico is placing extreme demands on all available water resources. Water diversion for irrigation and the construction of dams along the course of the Rio Pánuco have made an impact on many of the fish in this river basin. Although the Rio Pánuco is just south of the range of largemouth bass (*Micropterus salmoides*), this species—with the help of humans—has still found its way to the river. This poses an additional threat to the indigenous fish of the Rio Pánuco.

The reproductive strategy of goodeids is unusual but not entirely unique to fish. Instead of laying eggs that have to incubate and hatch in the water, goodeids give birth to live young. This requires a greater investment in each individual offspring, so each female produces much fewer young. The goodeid looks similar in appearance to fish such as the cachorrito, pupfish, and topminnow, but they have a number of anatomical differences that are associated with bearing live young (a process that is known as viviparity). Fossil records show the goodeids to be of ancient origin and that, millions of years ago, their ancestors were widely distributed across a large part of North America.

Donald Proebstel

SOLO GOODEIDO
North America

SPARROWS

Class: Aves

Order: Passeriformes

Family: Emberizidae

Subfamily: Emberizinae

Sparrows lead secretive lives in the dense vegetation of wetlands, shrub lands, and prairies. Many of them spend much of their time on the ground and few, if any, are truly arboreal.

North American sparrows are members of the family Emberizidae, but in other parts of the world members of the family Ploceidae are also called sparrows. Ploceidae sparrows are Old World birds, many of which are known as weaver finches. The ubiquitous house sparrow (*Passer domesticus*) belongs to this group. In North America the sparrow clan includes such birds as juncos (*Junco* sp.) and longspurs (*Calcarius* sp.).

The trick to caring for sparrows seems to lie not so much in eliminating the human presence, but in correcting past mistakes and restricting land use.

The Cape sable seaside sparrow, the Florida grasshopper sparrow, and the San Clemente sage sparrow were previously listed by IUCN, the former as endangered and the latter two as threatened, but were not evaluated by the time the Red List was compiled. Until more data is available, these species are included with other endangered taxa, because they may still be at risk according to IUCN.

Cape Sable Seaside Sparrow

(Ammodramus maritimus mirabilis)

ESA: Endangered

Length: 5 in. (12.7 cm)

Weight: ¾–1 oz. (19.8–27.4 g)

Clutch size: 3–4 eggs

Incubation: 12–13 days

Diet: Seeds, insects

Habitat: Marshes

Range: Monroe and Dade counties of southern Florida

The cape sable seaside sparrow has greenish gray upperparts streaked with darker gray-green. The underparts are dingy white, streaked with dull brown.

WHEN AMERICANS launched their first astronaut, Alan Shepard, into space, a small bird flitted through the grassy, marshy flats scattered about Cape Canaveral. As a rocket thundered John Glenn into America's first manned orbit, the bird sang its reedy trill. In the shadow of the mighty space craft that lifted Neil Armstrong and his crew to the first landing on the moon, the bird gathered insects to feed its young. A decade later that bird, the dusky seaside sparrow (*Ammodramus maritimus nigrescens*), was struggling to survive. Well before the twentieth anniversary of humanity's walk on the moon, the dusky seaside sparrow quietly became extinct. Away to the south the Cape Sable seaside sparrow awaits a similar fate.

Named for the curved peninsula of extreme southwestern Everglades National Park, the sparrow avoided detection until 1918. Somewhat greenish in overall appearance, the Cape Sable subspecies of the seaside sparrow has greenish gray upperparts streaked with darker gray-green. Dingy white underparts are prominently streaked with dull brown. A yellow lore gives the bird its only bright color, and it stands out in an otherwise plain face marked by a gray cheek and a white jaw line. The chin and belly are plain white; the wing and tail are washed with a faint brown. The gray beak differs in hue from the dull, fleshy pink foot and toe. The Cape Sable seaside sparrow is exquisitely colored and patterned for life in a grassy marsh.

The right plants are vital

Most seaside sparrows inhabit grassy coastal marshes from Massachusetts to Texas. The Cape Sable subspecies adapted to inland freshwater marshes. Occasional lightning fires naturally sculpted the plant communities of these marshes, creating a patchwork of marsh types. The Cape Sable seaside sparrow needs expanses of short, sparse grasses. Over time, the sparrow's populations probably shifted

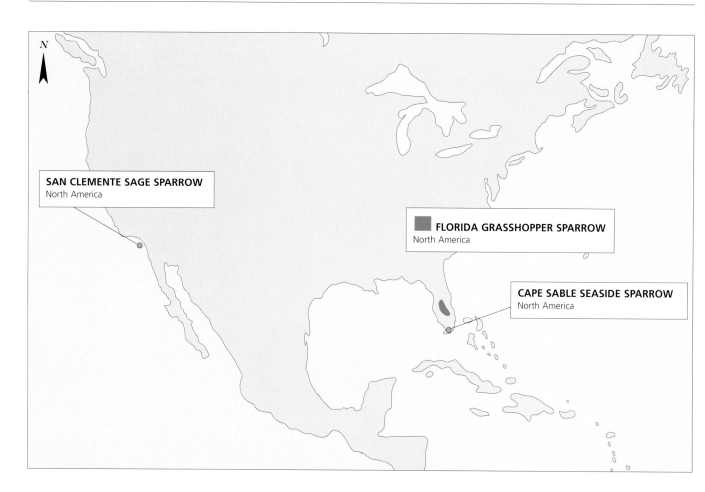

SAN CLEMENTE SAGE SPARROW
North America

FLORIDA GRASSHOPPER SPARROW
North America

CAPE SABLE SEASIDE SPARROW
North America

about as the character of plant communities within the marshes changed.

The Cape Sable seaside sparrow historically occurred on the Ochopee Plain southeast of Naples, Taylor Slough, and Cape Sable in Everglades National Park, and in the Everglades east of the park. The Ochopee and Cape Sable populations have either dwindled to such small populations that they have escaped recent surveys, or else they have disappeared altogether. Land development threatens the habitat of the sparrow in the eastern Everglades. The populations in Taylor Slough and the Big Cypress Preserve adjoining the park on the north number around 6,000 birds. This figure seems high enough to secure the sparrow's future, but its relative, the dusky seaside sparrow,

enjoyed a large population before its rapid decline.

The dusky seaside sparrow was devastated by mosquito-control projects, flooding, and burning. By the time anyone knew the dusky subspecies was in danger, it had dwindled to just a few birds around Merritt Island National Wildlife Refuge. The sparrow spent several breeding seasons without any successful nesting, so federal wildlife officials trapped all remaining live birds to attempt captive breeding. Unfortunately, all five of the dusky seaside sparrows taken into captivity were males. The subspecies became extinct with the last captive male. Ironically, an ample number of mosquitoes still live in the region.

The fate of the dusky seaside sparrow warns ornithologists not to take the status of the Cape

Sable seaside sparrow too casually. Tragedy can occur very quickly. The fire and water cycles of the Everglades have been severely disrupted by people. Restoring them to some natural level on behalf of the sparrow depends on understanding what that natural level might have been before all the disturbance began. If natural conditions are restored too quickly, the bird might experience more harm than good. Continued land development within and around the edges of the Everglades only makes natural cycles more difficult to restore. Most obvious are the occasional fires that are needed to maintain habitat for the Cape Sable seaside sparrow. Before too long these may become the responsibility of people instead of a random act of nature.

Florida Grasshopper Sparrow

(Ammodramus savannarum floridanus)

ESA: Endangered

Length: 5 in. (12.7 cm)
Weight: ½–1 oz. (13.4–28.4 g)
Clutch size: 3–4 eggs
Incubation: 12–13 days
Diet: Small fruits, seeds, insects
Habitat: Shrub lands
Range: A small area north and west of Lake Okeechobee, Florida

A BUZZING NOISE drones over the shrubs. A casual listener might easily dismiss it as just another insect, a grasshopper maybe. But it sounds too musical to be an insect. In fact, it is a small bird singing. The insectlike quality identifies it as the grasshopper sparrow.

As a full species, the grasshopper sparrow occurs over much of the United States south of Canada. Ornithologists recognize several subspecies, one of which lives only in central Florida. That bird, the Florida grasshopper sparrow, was declared an endangered subspecies by the U.S. Fish and Wildlife Service in July, 1986.

The Florida grasshopper sparrow appears noticeably darker than other subspecies. A white stripe runs from the forehead over the crown to the back of the head. A dark brown stripe separates the central crown stripe from a grayish stripe over the eye. The lore is orangish buff, not yellow. The tan cheek is narrowly bordered with dark brown. The dingy white chin and throat fade to a buffy tan breast faintly streaked with darker tan. The sides of the neck, nape, and back are darkly striped, roughly chocolate brown alternating with gray brown streaks. The wing and tail are brownish, the belly white. Short, dark streaks pattern the buff side beneath the folded wing. It inhabits slightly more shrubby habitats than other grasshopper sparrows. Habitat alteration has caused the bird's problems.

Saw palmetto (*Serenoa repens*), dwarf oak (*Quercus minima*), pawpaw (*Asimina* sp.), and other shrubs mixed with grasses, that form bunches instead of sod, strongly appeal to Florida grasshopper sparrows. Good sparrow habitat generally occurs in strips, bands, or patches between lowland marshes and upland forests and woodlands. The Florida grasshopper sparrow may actually inhabit one of the most botanically diverse areas in all of North America. The plant communities mix in various degrees according to the amount of soil, drainage, and age of the community. Most ecologists who have studied the area believe that periodic fires encourage some plants and discourage others.

After fires, small shrubs and grasses quickly establish themselves. Trees invade the burns more slowly, but they gradually take over to form woodlands and forests of pines (*Pinus* sp.), maples (*Acer* sp.), oaks (*Quercus* sp.), and other species. The Florida grasshopper sparrow does not use trees or tall shrubs. Rather, it prefers the shorter, younger shrubs with scattered grasses and ample bare ground.

Such shrub lands are only found in central Florida, mostly

Like all its relatives, the Florida grasshopper sparrow seems rather cumbersome with its short tail; large, flat-looking head; a thick, short neck; and a larger beak than most sparrows.

north of Lake Okeechobee. Some small shrub lands also occur west and southwest of the lake. These lands are mostly privately owned by people who operate cattle ranches. Typically, people remove the native vegetation to promote pastures that the grasshopper sparrows cannot use. In some localities pastures have gone unmanaged and native plants have crept back in. Sparrows do use such pastures, but only in low numbers. The U.S. Air Force maintains a bombing range of 100,000 acres (40,000 hectares) in Highlands County just northwest of Lake Okeechobee. A small portion of that range has been proposed for shrub land management to improve or preserve habitat for the grasshopper sparrow.

In the 1980s only 250 Florida grasshopper sparrows could be found. They all inhabited localized habitat in a five-county area including Osceola, Polk, Highlands, Okeechobee, and Glades Counties. Ornithologists currently believe that certain ranching practices such as periodic burnings may actually benefit grasshopper sparrows, if the practices are timed in a way that does not disturb nesting. To some degree, ranching may duplicate the effects of natural processes that originally formed the plant communities to which the sparrow has become adapted. Those natural processes will probably never be allowed to work at random again. Fires, floods, and changing plant communities do not favor the human lifestyle.

If people can match their land use demands with the needs of the Florida grasshopper

sparrow, this small bird will probably survive until well into the next century.

San Clemente Sage Sparrow

(Amphispiza belli clementeae)

ESA: Threatened

Length: 6½–7 in. (16.5–17.8 cm)
Weight: ¾ oz. (19 g)
Clutch size: 3 eggs
Incubation: 13–14 days
Diet: Seeds, insects
Habitat: Shrub land
Range: San Clemente Island, California

WHEN PEOPLE discovered San Clemente Island no goats lived there—but they do now. Because people put goats on San Clemente, they must accept responsibility for the consequences. One consequence of goats on the island has been the slow decline of the San Clemente Island sage sparrow.

This bird is notable among American sparrows for being attractively plain. Inland sage sparrows tend to be sandier with more stripes on their back and sides. Coastal sage sparrows are uniformly neutral gray and unstreaked above, and clean white below. A short, small, white line above the lore and eye highlights the face. A thin black line separates a broad white jaw line beneath a gray cheek from the white chin and throat. Small, pale gray streaks pattern the side. A black dot marks the white breast. The beak, foot, and toe are all dark gray. Sage sparrows in

general are about 6 inches (15 centimeters) long, but the San Clemente sage sparrow is larger. It is about 7 inches (17.8 centimeters) long.

The island's plant communities and the animals that depend on them have been grossly disturbed by the introduction of exotic animals to San Clemente. The goat (*Capra hircus*) is just part of a larger problem. Channel Islands gray foxes (*Urocyon littoralis*), house cats (*Felis sylvestris*), pigs (*Sus scrofa*), and rats (*Rattus* sp.) have all found their way to San Clemente. Only the fox was ever native there. The others arrived on the island's shores with the help of humans. Goats were intentionally released by the first European sailors to explore North America. No one intended to destroy unique species or subspecies by doing so. The idea was to stock goats on oceanic islands so that sailors could eat fresh meat occasionally, rather than completing entire voyages on a diet of salt pork.

Ships made regular stops at islands to explore, to improve their maps, and to resupply their firewood for cooking and fresh water for drinking. A few goats could be shot for food at such stops. What was a good idea for ancient mariners has proved a threat to island wildlife all over the world.

On San Clemente, as elsewhere, the goats survived by eating whatever vegetation they could reach. They reproduced without restraint from predators. As their populations grew, the goats foraged even more heavily on island plant life. In the 1970s approximately 5,000 goats occupied the 87 square miles

(226 square kilometers) of San Clemente Island. So many goats ate many parts of the island bare and severely grazed others. The San Clemente sage sparrow needs the shrub land habitat that has suffered from hungry goats. As the goats damage the shrubs, the shrub land thins. In the sparser cover sage sparrows are more vulnerable to cats and other predators, both natural and exotic. A thinning shrub land also means reduced food supply.

The U.S. Department of Defense administers the island through the U.S. Navy. Plans were drafted to exterminate the goats, but animal rights activists blocked the action because they objected to killing the goats. A court order allowed the group to live-trap the goats and remove them to private property on the mainland. Unfortunately, the goats reproduced so quickly that they could not be removed fast enough to make serious progress. As the environmental group's funds dwindled, the court rescinded the order and the Navy proceeded with its plans for killing the goats. Most of them had been eliminated by 1990. Cats and pigs also cause problems on San Clemente Island; before any meaningful recovery of island birds can occur, the other exotics must be eliminated as well.

As well as goat and predator control, there are calls to restore the island's vegetation. Deliberate action to restore the shrub community will stabilize the sage sparrow population by improving habitat quality. The U.S. Fish and Wildlife Service works with the Navy on the wildlife situation at San Clemente. Ornithologists with the USFWS have been able to respond to the sage sparrow's plight on San Clemente early enough to prevent it from declining into endangerment. Prevention always produces better results than recovery work. Other species on the island have suffered much more dramatically than has the sage sparrow. As botanists and ornithologists examine the problems of those species they can make recommendations and take action to improve the whole island at once, rather than just addressing individual species.

Many plants and animals will benefit from the eradication of the goats. Many birds will prosper once cats have been removed. Among them will be the San Clemente sage sparrow.

Kevin Cook

Spikedace
(Meda fulgida)

ESA: Threatened

IUCN: Vulnerable

Class: Actinopterygii
Order: Cypriniformes
Family: Cyprinidae
Length: 2⅘ in. (7 cm)
Reproduction: Egg layer
Habitat: Stream pools and riffles
Range: Gila River Basin, Arizona and New Mexico

THE ONLY MEMBER of the genus *Meda*, the spikedace currently occupies only about 6 percent of its former range and is considered to be a threatened species. It can be found at scattered locations in counties of eastern and central Arizona and western and southwestern New Mexico. At one time it was commonly seen in streams as far south as northern Sonora, Mexico.

The spikedace and all species of fish are important because they strengthen the biological diversity of the areas they inhabit. That is reason enough to protect them. Because of the spikedace's small size, other fish and animals count on its strong numbers for food.

Excellent hearing

The spikedace gets its common name from the protective spines carried on the dorsal fin of its back. Most members of this family lack these defensive devices. Cyprinids have a global distribution, with more than 1,500 species worldwide. All cyprinids, including the spikedace, have a peculiar organ called the Weberian apparatus. This internal body part is comprised of bones that connect the fish's gas bladder to its inner ear. It is apparently responsible for a cyprinid's keen sense of hearing. The gas bladder, which normally regulates the fish's buoyancy, acts as an amplifier of sound, just like a human eardrum, for the Weberian appa-

ratus. These amplified sounds are then carried by the Weberian apparatus to the ear.

The spikedace is small, with a slender body that is compressed from side to side, and a narrow tail section. The overall color is olive-brown on the back, sides, and the top of the head, with a yellow-white abdomen. The back and sides are sprinkled with dark spots and silvery flecks.

Breeding males develop a brassy appearance, and some observers have noticed a red or rose color. The spikedace breeds from March to May in shallow stream riffles. Females produce 100 to 800 eggs, and males provide some protection after the eggs are laid. They will often patrol the spawning area to deter predators. Irregular stream flows are essential to the well-being of the spikedace. These flows scour the streambed and loosen attached insects that the fish

The spikedace eats insects that inhabit the stream bottom and the water surface. It belongs with carps and minnows, to the family Cyprinidae.

SPIKEDACE
North America

(*Oncorhynchus mykiss*), small-mouth bass (*Micropterus dolomieu*), and channel catfish (*Ictalurus punctatus*) prey on the spikedace, and the aggressive red shiner (*Cyprinella lutrensis*) competes for feeding, breeding, and lounging sites.

The possibility exists for a major new dam to be constructed on the Gila River. The reservoir created by the dam would inundate many acres of prime spikedace habitat. Despite the potential for environmental damage, several special interest groups are in favor of moving ahead with the dam project. The U.S. Fish and Wildlife Service is lobbying for the protection of spikedace and other fish in this region, but their future is still very uncertain.

William E. Manci

otherwise might not find. This is one reason that changing water flow through the building of a dam can have a detrimental effect on certain fish species.

The spikedace is threatened primarily by habitat changes. Dams block migration and change seasonal water flow and chemistry patterns. Stream channelization that minimizes flooding alters these patterns too. The lowering of the water table, through irrigation and groundwater pumping, contributes to an environment that is unacceptably altered for the spikedace. Non-native fish also pose a big problem for this species. Fish such as the rainbow trout

SPINEDACES

Class: Actinopterygii

Order: Cypriniformes

Family: Cyprinidae

The small and unassuming spinedaces of the southwestern deserts of the United States can be found in Nevada, Utah, and Arizona. They are cyprinids, just like chubs, carps, shiners, minnows, and daces. Spinedaces, however, have not expanded their range as much as other cyprinids. In fact, the outlook for these fish is quite bleak.

Loss of vital habitat and water and the introduction of non-native fish are the primary reason for the decline of spinedaces. Demands on water and land for agriculture and urbanization, and the pollution and physical destruction that

usually follow, all contribute to the critical situation in which these fish find themselves today.

What spinedaces lack in size, they make up for with surprising adaptability. These diverse and versatile fish are designed to deal with a variety of habitats and environmental conditions. They can tolerate wide ranges in temperature and salinity. They are also opportunistic when it comes to food selection; that is, they eat whatever is most readily available. As an additional example of their distinctiveness, all spinedaces (similar to all cyprinids) have an organ called the Weberian apparatus, which contributes to their keen sense of hearing. The tiny bones of this organ are connected to the spinedace's gas bladder, which acts as an amplifier of sound in a similar way to an eardrum.

Little Colorado Spinedace
(*Lepidomeda vittata*)

ESA: Threatened

IUCN: Vulnerable

Length: 4 in. (10 cm)
Reproduction: Egg layer
Habitat: Stream pools
Range: Upper basin of the Little Colorado River, Arizona

TRUE TO ITS NAME, the home for this small minnow is the upper basin of the Little Colorado River in central Arizona, including Clear Creek and other tributaries. These streams are considered important sources of water for the region. As such they have been extensively dammed, and other dam projects are pending. This is a familiar story in the history of many threatened and endangered species. Blue Ridge Reservoir on Clear Creek and Lyman Lake on the Little Colorado River are just two examples of dam and reservoir projects that have had a severe impact on the Little Colorado spinedace and other native fish.

Altered habitat

Dams are probably the most destructive forms of human intrusion on fish habitat. They alter seasonal water flows and the water quality downstream from the dam sites. Overall, dams reduce the average downstream flow when they are used to divert water to other areas for crop irrigation or other human uses. The Little Colorado spinedace has adapted to the conditions that existed before the construction of these dams, when there was murky water, dramatic temperature fluctuations, and higher water flows.

Other disturbances within the streams, such as channelization for flood control, also damage spawning and feeding areas for this spinedace and other fish. Because of the dramatic changes in the river environment, opportunities exist for non-native fish to flourish.

This spinedace has a relatively unspectacular appearance and size. It is, however, suited to life in streams. Its body is slender and its snout is blunt. The body fins are triangular to minimize drag, and the tail fin is moderately forked to enable strong swimming in currents. Dorsal fin spines on the back help to protect

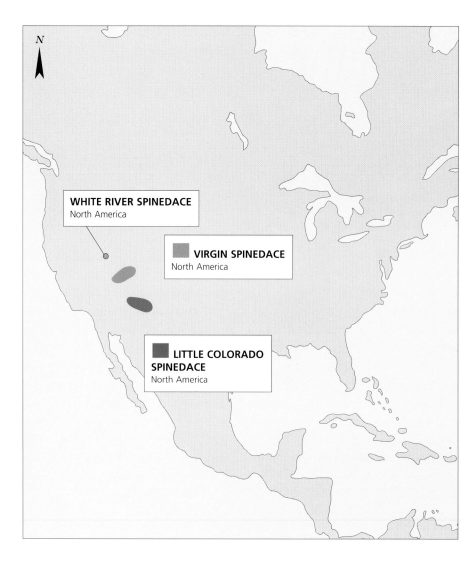

this fish from predators. Darker coloration on the back and the top of the head blend into lighter tones on the underside. There are also hints of darker horizontal stripes on the sides, as well as some silvery coloration. The mouth is set somewhat low on the face, and the eyes are not particularly large, but they do suggest that this spinedace is a visual feeder.

Reproduction

The Little Colorado spinedace breeds from early summer to early fall, but it is most active at the beginning of this period. Females produce from 600 to 5,000 eggs and deposit them over the river bottom or on aquatic

vegetation. Males change color slightly during this time, developing a weak orange or yellow at the base of the pectoral fins (just behind the gills) and the pelvic fins (on the belly). The favorite foods of this spinedace include adult insects and larvae and other aquatic invertebrates. This species also consumes algae when other foods are scarce.

Securing unaltered habitats is a priority for this fish. Fortunately, much of the land surrounding this species' range is owned by the federal government and is easier to protect from development. The needs of the Little Colorado spinedace will hopefully figure prominently in future development decisions.

Virgin Spinedace

(Lepidomeda mollispinis)

Length: 3 in. (8 cm)
Reproduction: Egg layer
Habitat: Moderate stream currents and pools
Range: Virgin River Basin, Nevada, Utah, and Arizona

THE VIRGIN SPINEDACE is found in the Virgin River Basin of Nevada, Utah, and Arizona. This range initially might sound fairly large, but like many western United States river systems, the Virgin River system is extensively dammed and used for irrigation and other purposes. Unfortunately for the Virgin spinedace, dams and the resulting reservoirs are impassable and severely restrict opportunities for migration and expansion of its natural range.

This fish is represented by two distinct subspecies, the Virgin spinedace (*L. mollispinis mollispinis*) and the Big Spring spinedace (*L. mollispinis pratensis*).

The Big Spring spinedace subspecies is found only in segments of the Meadow Valley Wash, a tributary of the Virgin River in southeastern Nevada. Before the construction of a water diversion at Big Spring, near the upper reaches of the wash, this stream carried much more water than it does today. During drought periods, the wash becomes so narrow at times that it nearly dries up completely before reaching the northern arm of Lake Mead. At present the Big Spring spinedace is forced to accept conditions within the

wash because it is blocked from upstream migration by dams and reservoirs, and from downstream migration into the Virgin River or Colorado River by Lake Mead.

Because it has access to more miles of stream than the Big Spring spinedace, the Virgin spinedace is in less danger. It has populations at several locations within the Virgin River Basin. Predators and competitors are the main threat to this fish. The brown trout (*Salmo trutta*), a voracious non-native predator, and the redside shiner (*Richardsonius balteatus*), an aggressive competitor for habitat, could ultimately overwhelm the Virgin spinedace, making it extinct.

Efforts are underway to protect both subspecies. The Nature Conservancy owns land along the Meadow Valley Wash and is working with the U. S. Fish and Wildlife Service to enhance habitat. They are also trying to find alternative secure sites for the Big Spring subspecies.

The back and top of this spinedace's head are somewhat dusky, but the sides are silvery and brass or copper colored. Some light blotches are present on the tail section, and speckles are randomly scattered over the

The Virgin spinedace is small and, by most standards, unspectacular. Its body is slender, with a blunt snout slightly above the mouth.

more forward sections of the body. The body fins are triangular, while the dorsal fin on the back has two protective spines. The tail fin is moderately forked, with each lobe quite pointed.

Spawning begins in mid-spring and continues through the early summer. While younger females usually spawn once per season, more mature fish may spawn twice. Males and females tend to spawn in a group within a stream pool over sand or gravel. Hundreds or thousands of eggs may be produced by each female. Both sexes prefer insects as their main food source, but will use algae and other vegetation during times when insects are scarce.

Though previously listed by IUCN–The World Conservation Union in the 1994 Red List of endangered species, the Virgin spinedace in now no longer evaluated. This means that it has not been assessed for the most recent Red List.

Until more data is available, the species is included with other endangered taxa, because it may still be at risk.

White River Spinedace
(Lepidomeda albivallis)

ESA: Endangered

IUCN: Critically endangered

Length: 5 in. (13 cm)
Reproduction: Egg layer
Habitat: Cool springs and outflows
Range: White River near Lund, Nevada

AT AN AVERAGE length of slightly over 5 inches (13 centimeters) the giant of the spinedace world is the White River spinedace. This species makes its home in the White River Valley of eastern Nevada. Technically, this spinefish occupies only Lund Spring and Flag Spring, which are parts of the White River waterway. These springs provide only a very restricted range.

In 1952 fisheries biologist Robert R. Miller realized that this species was in danger, and urged local residents to stop using the White River spinedace as a bait fish. However, water diversions, destruction of the instream and bank vegetation that provides cover for the fish, and groundwater pumping threaten to render its current range useless.

Introduced species

It is no wonder that this species has earned a status as endangered. Adding to its problems are several introduced non-native fishes such as the guppy (*Poecilia reticulata*), the goldfish (*Carassius auratus*), and the mosquitofish (*Gambusia affinis*), all of which prey on young spinedace and compete for food and habitat.

The face of this fish carries some red tones, and the dorsal and tail fins are greenish brown or pinkish brown. The pectoral fins just behind the gills bear shades of yellow, orange, and red, and the pelvic and anal fins on the belly are reddish orange and white. Other features, such as swept-back body fins, a forked

The White River spinedace is not only the largest in its genus but also the most colorful. The slender body is multi-hued, being olive-brass on the back and top of the head; brass and silver on the sides, and silver-white on the belly.

tail fin, blunt snout, and mouth positioned low on the face, are typical of other spinedaces.

Little is known about this fish's breeding habits, but it is most likely to spawn in the spring and summer as water temperatures rise. The White River spinedace spreads its eggs over a water bottom of gravel or sand. It feeds on insects and other aquatic invertebrates among bank vegetation and algae, eating algae when insects are scarce.

Steps have been taken to save this fish. Nearby Preston Big Spring, and Lund and Flag Springs, have been specified as critical habitat. Officials hope to reintroduce the White River spinedace into Preston Big Spring, which it used to occupy. Securing other habitats for this fish will further help to ensure its survival.

William E. Manci

SPINEFLOWERS

Class: Magnoliopsida

Order: Polygonales

Family: Polygonaceae

Chorizanthe is a genus in the family Polygonaceae, with 50 species distributed throughout dry western North America and southwestern South America. Of the 50 species of *Chorizanthe*, 41 are annuals. The plants are generally made up of a flower stalk that rises from a rosette of leaves. Flowers in this genus are tiny, and surrounded by a circle of leaves that can have papery margins and spike- or hook-shaped structures called awns. The leaves at the base of the flower may show more color than the petals. Some taxa in *Chorizanthe* are closely related and form taxonomically complex species groups.

Ben Lomond Spineflower

(Chorizanthe pungens Benth. var. hartwegiana)

ESA: Endangered

IUCN: Endangered

Height: 2–20 inches (5–50 cm)

Flowers: May to July, occasionally April

Habitat: Ponderosa Pine Sandhill

Range: Santa Cruz Mountains, California

THE BEN LOMOND spineflower is an annual herb with stems that grow nearly erect. The flower clusters are dense. Flower heads are 1 to 1.5 centimeters (⅓ to ⅔ inches) long. The six leaves at the base of the bloom are dark pinkish to purple and have papery margins. These leaves have hairs of two sizes: the larger are 2 to 3 millimeters long, alternating with smaller hairs that are 1 to 1.5 millimeters long.

Small flowers

The bloom itself extends beyond these leaves, and is 2.5 to 3 millimeters long. The base of the bloom is white, and the lobes are hairy and white to rose. The Ben Lomond spineflower has nine stamens. The seeds are small, dry, dark brown, and 2 to 2.5 millimeters long.

The flower heads of the Ben Lomond spineflower have dark pinkish to purple lobes and are densely spread. The stems are slightly erect.

The Ben Lomond spineflower is endemic to sandstone and mudstone deposits in the Santa Cruz Mountains, California. This is the only form of the Ben Lomond spineflower that occurs inland, which is the reason that this taxa has been upheld as a distinct variety. The difference between the inland and coastal forms of the Ben Lomond spineflower was first recognized by James Reveal and Clare Hardham in 1989.

The sandstone and mudstone deposits in the Santa Cruz mountains where this plant

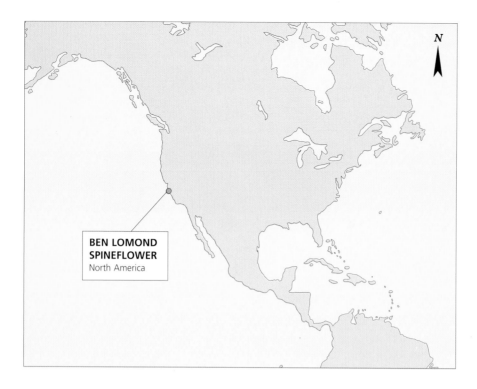

BEN LOMOND SPINEFLOWER
North America

N

Monterey Spineflower

Chorizanthe pungens Benth. var. pungens (Benth)

ESA: Threatened

IUCN: Vulnerable

Life form: Annual herb
Height: 5–50 cm (2–19 inches)
Stems: From 5–50 cm (2–19 inches) long
Leaves: Basal and oblanceolate, ¼–2 in. (1–5 cm) long, 4–7 mm wide
Flowers: White to rose. April to June
Habitat: Coastal strand, scrub
Range: Monterey and Santa Cruz counties, California

occurs make up pockets in the mixed evergreen and redwood forest that are more typical of the area, and act as biological islands.

The sandy soils of this region cover over 8,000 acres and make up 3 percent of Santa Cruz County. These soils are derived from Miocene Era marine sand deposits and are called the Santa Margarita Formation. They are deep, coarse-textured, and poorly developed soils.

Such soils, combined with a humid coastal climate, are rare in California and probably account for the unique flora they support.

Vegetation

The quickly draining sandstone and mudstone are predominantly vegetated by open ponderosa pine woods and northern maritime chaparral. Locally this vegetation is called Ponderosa Pine Sandhill. The sub-community where the Ben Lomond Spineflower occurs is called Ponderosa Pine Sand Parkland,

and it is characterized by widely spaced ponderosa pines, no shrubs growing underneath, and a sparse or absent grass cover. The soil is bare except for patches covered by lichen, and supports only small, ephemeral plants.

The parkland is scattered over 20 sites, half of which are located around the active Santa Cruz Aggregates Quarry near the town of Olympia. Most of the remaining parkland is proposed for sand quarrying in the future.

Threats

Sand quarrying is the most significant threat to this species. Other threats that face this plant arise from recreational activities, such as damage caused by the activity of off road vehicles, or trampling.

These spineflowers are bordered by the communities of Ben Lomond, Glenwood, Scotts Valley, and Felton, and would be affected if these towns were to increase in size.

THE MONTEREY spineflower is an annual herb. Its dense flower clusters arise from a circular base of leaves that are white (or rarely pinkish) and have dry, papery margins. The leaves at the base of the flower cluster have straight hairs of two sizes. The larger hairs are 2 to 3 millimeters, alternating with smaller awns, measuring 1 to 1.5 millimeters.

Corolla

The corolla, or flower cluster, extends beyond the leaf base, and is 2.5 to 3 mm long. The corolla tube is white, and the lobes are hairy and a white to rose color. The Monterey spineflower has 9 stamens. The seeds are small and dry, dark brown, and 2 to 2.5 millimeters long.

Little information is available about the breeding system or pollinators of the Monterey spineflower. However, the tiny,

The coast of Big Sur is a natural habitat of the Monterey spineflower. The species thrives in sandy soil, particularly in coastal scrub located at less than 1,475 feet (450 meters).

insignificant flowers seem unlikely to attract many pollinating insects, and it seems likely that these annuals self-fertilize.

A self-fertilizing breeding system could help explain the proliferation of many morphologically similar taxa in different regions, as occurs in this genus.

Distribution

The Monterey spineflower occurs in Monterey and Santa Cruz Counties of California, as well as inland into the Salinas Valley. It was first described by George Benthem in 1836, from a specimen collected in Monterey. Historically it was also reported to occur near San Simeon in the extreme northern part of San Luis Obispo County. Recently however, this species has not been found south of Monterey County. It grows at elevations from sea level to 200 feet (60 meters), and flowers from April to June. Today populations of the Monterey spineflower exist at Manresa State Beach and in the Dunes near Marina.

However, 70 percent of the range of this plant is on land belonging to the Fort Ord Army

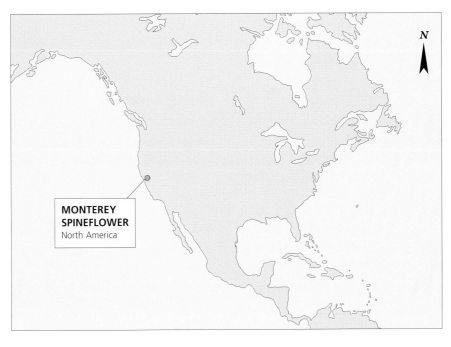

MONTEREY
SPINEFLOWER
North America

Base. In Fort Ord, the Monterey spineflower grows along road-sides, in fire breaks, and on other disturbed sites. The highest density of populations occur in the center of the firing range where the most disturbance takes place.

Location

In its increasingly rare natural chaparral habitats, the Monterey spineflower grows in the openings between shrubs. In the past the plant was most likely to be dependent on wild fires to create the disturbances necessary for it to survive. It prefers sandy or gravelly soil, and is limited to coastal regions, such as the borders between strand and chaparral, or coastal scrub at less than 1,475 feet (450 meters).

Climate

The climate in these coastal areas of California consists of hot, dry summers, and wet, mild winters. Frost seldom or never occurs. Heavy coastal fogs frequently occur during the summer months.

Threats

This plant is threatened by horse and foot traffic, development, and by a proposed realignment of Highway 101.

Some of the populations at Fort Ord were destroyed by the construction of an ammunition supply depot. Although Fort Ord set aside several small preserves in order to compensate, they are not likely to be large enough to be effective. Fort Ord was recently closed, and the future of this species will depend on who the new owners of the land will be, and how they choose to develop it.

Orcutt's Spineflower

(Chorizanthe orcuttiana)

ESA: Endangered

IUCN: Endangered

Life form: Annual herb
Height: ¼–6 inches (1–15 cm)
Leaves are narrowly spear-shaped and from 0.5–1.5 centimeters long
and 2–3.5 mm wide
Flowers: Densely hairy, yellow. March to May
Habitat: Coastal scrub
Range: San Diego County, California

ORCUTT'S SPINEFLOWER is an annual herb with stems that lie flat on the ground. Its leaves are thinly covered, top and bottom, in hair, giving them a grayish cast. The greenish floral bloom has three equal lobes, covered in hair. The hooked awns measure just 0.6 to 1 millimeters. The floral bloom is 1.5 to 1.8 millimeters long and is included within, or extends just beyond, the leaf base from which it grows. The corolla is yellow and densely hairy, and nine stamens are attached near its top. The small, dry seeds are a dark brown color and narrow, measuring just 2 to 2.2 millimeters long.

Self-fertilization

Pollination of this species has not been studied, and now too few plants exist for any such studies to be carried out. It seems likely that Orcutt's spineflower is self-fertilizing and rarely cross-pollinates.

Evolution

Orcutt's spineflower is an extremely distinct species. This species could possibly have arisen from the hybridization of the prostrate spineflower (*Chorizanthe procumbens*) and long-spined spineflower (*Chorizanthe polygonoides*). In some ways it resembles the prostrate spineflower, which also has densely hairy yellow flowers. It is possible to imagine the six involucral teeth (whorls of leaves below flower) of this spineflower being reduced to three by suppression of the minor teeth, and the stamen adhering to the floral tube. Research has not been carried out in this subject, however, so this is only speculation.

Habitat and distribution

This plant grows in sandy soil on mesas, or in coastal scrub from 200 to 410 feet (60 to 125 meters). It only grows on loose sand, which is probably not a permanent habitat.

However, all the historical sites for Orcutt's spineflower have been developed, and it was presumed to be extinct until it was rediscovered in 1991.

Twenty plants were discovered in an area measuring 5 by 5 feet (1.5 by 1.5 meters) at Oak Crest Park in Encinitas. They were growing in a chaparral clearing in loose sand downslope from eroded sandstone bluffs, south of a bike path, north of a grassy lawn, and west of a parking lot. Two specimens of Orcutt's spineflower were collected and put in the San Diego Natural History Museum. The site was revisited in 1992 and similar conditions and population size were reported.

Climate

The climate in this region is mild in the winter, with temperatures never dropping enough for frost. Summer and autumn are hot and dry, and there is sometimes coastal fog. There is seldom more than 20 inches (50 centimeters) of rain falling in one year, and this is mainly concentrated in the months between November and February.

Chance problems

A single site of this size could very easily be destroyed by chance events, and is threatened by park visitors walking through openings in the chaparral cover, and people crossing the border from Mexico who tend to sleep in the chaparral. It has been suggested that the site should be fenced off.

Orcutt's spineflower is also threatened by the negative effects of a small population size and by a lack of genetic diversity. However if this species has adapted to self-reproduction, then it is less likely to suffer from these negative effects.

Conservation

The conservation of Orcutt's spineflower is very difficult, because nearly all of its appropriate habitats have been developed. There are very few undisturbed coastal chaparral areas remaining in California that have the appropriate loose sand. This plant's rarity is due to lack of habitat, and this makes any reintroduction programs quite problematic.

Tiny problem

The tiny stature of this plant makes it particularly susceptible to chance destruction, and creates an additional conservation challenge.

Robust Spineflower

(Chorizanthe robusta)

ESA: Endangered

IUCN: Vulnerable

Life form: Annual herb
Height: 4–20 in. (10–50 cm)
Leaves: Spear-shaped, and ½–1¼ in. (1.3–5 cm) long by 2–5 mm wide
Flowers: Hairy, white to rose. May to September
Habitat: Coastal sand, scrub
Range: Alameda, Monterey, Santa Cruz, and San Mateo Counties, California

THE ROBUST SPINEFLOWER is an annual herb. Its stems may lie flat or stand erect. In the multiple flowers found on the main stems of these plants the terminal flowers are borne directly on the stalk rather than on secondary stalks. The flowers of this species are surrounded by six white-to-pinkish lobed leaves 2.5 to 4 millimeters long. This leaf structure is thinly covered with hair and has dry papery margins that extend only part way along the length of the awns (slender bristles). The awns are two sizes: the larger are 0.7 to 1.3 millimeters, alternating with the smaller awns, that measure 0.3 to 7 millimeters long. The robust spineflower has a flower cluster or corolla of 2.5 to 4 milimeters. The corolla tube is white, and the jagged lobes are white to rose, and hairy. This species has nine stamens, and light brown fruit (achenes) from 3.5 to 4 millime-

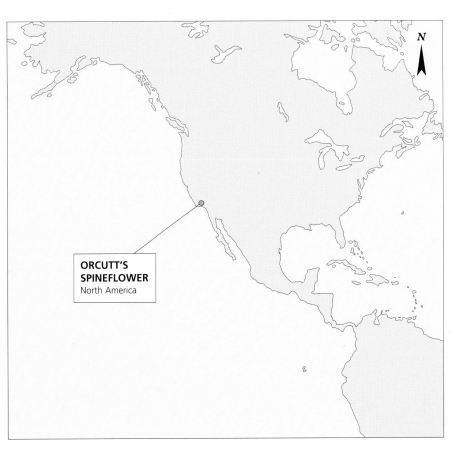

ORCUTT'S SPINEFLOWER
North America

ters long. This species was first described by Charles Parry in 1889. It is larger and more robust than other species of spineflower. The leaves at the base of the loom are also larger and tend to be a brighter white than the other species that inhabit the same region. Robust spineflowers have shorter awns than Monterey spineflowers.

Historically, the robust spineflower occurred in coastal sand and scrub at elevations of less than 980 feet (300 meters), in Alameda, Monterey, Santa Cruz, and San Mateo Counties, California. However, it is now exceedingly rare or extinct in San Mateo and Alameda Counties, where most of its sites have become urbanized. Sites where it was reported in the Salinas Valley have been converted to agriculture. It remains in the coastal ranges in Santa Cruz County, and near the coast in southern Santa Cruz and extreme northern Monterey Counties. Well-known populations occur northeast of Santa Cruz, on land that has been purchased by the University of California, near Sunset and Manresa State Beaches. There was estimated to

The coastal scrub situated just outside San Diego is a perfect habitat for Orcutt's spineflower. The plant only grows on loose sand or sandy soil.

be a total population of less than 7,000 individuals in 1990. These habitats are characterized by broad sandy beaches backed by extensive dune formations, and behind the dune formations, maritime chaparral. The robust spineflower is closely related to the Monterey spineflower. Like the Monterey spineflower, the robust spineflower has a coastal form, sometimes called *Chorizanthe robusta var. robusta*, and an inland form, sometimes called *Chorizanthe robusta var. hartwegii*. Both varieties are recognized by the IUCN as endangered. *Chorizanthe robusta var. hartwegii* is endemic to specific sandstone and mudstone formations and is in the Scotts Valley in the Santa Cruz Mountains of Santa Cruz County, California. It occurs in meadows, with species such as the toad rush (*Juncus bufonis*) and *Crassula erecta* both of which favor habitats with a locally high moisture content. Annual rainfall in the neighboring community of Felton averages 44 inches (112 centimeters), and nearby Ben Lomond receives 56 inches (140 centimeters). Summer fogs are common in this region. This variety of robust spineflower forms a population of about 6,000 individuals in Scotts Valley, north of Santa Cruz. It occurs on three parcels of privately owned land, and otherwise occurs only on land that has been proposed for a golf course. Along with the development of the Glenwood Estates golf course, this species is threatened by sand mining, dune stabilization, and competition from exotic species such as *Ammophilla arenaria* and *Mesembryanthemum* sps.

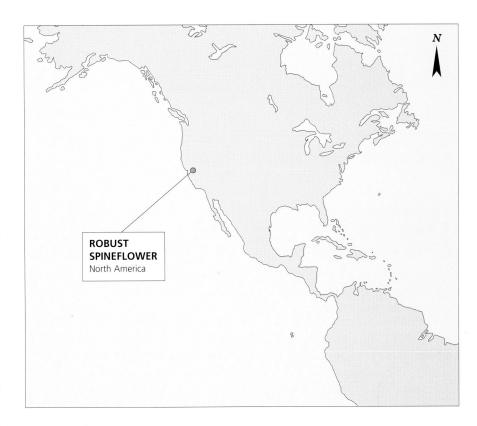

ROBUST SPINEFLOWER
North America

Sonoma Spineflower
(*Chorizanthe valida*)

ESA: Endangered

IUCN: Endangered

Height: 4–12 in. (10–30 cm)
Leaves: Broadly spear-shaped from ¼–1 in. (1–2.5 cm) long and 4–8 mm wide.
Flowers: White to rose or lavender, and hairy. Red involucres. June to August
Habitat: Coastal mesas, grassland
Range: Marin and Sonoma Counties, California

THE SONOMA SPINEFLOWER is an annual herb with erect stems. Its flowers are surrounded by six reddish whorled lobes, 3 to 4 millimeters long. This structure is called an involucre.

Appearance
Unlike the other species in the genus, the involucres of the Sonoma spineflower do not have obviously dry papery margins, instead they are inconspicuous and white. The straight, ivory-to-straw-colored awns (slender bristles) are two sizes, the long (0.7 to 1.3 millimeter) awns alternate with the shorter 0.5 to 1 millimeter awns.

Corollas
The flower clusters or corollas of the Sonoma spineflower extend well beyond the involucre and are 5–6 millimeters long. The corolla tube is white, and its lobes are white to rose or lavender colored, and hairy. The corolla lobes are unequal in size. This species has nine stamens, and dry, light

brown seeds 3 to 4.5 millimeters long. The Sonoma spineflower is closely related to the Monterey spineflower, and is part of the same species complex.

Color contrast

The red color of the Sonoma's involucres contrasts with its white or ivory awns, making this species easily recognizable. The contrast, the tight clustering of the flowers, and the relatively long corolla, hints that this plant may be more dependent on reproducing through pollination by unrelated blooms than is true for the other species in the genus. It has been observed that the flowers of the Sonoma spineflower have a very distinctive odor in the field, and attract numerous insects.

Insect interest

The honey bee (*Apis mellifera*), the yellow-faced bumble bee (*Bombus bosnesenski*), and the solitary ground nesting wasp (*Bembix americana comata*) have been observed foraging on the plant. When seeds were being collected, an unidentified wasp was found that resembles the seeds in size and color. It is possible that this wasp may have some sort of co-evolutionary relationship with the Sonoma spineflower, but further studies have not been carried out. The Sonoma spineflower has a history of growing in sandy soil on coastal mesas or grassland in

The Sonoma spineflower is a distinctive-looking member of the *Chorizanthe* species. It has red bracts and white to rose or lavender flowers that have contrasting white margins.

SONOMA
SPINEFLOWER
North America

N

Reyes Peninsula in Marin County was rediscovered. This site is situated on the Lunny Ranch, just south of Abbott's Lagoon, in the Point Reyes National Seashore. In 1988 it was reported to consist of over 2,000 individuals scattered over approximately 183,000 square feet (17,000 square meters). The climate in this area is mild, with very cool winters and warm foggy summers.

Cattle threat

This site contains the only known population of the Sonoma spineflower, and so is in need of careful protection. The site appears to be very well managed at this time, though a threat could possibly come from trampling by cattle.

Christina Oliver

Marin and Sonoma Counties, California. However, the Sonoma County occurrences near Fort Ross, Sebastopol and Petaluma have not been seen in very many years, as a result of human intervention. The coastal dune systems running along the west coast of the United States have suffered through coastal and river sand mining, residential and road development, invasive exotics, river damming and water diversion projects, as well as oil exploration.

The Sonoma spineflower was thought to be extinct at one time, but in 1980 a site on the Point

Black-faced Spoonbill
(Platalea minor)

IUCN: Critically endangered

Class: Aves
Order: Ciconiiformes
Family: Threskiornithidae
Length: 27½–29½ in. (70–75 cm)
Clutch size: Probably 3–5 eggs
Incubation: Probably 21–25
Diet: Probably small fish, crustaceans, insects, mollusks, and occasional plant material
Habitat: Wetlands
Range: Eastern China from Heilongjiang Province in the north to Fujian Province in the south; also North Korea and occasionally southern Japan

THE SPOONBILLS BELONG to the ibis family. Six species of spoonbill exist on six continents, where they use their specially adapted spoon-shaped bills for fishing.

The roseate spoonbill (*Ajaia ajaja*) ranges through the southern United States into South America. The yellow-billed spoonbill (*Platibis flavipes*) and royal spoonbill (*Platalea regia*) wander throughout the Australian region. The African spoonbill (*Platalea alba*) occurs in southern Africa and the island of Madagascar. The white spoonbill (*Platalea leucorodia*) inhabits broad areas of northern Africa, Europe, and Asia. The black-faced spoonbill once lived in eastern China, regularly migrated through Korea, and strayed to Japan and even to Southeast Asia and the Philippines.

Ornithologists know only a little about the rare black-faced spoonbill. A snow-white bird most of the year, it sports a shaggy, golden crest and breast patch in the summer breeding season. It loses this color when the breeding season ends. The leg, foot, and toe are all jet black. The face is bare around the eye and across the forehead, and this bare patch is continuous with the beak. The spoonbills get their name from their elongated beaks that gradually narrow, then abruptly flare out into a flattened disk, with a nail at the very end. Having a jet black, spoon-shaped beak and a bare, black face, the black-faced spoonbill is aptly named.

Spoonbills feed in the water. They use their peculiar beaks to both dabble and sweep side to side in big arcs as they walk. They consume a broad variety of foods caught in this manner, but as a group, their favorite is small fish. Some observers report seeing the black-faced spoonbill in the shallow waters and mudflats of tidal marshes. These are the preferred feeding habitats of all spoonbills. The exact diet of black-faced spoonbills has not been thoroughly researched, but considering their beak shape and habitats, it is probable that small fish and other aquatic organisms are just as important to the black-faced spoonbill as they are to other spoonbill species.

Asian distribution

The exact status of the black-faced spoonbill remains confusing because of incomplete knowledge about its natural history. The bird migrates annually to and from the northern reaches of its range in China, where ornithologists presume it nests. Whether the species also migrates in the southern part of its range is unknown, nor do ornithologists know how extensively the species nests there. A few black-faced spoonbills still nest on small islands off the coast of North Korea and in scattered localities of eastern China. Where those nesting colonies are, and how many nesting pairs they support, remains a mystery.

Several black-faced spoonbills were found at Lake Poyang in Jiangxi Province in 1986. Lake Poyang is a vast wetland complex. Its water levels fluctuate dramatically with the seasons. The area certainly offers ample habitat for the spoonbills, but no one has yet determined how extensively the species uses the area or how many spoonbills there might be.

At least 30 birds are known to occur in Korea, and 30 regularly winter in Hong Kong. Whether these are the same birds is unknown. Estimating population size on such scanty observations cannot be done with any accuracy. However, the lack of regular observations, the small numbers, and the absence of these spoonbills from areas they once used indicate that this species is in trouble. It is quite probable that the spoonbill suffers from habitat loss as China's huge population converts available land for food production.

Population estimates

Protecting the black-faced spoonbill will require surveying its historic range to determine its

In the closing decades of the 20th century, the black-faced spoonbill slowly but steadily disappeared from its historic range.

present distribution both in winter and summer. Basic natural history research must be undertaken to verify what the spoonbill needs for habitat, including nesting cover and food supply. Population estimates need to be compiled so that the species' numbers can be monitored over time. This will allow ornithologists to determine whether populations are increasing, decreasing, or holding steady. And finally, action must be taken to preserve the habitat in those areas where the black-faced spoonbill is known to occur. At present there is estimated to be a total population size of 323 individuals. They are known to breed only on four islands off the west coast of North Korea and in the Han Estuary in South Korea.

Kevin Cook

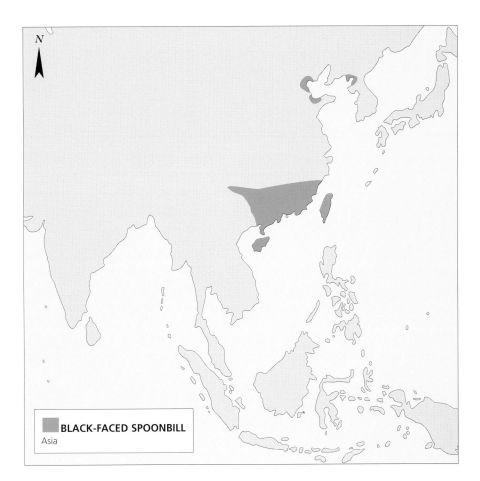

BLACK-FACED SPOONBILL
Asia

SPRINGFISH

Class: Actinopterygii

Order: Atheriniformes

Family: Cyprinodontidae

Springfish are part of the rather large and widespread group of fish called killifish (known as Cyprinodontidae and other families). Representatives of this family are found in temperate and tropical climates throughout most of the world. Killifish are found in North America, South America, Africa, southern Asia, southern Europe, and the East Indies, but are not native to Australia. Compared to most freshwater fish, killifish are able to inhabit some extreme aquatic environments. They are found in both salt water and fresh water, as well as in waters with a high mineral content. As a group, they show a tremendous range of temperature tolerance.

Killifish bear some resemblance to minnows (family *Cyprinidae*). In fact, the name of the killifish family loosely means toothed carp. Minnows and killifish are, however, quite different. The killifish tail is usually rounded. They have scales on the head (minnows do not) and, as the name toothed carp suggests, they have teeth in the mouth.

Springfish are solitary or live with only a few other species of fish. They are found in closed desert basins and often rely on springs or spring-fed environments (the habitat that gives them their name). Most springfish have evolved in isolated habitats that have remained relatively constant for thousands of years. This isolation has allowed changes to occur and, over time, these fish have evolved into unique species and subspecies.

Because springfish are small, they can occupy restricted habitats in significant numbers. This ability cannot save them, however, from severe changes in their spring environment brought about by human activities.

Their diversity is reason enough to study and preserve their populations. Yet some of their adaptations are so impressive that further study is warranted. Their biological mechanisms may have an important impact on human medical science. For example, springfish have the ability to live in water that is ten times more saline than seawater.

Railroad Valley Springfish

(Crenichthys nevadae)

ESA: Threatened

IUCN: Vulnerable

Length: 2¾ in. (7 cm)
Reproduction: Egg layer
Habitat: Warm spring pools and outflows
Range: Railroad Valley and Sodaville, Nevada

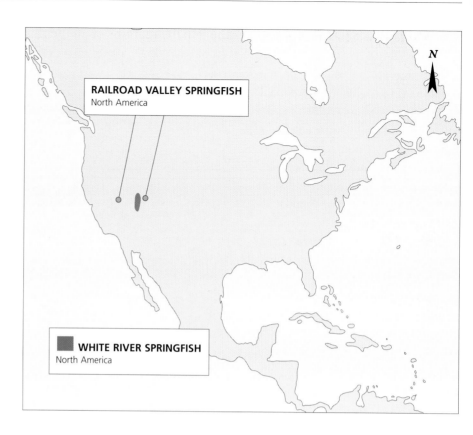

THE RAILROAD VALLEY springfish is native to a dry region in eastern Nevada and lives in isolated warm springs and their outflows. These springs are just west of the White River, home to other threatened and endangered springfish. Long ago, farmers and ranchers long ago took advantage of these springs to provide water for cattle and to irrigate crops and, as a result, have severely degraded the fish's habitat within these spring waterways. Cattle have trampled banks, and destroyed shading vegetation that is so important to the fish. Water diversions have dramatically altered water-flow patterns in the outflows. Nearby irrigators that pump groundwater have lowered local water tables and significantly reduced the output of free-flowing springs. Extra demands for water could cause the springs to fail.

Unwelcome visitors

There are also other problems. A number of introduced non-native fish such as the guppy (*Poecilia reticulata*) and the channel catfish (*Ictalurus punctatus*) have also had a significant impact on the springfish population in the Railroad Valley, through competition for habitat and predation.

The railroad valley springfish lacks pelvic fins on its belly like other springfish. It has a chunky appearance, its body being particularly broad near the head. It has a pointed snout, and a slightly upturned mouth.

Overall, the Railroad Valley springfish is green, with darker areas on the back and the top of the head and lighter shades on the sides. The belly and underside of the head are off-white and silvery. It has a distinctive row of black spots on each side that may or may not touch; the pattern suggests a stripe in some specimens. The dorsal fin on the back and the anal fin are positioned on the body toward the tail. Both are marked along their rounded tip with a band of dark pigment.

Because this species prefers warm spring water, spawning takes place throughout the year (but females produce more eggs in the summer). Females average 250 eggs per spawn in July and only 50 in January. The Railroad Valley springfish requires high-energy foods, such as aquatic invertebrates and other small animals, to meet its needs. However, during the summer, algae also provide an important component of the diet.

Special protection

In an effort to ease the threat to the Railroad Valley springfish, in 1947 some fish were moved to thermal ponds near Sodaville in western Nevada. The introduction was successful, but many of the problems that jeopardize the Railroad Valley population are also common to the Sodaville fish. The species as a whole is not endangered but, unless trends are reversed, the future of the Railroad Valley springfish at these locations is bleak.

White River Springfish

(Crenichthys baileyi baileyi)

ESA: Endangered

IUCN: Vulnerable

Length: 2¾ in. (7 cm)
Reproduction: Egg layer
Habitat: Spring pools and outflows
Range: White River and associated springs, Nevada

AT THE END OF the last glacial period, the White River was much larger and flowed into the Virgin River, a tributary of the Colorado River. Because of the warmer and drier conditions that followed the Ice Ages, water flow in the White River decreased substantially. Eventually, evaporation reduced the flow to zero. Forced to retreat to isolated pockets of springs and their outflows, separate populations of this springfish adapted to these altered conditions and evolved into several distinct subspecies, whose ancestors still survive today.

The White River springfish has a body shape much like that of its close relatives, the pupfish of the United States and Mexico. The body is robust, with a somewhat pointed snout. Scales cover most of the body, with the exception of the head. The dorsal fin on the back and the anal fin on the belly are set well back toward

An important factor in the White River springfish's survival is its adaptability. It is able to live in waters of high salinity and temperature. But even with these capabilities, the species cannot survive if its habitat is gone.

the tail; the margins of all the fins are rounded. One unusual trait is that all five subspecies lack pelvic fins on the belly. Their overall color is green, with a bold horizontal bar down each side. There are some dusky spots low on the tail section and lower sides.

Behavior

Because of their access to warm spring water on a year-round basis spawning continues throughout the year. Eggs are laid in warm pools and hatch within only a few days. Adults consume mainly insects, but they supplement their diet with algae and other plant material.

The various subspecies of White River springfish present biologists with a wonderful opportunity to study the processes of nature, especially the ways that a single species can splinter into subspecies when subjected to new conditions. Unfortunately, the total number of some species is low, occasionally less than 100 individuals. The diversion of water from springs of the White River and the pumping of groundwater pose real problems for their preservation. Despite their tolerance of high salinity

and high water temperature, these springfish will not survive in the wild if their springs fail. Compounding the problem is the presence of non-native fish that prey on the native White River springfish and compete for limited space. In particular, the convict cichlid (*Cichlasoma nigro-fasciatum*) and the mosquitofish (*Gambusia affinis*) present the greatest threats.

Efforts to save these subspecies have met with limited success. Securing habitat is particularly difficult when local landowners view these conservation efforts as unimportant.

Related subspecies

The White River springfish is related to four other subspecies, all of which are listed as vulnerable by IUCN-The World Conservation Union. These are the Preston springfish (*Crenichthys baileyi albivallis*), the Moapa springfish (*C. baileyi moapae*), the Moorman springfish (*C. baileyi thermophilus*) and the Hiko springfish (*C. baileyi grandis*), which is also listed as an endangered species by the U.S. Fish and Wildlife Service.

William E. Manci

Colorado Squawfish

(Ptychocheilus lucius)

ESA: Endangered

IUCN: Vulnerable

Class: Actinopterygii
Order: Cypriniformes
Family: Cyprinidae
Weight: Possibly more than 80 lb. (36 kg)
Length: Up to 6 ft. (1.8 m), average 3 ft. (0.9 m)
Reproduction: Egg layer
Habitat: River pools in murky water
Range: Upper Colorado River Basin, Colorado and Utah

THE COLORADO squawfish is considered to be a minnow and is part of the family Cyprinidae. But when people think of minnows, they think of small fish.

The Colorado squawfish, however, is the largest member of the family Cyprinidae in the United States. Known to live for as long as 50 or 60 years, the squawfish can reach lengths of up to 6 feet (1.8 meters) and weigh more than 80 pounds (36 kilograms). This fish is found in the upper Colorado River Basin at several locations above the Glen Canyon Dam at the Arizona-Utah border. All major tributaries in this upper basin, including the Green, Yampa, White, and San Juan Rivers of Utah and Colorado, hold at least some Colorado squawfish.

Before the construction of dams on the main stem of the Colorado River (and on other rivers in the basin such as the Gila, San Juan, and Green) this amazing river system was a great untamed water course. The rivers ran red with sediment, and the water flow and temperature varied greatly throughout the year,

depending on the amount of mountain runoff. During this period there were numerous Colorado squawfish throughout the river system. Early explorers and settlers used this species as a food fish and gave it the name of the "white salmon of the Colorado" because of its large size and white flesh. Then the construction of the Roosevelt Dam on Arizona's Gila River in 1913 started this fish on the road to disaster.

Deadly dams

After the Roosevelt Dam project came more than 20 others, including many on the main stem of the Colorado River such as the Hoover Dam and Glen Canyon Dam. These projects have changed the character of this 1,700-mile (2,735-kilometer) waterway forever. The Colorado River and its tributaries have become a series of dams and reservoirs, with downstream segments of river that bear little resemblance to their former condition. Dams have brought a variety of damage to the rivers and their native fish.

One type of damage caused by dams is the direct destruction of habitat through the creation of upstream reservoirs. These reservoirs inundate many miles of river, which become virtually unusable to river fish. Dams also block the migration of fish that traditionally move many miles up or down the river to spawn. They dramatically change the downstream water chemistry and quality by allowing sediments to settle out. Dams also alter the seasonal water flow and temperature patterns. This affects species' numbers: if a species is accustomed to cloudy or turbid

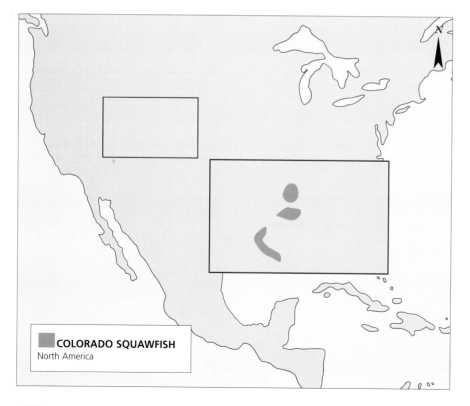

COLORADO SQUAWFISH
North America

water, clearer water can have an adverse effect, and vice versa. Finally, dams disrupt the food chain in the river, with native fish and other native animals replaced by more opportunistic, non-native species.

Some introduced non-native fish flourished in the altered surroundings. The lower Colorado River is now nearly incapable of supporting squawfish.

Appearance

The Colorado squawfish has a body shape that is typical of a river fish. As the total number of fish has diminished, the average length has decreased to about 3 feet (0.9 meter). It has a long tubular body, pointed snout, large mouth, and flattened head. All the squawfish's fins are light in color and a pointed triangular shape, except for the forked tail fin (indicating that it is a strong swimmer). The top of the head, back, and upper sides are a uniform olive green that lightens to white on the lower sides, underside of the head, and belly. The body is well scaled to prevent abrasion in the harsh river environment, but the head has relatively few scales.

Breeding

The Colorado squawfish reaches sexual maturity after six years and spawns in water at a temperature of about 70 degrees Fahrenheit (21 degrees Centigrade). River temperatures reach this in late spring and early summer. Eggs hatch a few days after spawning. The newly-hatched fish eat insects and aquatic invertebrates, but the adults eat other fish and sometimes aquatic mammals and birds.

During certain periods of the year, Colorado squawfish were so numerous that they were literally pitch-forked from the river and carted off to fields for use as fertilizer.

Despite the fact that the Colorado squawfish will never again enjoy the full extent of its historical range, biologists hope to repopulate the upper segments of the Colorado River Basin, as well as some segments of the lower basin. It is hoped that this will reverse the current trend toward extinction.

Efforts are underway to raise this species at state and federal fish hatcheries for restocking purposes, and some success has been achieved. Monitoring of the fish's progress after stocking is difficult, but data indicates that recovery, if at all successful, will be long and slow.

William E. Manci

SQUIRRELS

Class: Mammalia

Order: Rodentia

Family: Sciuridae

There are at least 260 species of squirrel, chipmunk, prairie dog, and marmot, and these live on most continents throughout the world. They come in a variety of sizes and shades of fur, but most are recognizable by their pointed, whiskered snouts, small forearms with four digits, and rather large tails, which are usually covered with hair.

Flying squirrels have a membrane of skin that joins their front and back limbs. By spreading this membrane, a flying squirrel can glide between trees. While flying squirrels and other species are mainly arboreal, many species are terrestrial, nesting on the ground.

All squirrels eat seeds, nuts, and other vegetable matter. Sometimes they damage crops with their burrowing, but they are also useful for eating harmful insects and weeds.

Carolina Northern Flying Squirrel

(Glaucomys sabrinus coloratus)

ESA: Endangered

IUCN: Vulnerable

Virginia Northern Flying Squirrel

(Glaucomys sabrinus fuscus)

ESA: Endangered

IUCN: Vulnerable

Weight: 6–14 oz. (170–390 g)

Habitat: Spruce-fir and hardwood forest

Range: Appalachian Mountains, North America

WHEN DARKNESS approaches across the northern portions of North America, most members of the family Sciuridae settle into their nests for the night. But this is not the case with the northern flying squirrel. One of two species of flying squirrel found in North America—the other being the southern flying squirrel (*Glaucomys volans*)—this species is just starting to gear up for another night of foraging when the sun goes down.

Each species of flying squirrel has its own habitat preferences: the northern flying squirrel ranges within coniferous forest, while the southern species prefers hardwood forest. In some areas these species overlap, and when this happens there appears to be some competition for both nesting sites and food. It is in one of these areas of overlap (the southern Appalachian Mountains) where two subspecies of northern flying squirrel are endangered. These are the Carolina northern flying squirrel (*Glaucomys sabrinus coloratus*) and the Virginia northern flying squirrel (*G. sabrinus fuscus*).

One of the first things to understand about flying squirrels is that they do not actually fly. The only mammals that can fly are bats, and these two species of squirrel would be more accurately known as gliding squirrels. Without a doubt, flying squirrels do manage to cover very large distances in the air, moving from tree to tree, but they do so in a way that is similar to hang-gliding.

A flying squirrel looks much like a squirrel, but with a few important differences. Its body is not very robust and is relatively long considering its weight. The tail is flattened, resembling a feather. The most distinctive physical trait is the patagium, a fur-covered gliding membrane which extends between the fore and hind limbs on each side of the body. By extending the limbs outward and using the flattened tail like a rudder, this species is able to glide up to 165 feet (50 meters).

Breeding

The northern flying squirrel produces one litter of two to four young each year, typically between late May and early July. While they prefer to spend the winter in hollow trees and other cavities (such as attics and sheds), members of this species often spend the summer and bear their young in leaf nests approximately 12 to 16 inches (30 to 40 centimeters) in diameter. The young weigh only about 5 to 6 grams at birth and do not open their eyes until they are about one month old. They are relatively inactive until they are eight to nine weeks of age, when they are weaned.

The diet of these squirrels, like many other squirrels, is quite varied. They eat nuts, seeds, buds, twigs, bark, lichen, fungi, fruit, insects, and occasionally meat. Flying squirrels remain in their nests during cold or harsh weather, but they do not hibernate. When food is plentiful, they are known to hoard supplies to use during the winter.

Since flying squirrels are active mostly at night, their major predators are nocturnal ones. In the range occupied by the Carolina and Virginia varieties, these predators include owls, house cats, foxes, and weasels.

Isolated populations

While the population levels of the Carolina and Virginia northern flying squirrels seem to have stopped decreasing since the 1980s, there is still much concern about their future. Together, both subspecies represent the southernmost populations of the Virginia northern flying squirrel (*G. sabrinus*) in the eastern United States. These populations occur on what are known as habitat islands. Since the squirrels prefer habitats that are dominated by conifers, they are isolated at high elevations ranging from 3,300 to 6,000 feet (1,000–1,830 meters), and live only on the north-facing slopes in the southern Appalachians. This isolation puts them in jeopardy for a great many reasons.

First, these areas have been logged in the past and are still potential sites for timber extraction. In addition, a number of high-elevation conifer forests in the Appalachians have shown deterioration. It is believed that this is due to climatic stress or atmospheric pollution.

Second, even if the habitat of these subspecies is protected

from logging and climatic assaults, there are other problems facing them. If their populations become too small, the potential for disaster is increased. For example, a severe storm or forest fire could wipe out all the members of a habitat island. In addition, small populations are always at risk of inbreeding. When there are too few breeding individuals, the quality of the gene pool is reduced. This lack of genetic diversity reduces a species' ability to respond to environmental change.

Also, there is some evidence that a parasitic nematode, or roundworm, carried by the southern flying squirrel (and apparently causing it no harm) is possibly lethal to the northern flying squirrel.

The watch continues

Surveys conducted during the late 1980s and early 1990s indicate that several new localities have been occupied by both the Carolina and Virginia subspecies, and that the use of nest boxes is high in several of the old localities. If this trend is to be encouraged it would mean a suspension of logging in the higher elevation coniferous forests so that the northern flying squirrels' habitat can be preserved. More study is needed to understand why these forests are deteriorating: it may be due to the climate, pollution, or a combination of both of these factors. The answers may help conservationists decide whether the Virginia and Carolina northern flying squirrels, as well as other members of these Appalachian habitat islands, require additional help in order to survive.

Delmarva Fox Squirrel

(Sciurus niger cinereus)

| IUCN: Lower risk |

Weight: 1½–2½ lb. (0.7–1.1 kg)
Head-body length: 9⅘–12⅓ in. (25–31.5 cm)
Diet: Omnivorous, primarily nuts and seeds
Gestation period: 45 days
Habitat: Mature mixed hardwoods
Range: Northeastern United States

IN WOODED AREAS of the eastern United States there are two species of squirrels in the genus *Sciurus*. They have similar nesting and feeding habits and seem to coexist mainly because they prefer slightly different wooded habitats. The gray squirrel (*S. carolinensis*) prefers woods with a shrubby undergrowth. The intricate network of branches provided by this undergrowth is probably their best defense against danger. By contrast, the fox squirrel (*S. niger*) prefers more open woods, especially those with clearings or open areas along streams. This species often takes to the ground when threatened, using impressive speed to outdistance its enemies.

It is these subtle differences in habitat preference that result in two species being affected in different ways by the arrival of the intensive, land-clearing agricultural methods of the European colonists. In this case, one species fared well, while the other suffered a decline. But even this reaction is not consistent across the range held in common by these two squirrels.

The Delmarva fox squirrel is one of the larger fox squirrels and was formerly found in southeastern Pennsylvania, south-central New Jersey, and the Delmarva Peninsula (containing portions of Maryland, Virginia, and Delaware). It has a large, bushy tail and small, round ears. The color of the fur varies from gray to reddish above, while the underparts are a dingy white.

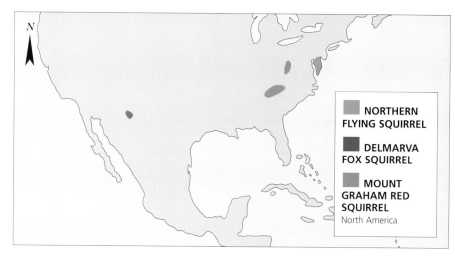

Nutrients

The Delmarva fox squirrel does not hibernate, preferring to survive the winter on its stored reserves of acorns, walnuts, beech, and hickory nuts. In the spring, summer, and fall it broadens its diet with the addition of buds, flowers, fruits, fungus, insects, and occasionally the eggs and young of birds.

The fox squirrel (*Sciuridae niger*) is part of the tree squirrel genus, but it forages on the ground and can outrun predators.

Fox squirrels have an extended breeding season, with peaks in activity occurring from late February to March and again from late July to early August. After a gestation period of about 45 days, females give birth—usually in a hollow den in a large tree—to a litter of two to four young. Females raise the young alone, while males attempt to mate with more than one female. The young open their eyes after about 5 weeks and are weaned between 9 and 12 weeks. Females have been known to produce two

litters a year. This is possible because of the relatively short gestation period, the young age at which their offspring are weaned, and the two breeding peaks each year.

Competition

This subspecies has suffered from a set of circumstances that, for reasons scientists do not fully understand, are different from those experienced by other subspecies of fox squirrel.

Elsewhere in the eastern United States, in areas occupied by both the fox squirrel and the gray squirrel, the clearing of land for agriculture has resulted in the fox squirrel expanding both its numbers and its range, often at the expense of the gray squirrel. One theory suggests that, after the forests in the Delmarva fox squirrel's range were extensively logged, the new growth had an abundance of brushy undergrowth that was then cut again before it could mature enough to provide the hollow den sites that are preferred by this species.

If this is the case then the gray squirrel, which uses predominantly leaf nests and eats many of the same foods as the fox squirrel, would have thrived and

added increased feeding competition to problems already affecting the Delmarva fox squirrel. Finally, the larger size of the fox squirrel relative to the gray squirrel, as well as its tendency to run across open ground, rather than hide in the branches, may have caused it to suffer greater losses to hunting in the late 19th and early 20th centuries.

Decline halted

Although the total population of the Delmarva fox squirrel may have been less than 1,000 in 1978, the recovery plan drafted at that time is apparently halting the decline and helping to stabilize the numbers of this particularly rare subspecies. The major thrust of the plan has been to provide nest boxes to squirrel populations in protected wildlife refuges and to relocate individuals from those areas to other suitable regions.

Delmarva fox squirrels were reintroduced to Chincoteague National Wildlife Refuge in Virginia in the late 1960s and early 1970s. The releases were successful, as were other releases in 1982 in Northampton County, Virginia, and in 1984 in Sussex County, Delaware. Individuals have also been released at the Prime Hook National Wildlife Refuge in Delaware.

The current recovery plan aims to establish a minimum of 30 colonies in areas that were formerly occupied by this fox squirrel. It appears that with acquisition of suitable habitat, placement of nest boxes, some brush removal, and occasional control of resident gray squirrels, this plan has a high probability of being successful.

Mount Graham Red Squirrel

(Tamiasciurus hudsonicus grahamensis)

ESA: Endangered

IUCN: Critically endangered

Weight: 5–11 oz. (141–312 g)
Head-body length: 6½–9 in. (16.5–23 cm)
Diet: Omnivorous
Gestation period: 33–35 days
Longevity: Up to 7 years
Habitat: Forests above 10,000 ft. (3,050 m)
Range: Pinaleño Mountains, southeastern Arizona

The ability to raise two litters a year may prove to be vitally important to the Delmarva fox squirrel.

THE RED SQUIRREL (*Tamiasciurus hudsonicus*) is a widely distributed member of the squirrel family. It is found throughout much of Alaska and Canada, as well as in many parts of the northern Midwest and New England. There are also several subspecies that occur at mid-to-high elevations within the Rocky Mountain region of the western United States. The population of one of these subspecies, the Mount Graham red squirrel, has been declining throughout most of the 20th century.

Although poorly studied, it is believed that the Mount Graham red squirrel produces a litter of from one to eight young, probably once or twice a year. This assumption is based upon knowledge of other subspecies. The squirrel does not hibernate, relying on its midden (a stash of food) to provide it with the food necessary to survive the winter. While the seeds from the Engelmann spruce (*Picea engelmannii*) and the corkbark fir (*Aibes lasiocarpa*) form the major part of the winter diet, the summer diet also includes nuts, fruits, bark, sap, buds, fungi, birds' eggs and fledglings, mice, and baby rabbits.

An unlikely enemy

Until recently, the decline of the Mount Graham red squirrel was, in most respects, similar to the decline of so many endangered organisms. Although common in the Pinaleño Mountains at the beginning of the 20th century, the loss of habitat to logging initiated a downward spiral in red squirrel numbers. Following the logging, there was further habitat disruption that followed the development of the area for recreation. Competition from the introduced tassel-eared squirrel (*Sciurus aberti*) is also believed to have played a part in the red squirrel's decline.

The Mount Graham red squirrel is a small rodent with the distinctive bushy tail associated with other members of the squirrel family.

While still threatened by potential logging and the expansion of recreational facilities such as picnic areas and campgrounds, the newest threat to the existence of the Mount Graham red squirrel comes from a most unlikely source: the University of Arizona. The listing of this subspecies as endangered in the summer of 1987 resulted in an outcry from astrophysicists, who had been counting on the development of a large telescope complex to be built within the range of the Mount Graham red squirrel (T. *hudsonicus. grahamensis*). Once a species is listed as endangered by the Department of Interior, that species' range is protected.

Officials at the University of Arizona and some Arizona congressmen began a campaign to rescue the economically attractive observatory complex. Despite the listing, many people wanted the project to proceed, even if it meant reducing the range of the red squirrel still further. A plan submitted by the university maintained that the observatory complex and the Mount Graham red squirrels could coexist on this high point above the desert. After a great deal of political maneuvering, the U.S. Congress overruled the listing and permitted the building of the observatory.

Population change

Midden counts indicate that squirrel numbers declined from around 200 in 1986 to around 50 in 1988. These were years of poor cone production by the corkbark fir and Engelmann spruce trees. However, good cone production during the years of 1989 and 1990 led to an increase in population numbers, so it appears that the squirrel's total population is at least partially determined by its food resources. It is still uncertain how much human encroachment will affect the squirrel, however, either through the loss of nesting habitat or the disruption of the squirrels' food supply.

Several unsuccessful attempts through the court system were made to delay the construction on Mount Graham. In September 1989, project construction began as planned. Construction has proceeded since that time, and even though legal efforts are still ongoing, the displacement of the endangered Mount Graham red squirrel is now an unavoidable fact.

Terry Tompkins

STARLINGS

Class: Aves

Order: Passeriformes

Family: Sturnidae

Subfamily: Sturninae

Starlings bully other birds at bird feeders, outcompete other birds for nesting space, and even evict other species from established nesting sites. They damage crops, gather in huge flocks to feed on cattle food, may spread disease to poultry, and create enormous messes with their droppings. If starlings can be so destructive, how is it possible that any of them might be endangered?

Not all starlings are the same. They comprise a large family of 111 songbird species, including the famous myna birds. The entire family occurs naturally only in the eastern hemisphere, excluding Australia. Many starlings are quite attractive and give calls and songs. The mynas, of course, amuse people with their ability to talk. They are actually capable mimics and repeat only what they often hear. They have no capacity for conversation.

Because people enjoy bird sounds, bright colors, and amusing tricks, they have captured and transported members of the starling family all over the world. Some of the birds have escaped captivity or have been deliberately set free. The European starling (*Sturnus vulgaris*) is the most recognizable starling, and it has survived well. Not all starlings have been so successful. Many species have declined dramatically, and several are extinct.

Bali Starling

(Leucospar rothschildi)

ESA: Endangered

IUCN: Critically endangered

Length: 10 in. (25.4 cm)

Clutch size: 3 eggs (in captivity)

Incubation: 10–16 days (in captivity)

Diet: Small fruits, insects, small reptiles

Habitat: Primary forests, woodland, savanna

Range: Bali in the Lesser Sunda Islands of Indonesia

THE BALI STARLING suffers due to two human factors: their passion for caging birds with pretty colors or songs, and their over-reliance on certain types of energy resources.

In the United States an energy crisis refers to inadequate supplies of petroleum for producing heating oil, gasoline, diesel fuel, and other similar fuels. In many other parts of the world an energy crisis means that there is too much demand for too small a supply of basics such as firewood. Many human cultures still use such resources for their living requirements. People in places such as Bali depend less on technology-based equipment for their day-to-day living and more on unrefined natural products. Wood provides fuel for cooking. Collecting firewood naturally becomes an important daily or weekly task.

Cut down

As the human population of an area grows, the demand for firewood grows accordingly. Quite often the demand for firewood exceeds a forest's or woodland's capacity to yield it. People cut down the trees and shrubs faster than these resources can grow back. The process eventually destroys forests or woodlands and displaces or destroys all the wildlife that depends on them. People ultimately suffer because they run out of firewood. The firewood dilemma has been growing on Bali for decades. Just 55 miles wide and 90 miles long (88 by 144 kilometers), Bali covers 2,243 square miles (5,832 square kilometers). Lying just east of Java, it is the westernmost island of the Lesser Sundas. The Java Sea washes its northern shores, and the Indian Ocean laps at its southern beaches. The original Balinese people produced fine works of carving and weaving. Dutch sailors found Bali in 1597 and set up trade with the Balinese. Access to Bali was rigidly controlled for centuries, but after World War II, approximately 13,500 islands of the East Indies were consolidated into the Republic of Indonesia. With the formation of Indonesia, the flow of Javanese emigrants to Bali increased dramatically. The population topped a million people in the 1970s. The island economy depends on crops of coffee, rice, and tobacco, as well as raising livestock and the processing of coconut into copra. Bali has also become a favored resort of the wealthy, and tourism is important to the economy.

Bali's growing human population forced changes during the

last half of the 20th century. The island's primary forests were cut to make space for people to live, and for agriculture. Additional forest area was scavenged for firewood. The habitat available for the Bali starling, which lives nowhere else except on Bali, shrank steadily. Other factors also worked against the bird.

Cage birds

Since its discovery in 1911, the Bali starling has been a prized cage bird all over the world. Two particular features distinguish it. First, it has an overall snow-white plumage, except for a black band across the tip of the tail and black tips across the outer flight feathers of the wing. The bare skin around the eye is a rich, cobalt blue. Second, the Bali starling has a large crest that grows from front to back and down, making the bird's head appear large and rather square.

Local interest

When bird populations decline because of excessive trapping for the cage bird trade, blame is usually aimed at a foreign demand for exotic species. In truth, local demand often matches or exceeds international demand. International treaties such as the Convention on Trade of Endangered Species of Flora and Fauna (CITES) make import and export of designated species extremely difficult. Even though illegal trading continues internationally, smuggling live birds into foreign markets has actually declined. That means that enforcement of local laws often fails to stop local trade. The people on Bali have always adored birds: many households

The Bali starling possesses an elegant, distinguished look. Trapping of the starling grew as the human fancy for birds in cages expanded.

keep many birds of several species.

The Bali starling now survives only in Bali Barat National Park. Despite national laws against bird poaching, trappers were living in the park as recently as the 1980s. Ornithologists estimated that the total Bali starling population was less than 1,000 in the 1970s, but in the 1980s as many as 16 were caged together in Bali villages, where anyone could buy them for the equivalent of $130 a bird.

Protection

Obviously, increased trapping in decreased habitat, coupled with unrestricted shooting, has led to a vastly diminished starling population. Specific recommendations for protecting the Bali starling have been made and some corrective actions have been taken. The bird prefers nesting in cavities of dead or partially dead acacia trees (*Acacia* sp.), which became scarce when forests were cut for firewood. Acacias have been replanted in certain areas. Also, nesting boxes suitable for Bali starlings have been hung in strategic areas. Other recommendations have included enforcing the trapping laws, expelling the resident bird trappers from the national park, and forbidding all forms of hunting for birds. The hunting ban would include firearms, nets, traps, bird lime, and blowguns, as well as other devices.

Since these recommendations have been proposed, captive populations increased from 50 birds in 1964 to 526 birds in 1974. By 1990 the captive population had grown to 1,000. Ornithologists hope that the ability to breed Bali starlings in captivity will produce a supply of birds that will eliminate the need to capture and smuggle wild birds. Captive populations keep individuals alive, but they are no substitute for wild birds in their natural habitat. On Bali, as the captive population grew, the wild population declined. In 1984 the wild population numbered less than

200 birds. Four years later, the Bali starling population had dwindled to less than 100.

Breeding program

An aggressive program to breed Bali starlings for release into the wild was undertaken in 1987. If successful, the program would bolster the wild population. However, if all the factors that caused endangerment and population decline remain active in Bali, the wild population cannot recover, no matter how many captive birds are released there.

The habitat set aside for the unique starlings of Bali must be protected from people who do not understand or care about the consequences of their actions.

The Bali starling would benefit from a stabilization or a reduction of the human population on the island. It would also be helped if an alternative source of cooking fuel was developed, to stop encroachment of its habitat.

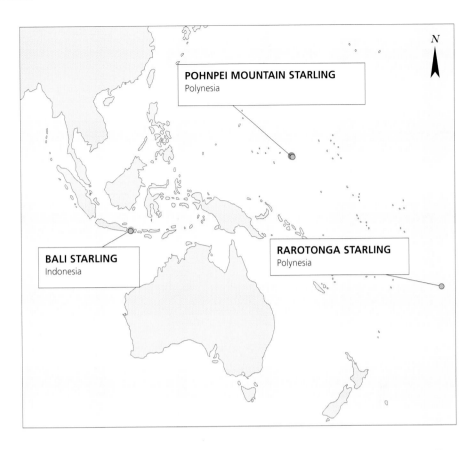

Pohnpei Mountain Starling

(Aplonis pelzelni)

ESA: Endangered

IUCN: Critically endangered

Length: 7 in. (17.8 cm)
Habitat: Forest
Range: Pohnpei of the Caroline Islands, western Pacific Ocean

A DOZEN small, dark birds move swiftly from the top of a tall tree at the forest's edge. They fly halfway across a clearing, turn sharply in unison, drop down a few feet, then resume their original course. Reaching the far side of the clearing, they rise up above another tree, circle back, then slow down before disappearing into the greenery. Against the tropical sky they almost look black. They might be Pohnpei mountain starlings, but their chunky body proportions, shiny plumage, thick beaks, and yellow eyes prove them to be Micronesian starlings (*Aplonis opaca*).

Coloring

Overall, the Pohnpei mountain starling appears to be a generally sooty color. Its eyes are a brown color, the wing shows more brown than the body, and the entire plumage lacks any kind of sheen.

While the Micronesian starling occurs commonly throughout the Mariana and Caroline Islands, the Pohnpei mountain starling may already be extinct.

Island life

Pohnpei was formerly known as Ponape. By global standards it is a small island of only 128½ square miles (334 square kilometers), but by Micronesian standards it is fairly large. Pohnpei is mountainous and retains some primary forests, especially at higher elevations. The Pohnpei mountain starling is a bird of the forest canopy. Being sooty colored, it can easily be missed in the shadows, especially if it occurs in small numbers.

Population reduction

Starling habitat still exists on Pohnpei, and Micronesian starlings still live abundantly on the island. Something on the island changed without seriously affecting the Micronesian species, but it did affect the Pohnpei mountain starling. At least 59 Pohnpei mountain starlings were collected in the early 1930s. The species was described as common in the mountain forests at the time, but those 59 specimens may actually have represented the bulk of the species' population. Ornithologists reported the species to be very rare by the 1940s. Since then, one specimen has been reported in the 1950s, none in the 1960s, one in the 1970s, none in the 1980s, and none in the early 1990s. Collecting may have worsened a decline that was initially started by rats.

Mountainous island
Both Polynesian rats and black rats (*Rattus* sp.) have colonized Pohnpei. Both rats are known to take eggs and nestlings. The Micronesian starling is bold and aggressive and may defend itself and its nests more successfully than the Pohnpei mountain starling. Although rats were probably depleting the population for decades, they may not be the only culprits.

Exotic threats
Other exotic species create problems all over the world. An exotic bird disease may possibly be afflicting the starling. An exotic plant may be out-competing native plants on which the starling depends for food. A very real possibility would be more than one exotic bird species, more than one exotic plant species, plus rats and disease all working simultaeously against the Pohnpei starling.

If such a combination of exotic species had been slowly depleting the population for a number of decades, a great collecting spree could have added one stress too many.

Disappearance
As yet, ornithologists do not clearly understand the disappearance of this starling. Some contend it may still live in small numbers high in the island's remote montane forests. Other birds have survived undetected for long periods. Single observers, even small teams of them, cannot cover all habitat simultaneously. Short search periods are also a problem. Finding birds can be a matter of searching at the right time of day in the right season. The Pohnpei mountain starling will, quite possibly, eventually prove itself among the survivors.

Rarotonga Starling
(Aplonis cinerascens)

IUCN: Vulnerable

Length: 8 in. (20 cm)
Habitat: Forest
Range: Rarotonga in the Cook Islands of the central Pacific Ocean

BY THE TIME people found Rarotonga Island, birds were already well established there. Many birds are specially adapted for life at sea and can survive extreme water and weather conditions. Yet even land birds ill-equipped for ocean life fly towards the horizon and end up on islands. Most of them perish, a few return, and far fewer find islands where they can settle. When individuals find islands, the eventual outcome is death. If flocks of birds find them, or if islands are positioned so that regular invasions can occur, then those birds can reproduce. Given adequate water, food, and cover, the birds may survive. Isolated over time and pressured to survive on the meager resources of the island, those birds may specialize into unique species. The Rarotonga starling is probably such a bird.

At least a dozen land birds found Rarotonga long before the first people arrived. Asian peoples pioneered the islands of the East Indies around 1500 B.C.E. They quite probably found New Guinea and lived there for a while as their population grew. People departed New Guinea in many ways. Many intrepid explorers no doubt suffered the same fate as the first land birds caught upon a stormy sea. Others found their way to islands, and eventually most of the Pacific islands became inhabited by people, including Rarotonga.

Largest of the Cook Islands, Rarotonga barely covers a droplet of the great Pacific Ocean. Just 6 miles long by 4 miles wide (9.6 by 6.4 kilometers), it covers 26 square miles (67 square kilometers). Most of Rarotonga's early settlers lived in the coastal lowlands, where they pursued a lifestyle that met their needs. Colonialism introduced the concept of producing goods for international trade. Soon Rarotonga was producing oranges, bananas, coconuts, and vanilla for the benefit of world trade. Developing plantations required cutting down native forests that were home to the

The passion for birds is not limited to keeping them in cages. Some people find greater delight in shooting birds. Wealthy tourists on Bali enjoy a good hunt in the countryside, where they shoot whatever they find.

birds that had found Rarotonga long before the first humans arrived.

Birds in danger

Converting the lifestyle of the island to fit a global economy has reduced the habitat available to these birds. Among the dozen bird species were three pigeons, two kingfishers, two starlings, and one each of a parrot, cuckoo, swiftlet, warbler, and monarch. Almost without doubt the same problems of exotic species that befell other islands afflicted Rarotonga, too. People brought pets and livestock to the islands, and rats probably came along by accident. Pigs and goats can radically alter natural plant communities by the way they feed. Cats and dogs can affect wildlife through their predatory habits. Rats also severely affect wildlife by their ability to climb trees and hunt eggs and nestlings.

The Rarotonga monarch (*Pomarea dimidiata*) has dwindled to just a few birds, and the Rarotonga starling has also declined.

Appearance

The Rarotonga starling has plumage that is ashy gray overall, with a pale brown wash and a bright white undertail. The body feathers are paler at the edges and darker in the centers so the bird appears faintly scaled or spotted. At only 8 inches (20 centimeters) long, with a short tail and modest beak, the

Rarotonga starling has the same physique as the commonly known European starling (*Sturnus vulgaris*). However, unlike the European starling that has thrived worldwide, the Rarotonga starling lives nowhere else except on this speck of land in the Pacific Ocean. Described as common in decades past, the Rarotonga had declined to fewer than 100 birds by the 1980s.

Ornithologists have offered no thorough explanations for the species' survival problems. Worldwide, however, the combination of habitat loss, growing human populations, exotic mammals, and the natural isolation of an island creates a lethal formula for endangering birds.

Danger

The Rarotonga starling may perish altogether before its problems can be specifically identified and corrected.

Kevin Cook

1387

STICKLEBACKS

Class: Actinopterygii

Order: Gasterosteiformes

Family: Gasterosteidae

Sticklebacks have been the subject of scientific curiosity for many decades. Film documentaries have been produced and volumes of behavioral data collected for many of the species in this group.

Their stylized courtship ritual, which involves the construction of a tunnel nest by the male and precise body movements and courtship positions, has been studied by behaviorists who hoped to understand the development of this evolutionary adaptation.

The common name for these fish is well deserved. All sticklebacks wield a varying number of stout defensive spines on their back and belly, and most have protective armor plates in rows along the sides instead of scales. Despite this formidable array of defensive weapons, sticklebacks are preyed on by the many larger fish that have mastered the art of eating a stickleback head first, minimizing damage to the predator's mouth and digestive tract.

These small, curious fish occupy primarily temperate and polar marine environments throughout a large portion of coastal North America, Eurasia, and even northern Africa. Those populations that have moved inland to freshwater environments have been successful and have penetrated the continents for thousands of miles. In North America sticklebacks can be found as far inland as the upper midwestern states, and in Asia they can be found in central Siberia. Given this range, it is not surprising that sticklebacks readily adapt to different environments, even within the same species.

Despite their remarkable ability to colonize new areas and expand their range, sticklebacks are sensitive to changes in water quality. Chemical pollution, siltation, and other physical and chemical disturbances severely disrupt the stability of stickleback populations. Those species that are threatened or endangered have been adversely affected by diminished water quality.

The Enos stickleback and the giant stickleback species were previously evaluated by IUCN as threatened, and the Santa Ana and unarmored threespine was ranked as endangered, but these were not evaluated by the time the Red List was compiled.

Until more data is available, the species is included with other endangered taxa, because it may still be at risk.

Enos Stickleback
(Gasterosteus sp.)

Giant Stickleback
(Gasterosteus sp.)

Reproduction: Egg layer
Habitat: Pristine lakes and streams
Range: British Columbia, Canada

LITTLE IS KNOWN about these members of the genus *Gasterosteus* because they are undescribed by ichthyologists (scientists who study fish). Without an accurate description of a real specimen, it is hard to tell anything about the physiology and natural habits of a species.

Environmental threat

Both the Enos stickleback and the giant stickleback occupy a severely restricted range within British Columbia, Canada. Reports indicate that these fish are threatened by the destruction of habitat that is critical to their survival. In all probability, it is changes in water quality caused by human activities and development that have threatened these species.

Recommendations

Without knowing the causes for certain, however, little can be recommended in the way of protecting either the Enos stickleback or the giant stickleback, other than recommending that their habitat be left undisturbed.

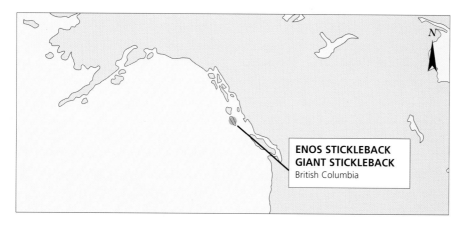

**ENOS STICKLEBACK
GIANT STICKLEBACK**
British Columbia

Santa Ana Stickleback

(Gasterosteus aculeatus santaeannae)

Unarmored Threespine Stickleback

(Gasterosteus aculeatus williamsoni)

ESA: Endangered

Length: 2½ in. (6 cm)
Reproduction: Egg layer
Habitat: Clear and clean stream pools
Range: Santa Ana River Basin and Santa Barbara County, California

THE SANTA ANA stickleback and the unarmored threespine stickleback are two of several subspecies of threespine sticklebacks present on the North American continent.

The Santa Ana stickleback used to be found throughout the Santa Ana River of Orange and Riverside Counties in southern California. However, given its extreme sensitivity to even slightly degraded water quality, today this stickleback is found only at scattered locations within the river. Urbanization and the accompanying pollution and destruction of habitat in the lower reaches of the river quickly eliminated the Santa Ana stickleback from many segments of the river. Additionally, predators such as the introduced African clawed frog (*Xenopus laevis*) and the rainbow trout (*Oncorhynchus mykiss*) can easily consume this weak-swimming fish. The use of

frogs in laboratories and as pets means that there is a constant threat of introduction, despite efforts to rid the area of this pest. Competitors, such as the mosquitofish (*Gambusia affinis*), could adversely affect the remaining populations.

In addition to keeping the existing habitat free of predators and competitors, there is an effort on the part of conservation officials to maintain minimum stream flows. Water diversion and groundwater pumping could deplete the Santa Ana River to dangerously low levels. Such diversions and pumping would not be unusual in an urban area.

During most of the year the Santa Ana stickleback is olive or green on the back and silvery white on the belly. However, during the breeding season the male changes dramatically, and its belly becomes bright red. The female changes color as well, but in a much less dramatic fashion: her belly and throat turn pale pink. Both sexes wield protective spines, not only on their backs but also on the belly in front of

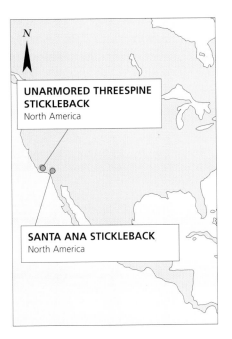

the pelvic and anal fins. The pectoral fins just behind the gills are broad and square and the dorsal fin on the back is set behind the three defensive spines. The tail section of the fish is unusually narrow, which partly accounts for its poor swimming performance. The tail fin is triangular to accommodate its narrow base.

The breeding behavior of sticklebacks is highly stylized and elaborate and has been well documented for many stickleback species. After building a tunnel-like nest from pieces of vegetation and debris, the female is lured into the tunnel and coaxed to release her eggs. The male follows quickly to fertilize the eggs and protect them from predators. The male also fans the nest with his large pectoral fins to keep adequate amounts of oxygen flowing through this tunnel.

After the eggs hatch and the young fry absorb their yolk sac, they feed on plankton until they are large enough to eat their favorite foods, which include snails and insects.

The threespine stickleback has the same protective spines on its back as other sticklebacks. Unlike other sticklebacks, however, this variety lacks the armor plating that provides extra protection against predators and so is called unarmored. In every other respect the unarmored threespine stickleback shares the same appearance and breeding behavior as the Santa Ana variety.

This subspecies used to be found throughout both Los Angeles and Santa Barbara Counties of southern California. The Los Angeles River and other rivers that flow through the heart

The unarmored threespine stickleback is closely related to the Santa Ana stickleback.

of the city used to carry large populations of this fish. However, given its extreme sensitivity to even slightly degraded water quality, it is no surprise that today it is found only in the headwaters of the Santa Clara River and in San Antonio Creek, both in Santa Barbara County. Urbanization, and the accompanying pollution and disturbances to natural systems, very quickly eliminated the unarmored threespine stickleback from Los Angeles County waterways. In San Antonio Creek this fish is threatened by interbreeding with another threespine stickleback (*Gasterosteus aculeatus microcephalus*). Fortunately, the Santa Clara River population is somewhat secure.

Presently, the area is not highly developed, and interbreeding with other species of sticklebacks does not seem to be a particular concern. However, there is very little doubt that introduced predators, such as the African clawed frog, and competitors, such as the mosquitofish (*Gambusia affinis*), could adversely affect the remaining populations of unarmored sticklebacks.

Conservation

Keeping existing habitat free of predators and competitors is the goal of conservation officials, who are also trying to maintain the minimum stream flows. Water diversion and groundwater pumping could deplete the Santa Clara River to dangerously low levels.

William E. Manci

STILTS

Class: Aves

Order: Charadriiformes

Family: Recurvirostridae

Stilts stand tip-toed on long, skinny feet. Spindly legs give them their common name, but most of their leg is actually a foot. A bird's upper leg is entirely concealed under its body feathers where it cannot be seen. The lower leg extends downward from the hidden knee. The part of the leg that looks like a backward knee is really the bird's ankle. The leg located between the ankle and the ground is actually the bird's foot. All birds actually walk on their toes all of the time.

The stilt family includes two species groups, stilts in the genus *Himantopus* and the avocets (genus *Recurvirostra*), plus the unique banded stilt (*Cladorhynchus leucocephala*) of Australia. Some ornithologists recognize that there are as few as three stilt species, others recognize as many as eight. A recent attempt to revise general bird taxonomy proposes five species. Most ornithologists agree on four avocet species.

All the stilts inhabit wetland habitats. Their long legs and feet elevate them for wading in shallow water, especially shallow water with plant life that grows a few inches above the water surface. They all build nests near the water's edge. When the chicks hatch, they have a complete coat of downy feathers and soon walk and run very proficiently. The young feed themselves, and the parents protect them by distracting predators and herding them into cover.

The availability of nesting cover, escape cover, and feeding areas determines the abundance of any species. Unfortunately, because wetlands have been destroyed all over the world, wildlife that depends on such environments has been in decline worldwide.

Black Stilt
(Himantopus novaezelandiae)

IUCN: Critically endangered

Length: 15 in. (38 cm)
Clutch size: 4 eggs
Incubation: 25 days
Diet: Small aquatic animals including worms, insects, mollusks, fish, plus dryland worms and insect larvae
Habitat: Mountain ponds, shallow streams, lagoons, estuaries
Range: Mackenzie Basin of South Island, New Zealand

AN INCESSANT, shrill yapping in a wetland during summer could mean that a stilt nest lies close by. In New Zealand the irritated bird could be a pied stilt *(Himantopus himantopus)* or the much rarer black stilt. They are easily distinguished by their appearance and behavior.

The pied stilt has a clean white head, breast, and belly, with a black neck ring and black back, wing, and tail. The black stilt wears solid black plumage. A bit of sheen accents the wings and back, and the head and neck often appear sooty or brownish black. Both species have long patches of a rose red color on the leg and foot. The pied stilt has longer legs; the black stilt is plumper.

When it comes to its behavior, the pied stilt is the more animated and nervous of these two species. Disturbances can lead to hysterical displays and extremely agitated calling. The black stilt appears more patient, less excitable, although it does call

As an island species, the black stilt is particularly vulnerable to changes in its environment. When humans came to South Island, New Zealand, the degradation of this bird's habitat began almost immediately.

when it is annoyed. Ornithologists generally interpret the behavioral differences to indicate that the black stilt has been isolated on New Zealand far longer than the pied stilt. In fact, the pied stilt is part of a species complex that occurs widely throughout the Old World. The black stilt occurs nowhere else except in New Zealand, and there its population is in great jeopardy.

When ancestors of the Maori people first settled onto the islands of New Zealand, around C.E. 900 to 1000, the black stilt occupied both North and South Islands. Through successive waves of immigration, settlement, and population growth, the total Maori population grew to about 200,000. British navigator James Cook visited New Zealand in 1769, 1772, and 1777. He initiated European exploration of these isolated islands, and in 1840 Great Britain claimed New Zealand as a colony. British colonists began an almost immediate remake of the island. Acclimatization societies were developed dedicated to bringing better game and fish to New Zealand. They did this because the islands had no mammals or fish valued by the settlers. Colonists also imported livestock, pets, and agriculture. The result of this was significant habitat alteration and a disastrous growth of certain exotic species.

Among the exotic species were predators that soon discovered the nutritional value of native birds. Rats (*Rattus* sp.), house cats (*Felis sylvestris*), short-tailed weasels (*Mustela erminea*) or stoats, and European ferrets (*Mustela putorius*) proved a lethal combination for black stilts. They devour nests, chicks, fledglings, and adults when they can catch them. Unlike the pied stilt that lives where predators are a normal hazard of life, black stilts developed in an area without predators. Pied stilts nest in colonies. They react hysterically to predators or other suspicious disturbances, and raise their chicks to fledgling age in a shorter time. Black stilts aggressively defend territories against other black stilts, so they nest in

pairs. Their chicks take two weeks longer to reach flying age than pied stilts, and the adults are more tolerant of intrusion.

Decades after the British arrived in New Zealand, the black stilt began to disappear from many of its native haunts. The twilight of the black stilt began with the 20th century. Mostly gone from North Island by 1900, it disappeared as a breeding species from the island within a century of British settlement. By 1990 only 50 black stilts survived. They breed in a small area of south-central South Island. After nesting ends and the chicks have fledged, the black stilts wander to the seacoasts and drift as far north as southern North Island.

Not all of the decline can be attributed to exotic predators. New Zealanders built dams and reservoirs along rivers where black stilts nested and raised their young. They also drained and filled marshes to develop farmland. In addition, the island's human population is growing (it is currently over two million). Together, these factors applied more pressure to the black stilt than the species could handle.

To protect the remaining black stilt population and perhaps recover the species, New Zealand wildlife officials have begun three corrective actions: they now take black stilt eggs into captivity for hatching so weasels, rats, and ferrets cannot get to them first; they have erected electric fencing around stilt nesting sites to exclude predators from finding nests and chicks; they have also initiated an aggressive trapping program to eliminate

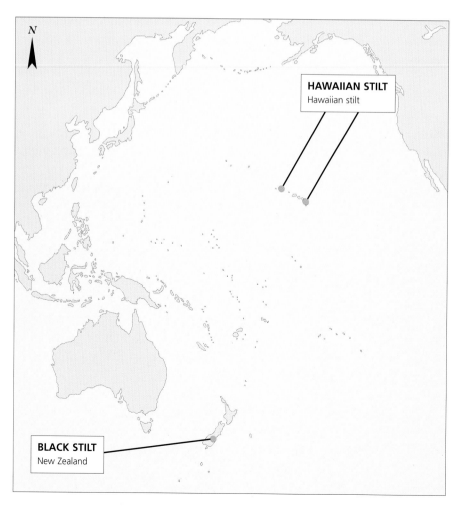

HAWAIIAN STILT
Hawaiian stilt

BLACK STILT
New Zealand

exotic predators, or at least to suppress their populations in stilt nesting areas. These programs are too new for long-term results to be available, but to save the black stilt, the corrective actions must work.

Hawaiian Stilt

(Himantopus mexicanus knudseni)

ESA: Endangered

Length: 14–15 in. (35–38 cm)
Clutch size: 4 eggs
Incubation: 24 days
Diet: Small aquatic animals including worms, crustaceans, insects, mollusks, and fish
Habitat: Wetlands
Range: Hawaiian Islands of the Pacific Ocean

ORNITHOLOGISTS measure the length of a bird from beak to tail tip when a relaxed specimen is positioned on its back. The black-necked stilt measures about 14 to 15 inches (35 to 38 centimeters), but it stands on gangly legs and feet that elevate it to a height of 18 to 20 inches (46 to 51 centimeters). These peculiar legs and feet give the bird a wonderful grace as it moves across shallow marshes.

Location
The black-necked stilt ranges from the United States into northwestern South America. It is most abundant around the marshy areas of the Great Basin, particularly the Great Salt Lake region. At some time in the distant past, a few black-necked stilts found their way across the

Pacific Ocean to the Hawaiian Islands. They survived and stayed there without migrating back to the continent. Isolation over time molded them into a recognizable subspecies now known as the Hawaiian stilt.

Color
The Hawaiian stilt has three simple colors: the upperparts are black, the underparts are white, and the leg and foot are bright rose. The female differs from the male in having a back that is browner in color, and not so deep black. The Hawaiian stilt differs from the mainland black-necked stilt in having less white on the forehead, more black on the neck, and a longer foot and tail.

This bird can be found in both freshwater and coastal wetlands where fresh water and salt water mix to form brackish water. The stilt population began to decline with modern settlement of the islands. Ameri-

Because it is not particularly fussy about its home environment, the Hawaiian stilt readily occupies a variety of open wetlands.

can missionaries arrived in the Hawaiian Islands in the 1820s. Their presence opened the way for other settlers. They imposed a new lifestyle on the islands, which included new types of agriculture, growing different kinds of crops. The new agriculture required vast areas, so many tracts of wetland habitat were drained or filled. Some people have claimed that the decline of taro (*Colocasia esculenta*) farming caused the Hawaiian stilt to decline. But this theory is subject to interpretation.

Habitat
If the taro fields were artificially grown by the Polynesian settlers, then the habitat those fields provided inflated the stilt population. Retiring those fields

would theoretically return the islands' wetlands habitat to more natural levels. The stilt population would be expected to decline accordingly. If the taro fields were naturally occurring and the Polynesian settlers simply harvested them, then the loss of those fields would amount to habitat destruction. As the taro fields were replaced with more profitable sugarcane and pineapple fields, natural wetlands were also being converted. Not all the wetlands were lost to agricultural development: people also need houses, schools, places to shop, and so on, all of which occupy areas of land.

The Hawaiian stilt historically lived on all the large Hawaiian Islands that offered wetland habitat. Lanai and Kahoolawe had little suitable habitat and so stilts were rare on those islands. Many of the stilt's neighbors disappeared from the islands as rats, house cats, and Indian mongooses (*Herpestes auropunctatus*) became established. These predators take eggs and nestlings. The stilt's broad distribution, watery habitat, ability to fly, and protective habits toward its nest and chicks probably helped it to survive the onslaught of exotic predators that people introduced to the islands. Still, the stilt dwindled in numbers.

Population

By 1940, probably only 300 birds survived. The population hit a low of 253 in 1960, but recovered to as high as 1,476 birds in 1977. The numbers of the Hawaiian stilt naturally fluctuate, as do those of the black-necked stilt on the continent. The U.S. Fish and Wildlife Service has established a goal of maintaining 2,000 Hawaiian stilts for at least three consecutive years. If this is reached, the stilt will be considered for upgrading from an endangered to a threatened status, but this may be difficult to achieve.

Although exotic predators have not devastated the stilt as much as they have other native Hawaiian birds, predators remain a problem. Exotic plants also pose a serious hazard. Many exotic plants grow so prolifically that they change the character of wetlands so that stilts will no longer use them.

Recovery efforts call for managing wetlands to maintain stilt habitat. This means that exotic plants and predators need to be controlled. Artificial nesting platforms that float have also been successful.

The only way to recover and protect Hawaiian stilts is to maintain these efforts and expand them to other wetland areas around the islands.

Kevin Cook

STORKS

Class: Aves

Order: Ciconiiformes

Family: Ciconiidae

In European folklore the white stork (*Ciconia ciconia*) gets credit for delivering babies. Although Americans have adopted the tale, it has never really caught on, probably because white storks do not live in North America.

Seventeen species have traditionally made up the stork family, just one of five or six families in the stork order (Ciconiiformes). For many years ornithologists have recognized that storks and New World vultures—such as California condors (*Gymnogyps californianus*) and turkey vultures (*Cathartes aura*)—share certain features of anatomy and behavior. In particular they share the remarkable behavior of defecating on their feet and toes as a way of cooling themselves down when they are hot. The evaporating liquid carries off body heat much as perspiration does on humans.

Unlike the mythical role of storks as bearers of babies, in real life they are the bearers of bad news. Many storks depend on wetlands, and wetlands are badly abused by people. As wetlands disappear, storks vanish as well. Several species have declined, but some species are more seriously affected by human activities than others.

Greater Adjutant Stork

(Leptoptilos dubius)

IUCN: Endangered

Length: 57 in. (148 cm); stands 4–5 ft. (1.2–1.5 m) tall
Diet: Large invertebrates, all vertebrate groups, carrion
Habitat: Mainly fields and marshes
Range: Formerly northwestern India into southern Vietnam; now nests only in Assam, India

THE GREATER adjutant stork is not the most attractive of birds: its black upperparts contrast with

dingy white underparts; a broad gray band marks the inner wing; the head and neck are usually bare and dull yellowish to pale brown most of the time, but pink during breeding season; a yellow pouch hangs from the throat like a goiter. The massive beak dominates all the other features of this bird. Roughly square, the four-sided beak opens up into a cavernous mouth. The bird's tongue probably weighs more than its brain. Such a cavernous mouth allows the greater adjutant stork to swallow almost any animal it can grasp, including birds as large as ducks.

Movement

Greater adjutant storks prowl about flooded fields and wetlands searching for their prey. They often congregate in sizable groups. When they walk around a field, they do so with an eccentric gait that appears rigidly militaristic, which possibly accounts for their unusual name. Alt-

ernatively, the bird may have been named for its valuable services. Because they eat almost anything, including carrion, these storks gather on the rooftops and periphery of many villages to await handouts of garbage and livestock carcasses. In a country as populated with humans as India, garbage was never in short supply. Consuming great quantities of it was a valuable service to the villagers and made the storks important assistants, or adjutants.

Disappearance

It took a long time for ornithologists to realize that the greater adjutant stork was in trouble. Known to be widespread and abundant as a species, the greater adjutants slowly dwindled away. They disappeared from most of their historic range in India. They are now completely gone from Bangladesh, where people simply hunted them to extinction. They have also

Reaching 5 feet (1.5 meters) from the ground to the top of its head, the greater adjutant stork of India stands taller than most children.

vanished from most of Southeast Asia. Vietnam and Thailand now see only vagrant wanderers. Political conditions in Cambodia and Myanmar have not permitted ornithologists to study freely in those countries. Myanmar (formerly Burma) once hosted the largest number of greater adjutant storks. The breeding colonies were so large that some ornithologists suspect that the greater adjutants from other countries returned to Myanmar to nest. The huge Burmese colonies are all gone now. Kaziranga Wildlife Sanctuary in Assam, India, hosts the only known remaining population of nesting greater adjutant storks.

Significant recovery work has yet to be undertaken for this bird. Besides hunting pressures, the

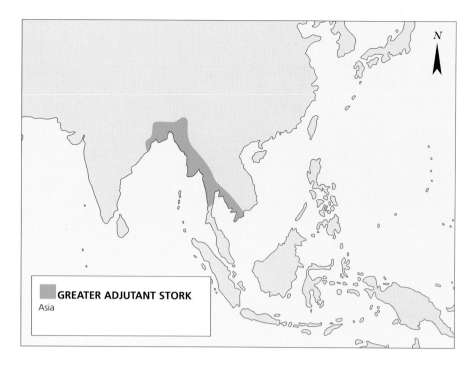

GREATER ADJUTANT STORK
Asia

species no doubt suffers from habitat loss. Former nesting and feeding areas have been converted to farmlands, and in many situations they have been engulfed by cities. Vietnam has conducted surveys to locate colonies of the greater adjutant, but without success. The Vietnamese government has, nevertheless, extended some protection to stork habitat.

Protection

Recommendations for protecting the greater adjutant include an expansive education program among local citizens and the hiring of wardens to protect known stork nests from disturbance. Guarding individual nests may seem an extreme measure, but so few nests remain that guarding them may be the species' best short-term hope for survival.

Some ornithologists now believe that the greater adjutant stork ranks as the rarest, and probably the most endangered stork in the world.

Lesser Adjutant Stork

(Leptoptilos javanicus)

IUCN: Vulnerable

Length: About 40–45 in. (102–114 cm); stands 3½–4 ft. (1.1–1.2 m) tall
Clutch size: Probably 3–4 eggs, as in related species
Diet: Large insects, crustaceans, and small vertebrates
Habitat: Wetlands, particularly swamps and wet forests
Range: India, Nepal, and Sri Lanka through Bangladesh into Southeast Asia, parts of Malaysia and Indonesia

ALONE IN THE swamp, the lesser adjutant stork stands motionless, like a carved artifact. Unfortunately, this sight is becoming rarer in the swamps and marshes of southern Asia.

The homelands of the lesser adjutant stork are also attractive to humans. They cut the trees, drain off the water, and plant bananas, coconuts, or other commercially valuable crops. Some marshes are kept wet but have been converted to rice production. Whereas the greater adjutant (*Leptoptilos dubius*) stork has made an effort to accept and tolerate people, the lesser adjutant shuns people and their habitations. This might explain why the lesser adjutant species has survived in greater numbers than its close relative. The two species differ in other ways, too.

Appearance

The greater adjutant stork stands about 12 inches (30 centimeters) higher than the lesser adjutant stork. The lesser adjutant stork has plumage that is blacker across the back. Both species have sparsely feathered heads and necks, which are mainly a mottling of reddish pink and dirty yellow, but the lesser adjutant lacks the conspicuous throat pouch of the greater adjutant stork. The differences in habitat preference, general behavior, and subtle traits of appearance make distinguishing the two storks fairly simple, but actually locating the storks presents more of a problem.

Decline

No estimates of the total population have been made, but separate surveys in different countries strongly indicate a species in decline. The lesser adjutant stork once wandered over much of India and Nepal, and as far south and east as Java and Bali in Indonesia. Individual storks no longer wander over such a large area because the species' population has become fragmented into smaller, and more scattered colonies.

The lesser adjutant still occurs as a breeding species in Sri Lanka, India, possibly Bangladesh, Vietnam, Malaysia, and Indonesia. The Bangladesh population declined steadily and sharply through the 1970s and 1980s, so its status in the 1990s is doubtful. Myanmar and Thailand once hosted great numbers of lesser adjutant storks, but neither country held a breeding colony in the mid-1980s. No information is available from Laos or Cambodia. Ornithologists surveying in Sumatra found 579 storks in 1984, followed by 1,095 in 1985

By staying away from people, the lesser adjutant stork very likely avoids the hunting pressure suffered by the greater adjutant stork.

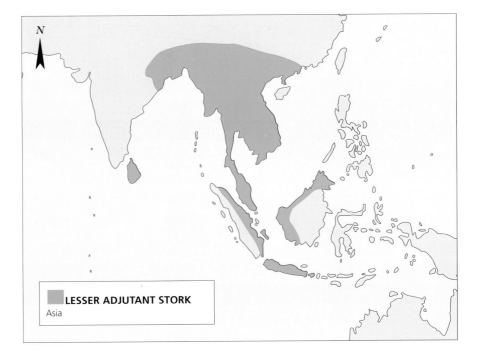

LESSER ADJUTANT STORK
Asia

and 686 in 1986. However, the rate of habitat destruction in Sumatra gives little hope for any long-term stability for the lesser adjutant stork population there.

No specific action has been taken to help the lesser adjutant stork, but efforts to preserve habitat for other endangered or threatened species may also ultimately benefit the stork.

Recommendations

The few specific recommendations for recovering the lesser adjutant echo those of the greater adjutant. Poaching must be stopped, nests must be protected, habitat must be preserved, and the local people need to be educated to care about their wildlife. Also, the lesser adjutant stork should be protected from international trade.

Recovery

Anything less than these measures will allow the lesser adjutant stork to decline into the same endangered status as its larger relative.

Milky Stork
(Mycteria cinerea)

IUCN: Vulnerable

Length: 38 in. (96.5 cm)
Weight: Probably 4–4½ lb. (1.8–2 kg) based on comparisons to related species
Clutch size: Probably 2–3 eggs
Incubation: About 28–32 days
Diet: Probably large crustaceans, small fish
Habitat: Wetlands
Range: Java and Sumatra of Indonesia, peninsular Malaysia, coastal lowlands of Cambodia and southern Vietnam

LAWS CANNOT protect a species, and the milky stork proves it. Malaysian law prohibits the hunting or killing of milky storks except by certain tribal peoples. Despite the law, milky storks have been hunted so heavily that the species has nearly vanished from that country. A few individual birds still wander into

Malaysia, but the stork no longer occurs as a breeding species there.

Appearance

The front half of the milky stork's head is bare, from the base of its beak to a distinct line running from the mid-crown down the cheek and under the chin. During the breeding season, this bare face turns bright red. The leg, foot, and toe are also red. The stout beak is long and slightly curved downward. The combination of long legs and feet, plus a long neck and beak serve the milky stork well as it prowls shallow marshes for its meals. Spending much of its time in coastal areas, the milky stork works the mangrove swamps, where it snaps up small fish and large crustaceans. Milky storks also visit freshwater marshes found in the coastal plains of the countries where they occur.

All the coastal wetlands are threatened within the stork's range. Many of them are developed into commercial production facilities for raising shrimp and various food fish. Many are converted to rice production.

Hunting

Habitat loss is not the milky stork's only problem. People hunt it for food and for sale on the cage bird market. Hunting pressure can often be quite intense. The species probably tolerated some hunting for hundreds, or even thousands, of years. As the human population has increased, however, the numbers of people hunting milky storks has exceeded the species' ability to reproduce fast enough to replace itself. Where hunting laws prohibit the killing of milky storks, people ignore the law. Poaching is done both openly

The milky stork wears pure white plumage except for black flight feathers in the wing.

and secretively. Circumstances in Malaysia more than adequately prove that laws alone are not enough: laws must be enforced to be effective.

Distribution

Surveys conducted in the 1980s showed that milky storks had almost completely disappeared from Vietnam and Cambodia. They were also drastically reduced in peninsular Malaysia, and no nesting colonies could be found there. The species seemed to be surviving in fair numbers in Sumatra and Java, Indonesia. The Sumatran population may have numbered between 5,000 and 6,000 birds in the mid-1980s, and the Javan population around 400. More than half the Sumatran population was found

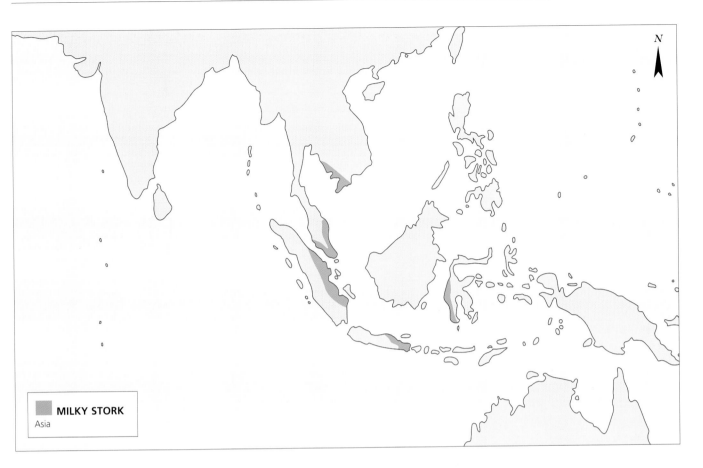

MILKY STORK
Asia

on the eastern side of the island, where the stork habitat was vulnerable to human settlement.

Land

The Indonesian government has long pursued a policy called transmigration that was developed to relieve the enormous human population on Java. Basically, the policy relocates Javan people to other Indonesian islands. Many of these people are relocated to Sumatra. To accommodate the resettled peoples, vast tracts of land must be developed into housing, farmland, and so on. Each new wave of transmigration brings more change to the Sumatran landscape and leaves a little less habitat for the milky stork.

The surveys provided an essential first step in preserving the milky stork. By themselves, however, surveys mean little.

Ornithologists have recommended a specific management plan for the stork. The recommendations include preserving habitat, banning hunting, prosecuting poachers, protecting nesting colonies, and developing education for local people. Education may well be the most important step. As long as local people believe that they can hunt birds such as the milky stork without consequence—probably because they presume that more storks live somewhere else— no other recovery work will actually succeed.

Action

The milky storks in Malaysia have proved that laws alone do not protect species. People must take action on the problems that cause endangerment. If action is delayed too long, the milky stork will continue to decline.

Oriental (White) Stork
(Ciconia boyciana)

ESA: Endangered

Length: 43–45 in. (110–115 cm)
Weight: 5½–99 lb. (2.5–45 kg)
Diet: Mainly fish; some amphibians, mammals, even small birds
Habitat: Marshes with scattered clumps of trees
Range: Breeds in southeast Siberia and parts of northeast China; winters mainly in southeast China

THIS IMPRESSIVE BLACK and white bird of the wetlands was an abundant breeder in Japan and South Korea 150 years ago, but heavy hunting pressure in the later years of the 19th century greatly reduced its numbers. Eventually its Japanese population was reduced to just a few pairs on Tsuruyama Hill in the west-central part of Honshu island. More enlightened attitudes meant that it was protected there. The numbers slowly started to increase until by the late 1950s there were 50 birds, and the future looked brighter.

However, from 1957 pesticides containing mercury were used extensively on crops in Japan. This chemical got into the food chain and contaminated the loach, which was the storks' favorite fish prey. In due course the mercury affected the storks, either slowly poisoning them or causing reproductive failure. As a result, the last successful breeding of Oriental (white) stork in Japan occurred in 1970. This sad episode demonstrated how the protection of a species is not enough to save it if its habitat or food supply are not protected.

As if these problems were not enough, this species has also suffered from widespread hunting, the draining of wetlands for agriculture and disease control, and the burning and cutting of nesting trees.

Unlike many endangered species, the threats to Oriental (white) stork populations have been known for years, and efforts have been made to bolster its populations in the wild by various captive-breeding programs. Although early efforts at breeding in captivity for later release in the wild proved to be unsuccessful in China and Japan, with most of the chicks dying young, more recent projects have produced better results. The first successful captive breeding was

in Germany in 1987, when there were 38 known captive birds. The aim is to be able to reintroduce birds into China and Japan.

In the past the Oriental (white) stork was often thought to be just a race of the European white stork, but it is different in a number of ways. For a start, it is considerably larger—up to 45 inches (115 centimeters) long—while the European stork is 40 inches (102 centimeters) long, and its bill is black, not red.

It appears not to be adapted to life close to human settlement in the same way as its close European relative, perhaps because of a long history of persecution. It was the increased use of guns for hunting in the 19th century that set in motion its catastrophic drop in numbers. Unfortunately, the problem has persisted much more recently: a pair was found nesting in South Korea in 1971, with villagers saying that the

species had been present for 40 years, but within three days of the news breaking the male bird had been shot by a poacher; the female was taken into captivity.

Like other members of its family, the Oriental (white) stork can be very long-lived, with the record going to a bird in captivity which survived to the grand old age of 48 years. Like other storks, it is magnificent looking, and has a wingspan of about 70 inches (180 centimeters). It has a white body, head, neck, tail and wing coverts, contrasting starkly in flying birds with black primary and secondary flight feathers, as well as long red legs and a powerful long bill.

The latter is well adapted for taking a wide variety of prey: mainly fish, but also frogs, voles, and vegetable matter. Its varied diet means that it is not tied to estuaries and marshes, but can also feed in wet grassland and

ORIENTAL (WHITE) STORK
Asia

Breeding range

Winter range

along river banks. When it was a common bird in Japan it could be seen in cultivated areas, such as paddyfields.

Unlike its close relative the European white stork, which nests on church towers in towns and villages, the oriental stork usually breeds away from human habitation; dead trees with good visibility over the surrounding countryside are particularly favored. It is loosely colonial, with several pairs often nesting quite close together. A total of 700–800 pairs was counted in the Amur and Ussuri River regions of southeast Siberia in the mid-1970s, and this population, together with populations in parts of northeast China, are the core breeding areas.

One way that the fortunes of this stork have been judged has been by counting migrants as they move south to their wintering grounds in the autumn. In 1986 a total of 2,729 were logged at the migration watchpoint of Beidaihe on the Chinese coast, with slightly fewer noted in subsequent years. Most of these birds spend the winter months in the wetlands of the lower Yangtze Valley, but since 1990 there have also been some quite large numbers in Hong Kong. For example there were 121 in January 1991.

Campaigns involving the display of public awareness posters have been tried in both China and Siberia in order to discourage hunting of the storks and the felling of nesting trees. However, as the history of the species has already demonstrated that habitat protection is the most important factor in its long-term survival; it is vital that the wetlands it needs to feed in are conserved.

The wood stork is very particular about its nesting habitat; the slightest degradation or disruption can stop this bird from reproducing.

In addition, a better understanding of where the whole population breeds and winters, along with migration stop-over sites, is crucial to selecting conservation priorities. It will be a bonus if the wild population can also be topped-up with individuals from captive-breeding programs.

Hopefully, as a result of more enlightened attitudes and hard work on the part of conservationists, in the not too distant future Chinese villagers will once again be able to witness large flights of these magnificent storks heading northeast toward breeding grounds across Japan and the Koreas every spring.

Tim Harris

Wood Stork
(Mycteria americana)

ESA: Endangered

Length: 34–47 in. (86.4–119.4 cm)
Weight: 4½–6 lb. (2–2.7 kg)
Diet: Mostly small fish but also crustaceans, large insect larvae, and amphibians
Habitat: Wetlands
Range: Coasts of Mexico south into South America east of the Andes Mountains and south to Argentina; in the United States from Virginia, south along the coast to Florida and around the Gulf of Mexico to Texas

SOMETIMES HAVING a place to live is not enough. Sometimes the place must be perfect at just the right time. For the wood stork, water conditions must be just right in the spring or it cannot breed successfully. Sometimes it simply cannot feed its nestlings; other times it fails to nest at all.

The wood stork is the only stork species that nests in the United States. Another stork, the jabiru (*Jabiru mycteria*), occasionally wanders into Texas from Mexico, but it has never nested there. The wood stork also wanders. Observers have reported sighting it from New Brunswick, Canada, and most of the eastern states to Montana, Wyoming, Colorado, Idaho, and many places in California. Wood storks that nest along Mexico's west coast often disperse northward and were once regularly found in Arizona and southern California. Sightings have become more

infrequent, and the wood stork populations in the southeastern United States have also declined.

Estimating historical numbers of a species provides some clue to population trends. Best estimates put the America wood stork population at about 20,000 to 30,000 breeding pairs in the 1930s. Adding non-breeding birds to the figure brings the total population to somewhere just under 100,000 wood storks. A steady population decline brought the American population down to 5,000 breeding pairs in the early 1980s, with a total possible population between 11,000 and 12,000 birds. Although such imprecise statistics have little scientific value, for discussion purposes they represent an 80 to 90 percent population loss for the wood stork.

A bald bird
The neck and head of the wood stork are completely bare. The black skin appears warty. The large, slightly downward-curved beak is a dull grayish horn color.

This stork has an interesting way of feeding. Walking through water only a few inches deep, it probes submerged vegetation and debris with a partly opened beak. It frequently stops walking and brings a foot forward to shake its toes in debris. Anything hidden in the debris usually darts out. If it bumps into the stork's beak, the bird snaps it up.

Lightning reaction
The stork's reflex is lightning fast. It depends on feeling its prey to catch it. If the water is too deep or too shallow, the wood stork's feeding technique does not work efficiently enough, so the bird moves around to find better feeding waters that have the conditions it prefers.

One of North America's largest resident birds, the wood stork stands about 4 feet (1.2 meters) tall. It has all-white plumage except for black flight feathers in the wing and a black tail.

The wood stork's decline corresponds almost exactly to an era in American history when wetlands came under deliberate attack. Citing every conceivable reason from flood and mosquito control to crop irrigation, navigation, recreation, domestic consumption, economic growth, jobs, and resource management, one government agency or another turned its attention to improving America's water situation. Wetlands were viewed largely as wastelands. Swamps and marshes were filled and drained. Rivers were straightened, or dammed, or changed in both ways.

Water management

The consequences of America's water management policy were staggering. The country lost roughly half its wetlands in the 20th century. The exact figure cannot be determined because no one ever calculated the total wetland area before the draining, filling, and damming began. As a further complication, some artificial wetlands have been created. These never match the full character or quality of natural wetlands.

The right stage

For successful nesting, wood storks need wetlands that are in a drying stage. This concentrates fish in a smaller area so the parent birds can catch enough fish quickly enough to keep their chicks fed.

During the 20th century wood storks often found their traditional feeding waters regulated by people. Either too deep or completely dry, the wetlands no longer met the storks' needs.

WOOD STORK
North and South America

- Historic range
- Present range

Successive years of nesting failure understandably led to a dwindling population. The failure eventually caused the wood stork to disappear as a breeding species in Texas, Louisiana, Mississippi, Alabama, and North Carolina. By the early 1990s, the wood stork nested only in Florida, Georgia, and South Carolina.

Wood stork populations in Mexico have also been declining. Coastal wetlands where the storks both nest and feed are being developed for fish and shrimp farms and for tourist developments. The Mexican people have hunted wood storks and collected their eggs to use as food for centuries. However, Mexico's human population has grown so enormous that the wood storks can no longer fully support human food needs. Other wood stork populations distributed all around areas of Central and South America face quite different degrees of human intrusion. Some colonies of wood storks appear to be quite secure, while other colonies have been almost completely devastated.

Intensively studied

Wood storks have been intensively studied. Their natural history is well documented. The only step remaining is the decision to save them. Some measurable progress has been made toward that goal. A nuclear power facility near Augusta, Georgia, threatened to destroy the feeding habitat that the wood storks need.

Collaboration

A collaborative effort developed among several government agencies, private businesses, and environmental groups brought about a new, artificial feeding area for the storks. When the wood storks actually accepted the area of Kathwood Lake, plans for additional feeding sites were developed for other areas that were also situated within the wood stork's range.

The work to preserve the wood stork has the added benefit of protecting other wildlife species, many of which also depend on wetlands.

Safe future?

The wood stork's future in the United States cannot be considered safe. However, the intent to preserve the wood storks is firmly established.

Kevin Cook

Streber

(Zingel streber)

IUCN: Vulnerable

Class: Actinopterygii
Order: Perciformes
Family: Percidae
Length: 7 in. (18 cm)
Reproduction: Egg layer
Habitat: Fast-flowing streams over clean gravel
Range: Southeastern Europe

AS A MEMBER of the clan known as European strebers and a close relative of the endangered asprete (*Romanichthys valsanicola*) and the asper (*Zingel asper*), the streber has been subjected to many of the same kinds of environmental insults. This fish occupies major river systems such as the Danube, Prut, and Dniester throughout southeastern Europe including Hungary, Romania, Bulgaria, Greece, and the Ukraine. Years of abusive pollution and disregard for wildlife have decimated populations of this fish. Literally poisoned and smothered in its home, the streber faces an uphill struggle to avoid extinction.

River fish that must stay in one place in order to breed and feed require some method for overcoming the natural current besides constantly swimming. The streber's solution is to have no swim bladder, which is extremely uncommon for many other fish such as minnows and salmonids. If the streber had a swim bladder, it would be able to regulate buoyancy (its depth in the water) using this gas-filled bladder. Because it does not have a swim bladder, however, the streber sinks to the bottom and is not forced to swim against the stream to maintain its position.

Locally, depending on the country in which it is found, this fish is called a *fusar, upiravec,* or *malyi tschop.* It bears a resemblance to the North American yellow perch (*Perca flavescens*) and the European perch (*Perca fluviatilis*) and is included in the same family, Percidae. The streber has the same thin and narrow body. On its back are two dorsal fins: a short, protective spiny fin at the front and a longer, soft fin directly behind it. The mouth is low on the snout. Like some fish known as suckers and other bottom feeders, this position of the mouth permits the streber to catch insects, bottom-dwelling invertebrates, and small fish.

The streber's body is brown on the back and sides, with a lighter chin, throat, and belly. Several dark vertical bars mark the sides, and the pectoral and pelvic fins just behind the gills

STREBER
Europe

and the tail are banded with narrow, dark stripes. The body behind the head is heavily scaled, but the head and gill covers have few scales. Some patches of this fish are completely nude.

Reproduction

Fisheries biologists believe that the streber is primarily nocturnal, feeding at night. It breeds in the spring and hides its eggs among the bottom gravel where the eggs cling. This gives the eggs protection against predators. During the breeding period both sexes develop nodulelike tub-

ercles or bumps on their bodies and fins. This adaptation is a visual cue to other strebers that they are ready to spawn.

Politics and endangerment

When eastern Europe was dominated by Communist governments, official public policy was almost entirely geared toward commercial and industrial development, with no thought given to any environmental consequences. As a result, much of the land and water in this part of the world was seriously damaged by agriculture and heavy industry.

This activity either killed streber populations directly or left spawning areas filled with silt and therefore totally unusable for reproductive purposes.

Now that these countries are in transition, changing their governments and re-examining their priorities, perhaps the extent of the damage will be recognized and halted. Hopefully, a plan to help restore formerly habitable areas will be implemented, and species such as the streber can again have clean waters in which to swim.

William E. Manci

STURGEONS

Class: Actinopterygii

Order: Acipenseriformes

Family: Acipenseridae

Some of the most unusual and primitive fish on our planet, the sturgeons have lived and survived for over 200 million years. The 25 to 30 species of sturgeon that live today all inhabit the Northern Hemisphere and live in a variety of environments, from arctic seas to temperate freshwater lakes. Sturgeons grow slowly to a very large size and live for many years; some survive up to the age of 60 or even older.

When North America was first being colonized by Europeans, Native Americans had routinely used sturgeons as a food source. Some European and many Asian cultures had been using sturgeons as food for centuries. Yet these fish were originally shunned as food and were known as trash fish by the first European colonists of North America, but they quickly grew to appreciate the importance of sturgeons as food fish (both in terms of quality of the meat and the eggs).

The antiquity of sturgeons is not difficult to discern. Their appearance, with rows of protective plates on their back and sides, makes them resemble alligators, crocodiles, or other reptiles that have lived relatively unchanged for millennia. Less noticeable is the primitive nature of their skeletons. While sturgeon are considered bony fish and members of the class Actinopterygii, much of their structural frame is flexible cartilage, like that of sharks and other cartilaginous species.

Typically, spawning occurs only once every several years. Some older female sturgeon produce over three million eggs per spawning year. Because of their slow growth and the time it takes them to reach sexual maturity, sturgeons are extremely vulnerable to overexploitation by humans.

An analogy can be made between sturgeons and the ancient, old-growth forests of the Pacific Northwest. Once these trees are gone they are, for all practical purposes, gone forever. While the same is not exactly true for the sturgeon, it is impossible in nature to quickly regenerate a

population after it has been overfished or ravaged by pollution and other factors that destroy habitat.

Many sturgeon species are considered threatened or endangered within their native ranges. The domestic and international trade in sturgeon products is a major factor in the cause of the decline in wild sturgeon populations. The Convention on Trade in Endangered Species of Wild Fauna and Flora (CITES) now controls the trade in all sturgeon species and their products.

When fisheries biologists first realized that sturgeon populations were declining, efforts were undertaken to culture or raise sturgeon and replace the fish taken from the wild.

Unfortunately, most of these early efforts to conserve sturgeons failed because of the use of inappropriate technology and a lack of understanding of the basic biology of these particular animals. Only today are scientists beginning to successfully produce certain species of sturgeon in large enough numbers.

Alabama Sturgeon

(Scaphirhynchus suttkusi)

IUCN: Critically endangered

Length: 30 in. (75 cm)
Reproduction: Egg layer
Habitat: Large rivers and estuaries
Range: Tombigbee and Alabama River Basins

SIMPLY PUT, the principal threat to the Alabama sturgeon is destruction of its habitat within the Tombigbee and Alabama Rivers. For many decades, the U.S. Army Corps of Engineers, in an effort to minimize flooding and its effects, has modified vast stretches of streambeds through channelization (the improvement of existing waterways), removal of vegetation, and other destructive techniques. The Corps achieved its goals and deepened and narrowed stream channels to the point where significantly less suitable streambed was available for feeding and reproduction. Dams built to control flooding destroyed many miles of stream and dramatically altered the downstream water chemistry and flow patterns. Dams also prevent upstream spawning migrations and, as a result, spawning success is drastically reduced.

Rapid, or even moderate, rates of recovery will be impossible for this species. Even if habitats can be restored, the low reproductive rate of the Alabama sturgeon precludes a swift return to its former numbers. Juveniles can take over a decade to reach sexual maturity, and females spawn only once every several years. When spawning does occur, large numbers of eggs are produced but many are lost to predators. The development of culture techniques for the Alabama sturgeon in an artificial hatchery setting may accelerate its recovery.

Appearance

This species was only described in 1991. It is very similar to the Shovelnose sturgeon (*Scaphirhynchus platorynchus*) and some biologists do not recognize it as a separate species. Like its close relative the pallid sturgeon (*Scaphirhynchus albus*), the Alabama sturgeon is light brown and tan in color on the back and sides; the belly is cream. The snout and tip of the tail are both pointed and long, and the tail section is very narrow and slender. If not for the more robust body, the fish could almost be called petite. The bony plates on the back and sides, called scutes, are much smaller when compared to other sturgeons and do not cover as much skin area. The Alabama sturgeon displays typical characteristics when it comes to other physical features. The fins, except for the pectoral fins just behind the gills, are set far back on the body; the eyes are small; and the barbels or whiskers and mouth are set back from the tip of the snout on the underside of the head.

Little is known about the biology of this fish, but it is known to spawn in the spring in swift river currents. In all probability, adults mature slowly, have a long life span, and spawn only once every three to six years. The Alabama sturgeon feeds on insects and other aquatic invertebrates. Interestingly, the Alabama sturgeon had been caught by fishers using poultry parts, fish, and other commercially prepared baits.

Amur Sturgeon

(Acipenser schrenckii)

IUCN: Endangered

Length: 54 in. (135 cm)
Reproduction: Egg layer
Habitat: Large rivers and estuaries
Range: Amur River basin, Russia and China

FOR MANY YEARS the Amur sturgeon was the prized catch of commercial fishers along the Amur River in eastern Asia at the border between the Commonwealth of Independent States (formerly the U.S.S.R.) and the People's Republic of China. The Amur sturgeon's large size, delicate flesh, and large number of eggs mean that each fish is worth a small fortune. Indeed, the monetary incentive to capture this fish is so great, that it is now threatened with extinction. A population estimate in 1996 showed that around 288,000 individuals inhabited the Amur River basin. Restrictions on commercial fishing for the Amur sturgeon were imposed by Russia in 1958, but the river forms part of the border with China, and this country does not impose similar controls. The high price of caviar is still contributing to the legal and illegal exploitation of this species.

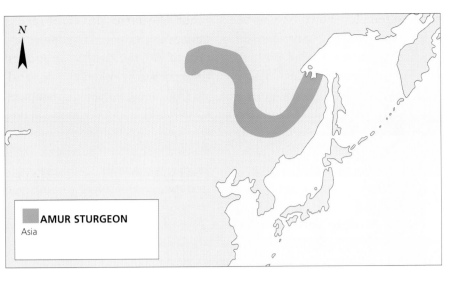

AMUR STURGEON
Asia

like a paddle, and beneath the snout is a set of barbels or whiskers to sense chemical cues and aid in the search for food.

Coloring

The back and sides are uniformly colored dark gray and the belly is a much lighter cream or white. The fleshy-based, triangular dorsal fin on the back is set well toward the tail, much like the pelvic and anal fins on the belly. The pectoral fins just behind the gill covers are fleshy as well, showing fin rays, but they have less flexibility. The forked tail fin has two lobes; the upper lobe is pointed and much larger than the lower lobe, which is much like the tail of a shark.

The Amur sturgeon spawns in the spring over sand and gravel in fast-flowing river water. Females lay from 30,000 to 430,000 eggs during a spawning event, numbers that seem large but are small relative to other sturgeon that can lay well over three million eggs. The eggs stick to the bottom and to vegetation, preventing their downstream movement. After hatching, the offspring feed on plankton until they are large enough to begin scouring the river bottom for insect larvae and other aquatic invertebrates.

Since the commercial fishing ban was put into effect so many decades ago, one might at least hope that the species would have recovered in part from this historic devastation. The problem with the Amur sturgeon is in its lifespan and reproductive cycle. Some species cannot recover as rapidly as others when their populations are devastated. While recovery of the Amur sturgeon is not impossible, it is difficult given the fish's long cycle from hatching to sexual maturity (nine to ten years), and the female's reproductive cycle that allows only one spawn every several

Like other sturgeons, the green sturgeon has protective bony plates along its body and sensitive whiskers on its mouth.

years. The result is that every female becomes very important to the survival of the species as a whole. When large numbers of fish are captured, the recovery period becomes very long indeed. There are plans in China to construct a large dam on the Amur River. This will inevitably have an impact on the development of spawning sites for the Chinese sturgeon.

This fish and all sturgeons have an unusual appearance; most notable are the rows of armorlike scutes or bony plates that can be found along the middle of the back and on each side. The shape of the scutes varies from species to species and is used as a means to identify them. The head and snout of the Amur sturgeon are quite long and flat,

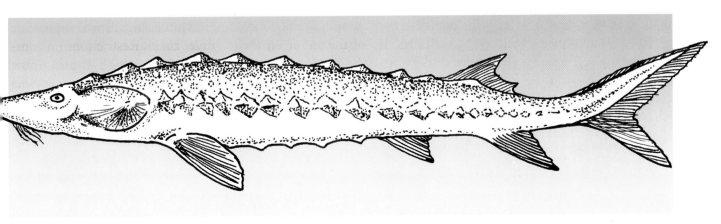

Beluga Sturgeon

Huso huso

IUCN: Endangered

Length: 19¾ ft. (6 m)
Reproduction: Egg layer
Habitat: Large rivers, and inland seas
Range: Caspian, Black, and Azov Seas. Ural, Kural, Sefid-Rud, Terek, Rioni, and Danube Rivers

---

THE BELUGA sturgeon is the largest of all the sturgeons, growing to 19¾ feet (6 meters) in length and weighing more than 2,200 pounds (1,000 kilograms). Unfortunately, such giants are rarely encountered today, as this mighty sturgeon is being fished to the brink of extinction. The main reason is due to Beluga caviar: the unfertilized eggs of the female, which are highly prized as an exotic delicacy.

Sturgeons are very slow growing and the Beluga sturgeon takes fifteen to twenty years to reach maturity. A mature female can produce up to 39.7 pounds (18 kilograms) of caviar at one time and live for one hundred years or more. The diet of the Beluga sturgeon consists of fish and invertebrates.

The Beluga sturgeon is primarily found in the Caspian Sea, migrating up large rivers such as the Volga River to spawn. A few Beluga sturgeons can still be found in the rivers bordering the Black Sea. The species is listed as critically endangered in the Sea of Azov, with few now being caught. Historically the Beluga sturgeon was found in the Adriatic Sea, but is now presumed to be extinct in this region.

There is no information on the total size of the Beluga sturgeon population. The Caspian Sea and the Volga River are thought to have the largest populations. In 1996, it was estimated that between 8,000 and 9,000 adult fish were breeding in the Volga River, of which less than 25 percent were female. The low numbers of females is cause for concern as the eggs they carry are critical for the future survival of the species.

The Beluga sturgeon is a very valuable fish. It is good to eat, and its swim bladder is used to make a variety of products, such as glue. However, it is the eggs that give it real value. The Beluga sturgeon, the Russian sturgeon (A. *gueldenstaedtii*), and the Stellate sturgeon (A. *stellatus*), produce 90 percent of the world's caviar. This is exported all over the world, including the United States, Europe, and Asia.

The Beluga sturgeon is being fished to extinction. Before 1991, the then Soviet Union and Iran tightly controlled the sturgeon fishery and the world trade in caviar. After the dissolution of the Soviet Union in 1991, the market opened up as several newly independent countries bordering the Caspian Sea began catching sturgeon for themselves. Fishing also began to be carried out illegally by organized groups. Sturgeon were being fished indiscriminately in the open sea, and females were caught well before they were mature enough to produce eggs. In 1996, countries bordering the Caspian Sea agreed to ban fishing in the open sea to protect juvenile fish, and a fishing quota was set.

The Beluga sturgeon is not only threatened by overfishing. Dams built along crucial rivers have destroyed the spawning areas. These constructions restrict the movement of fish up the river to spawn, and juvenile fish cannot get back down to the sea. Only 10 percent of the traditional spawning grounds remain, and the Ural River in Kazakhstan is

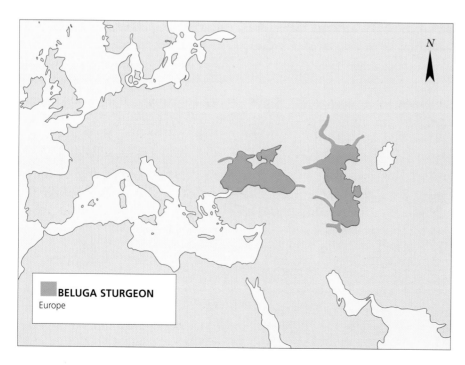

BELUGA STURGEON
Europe

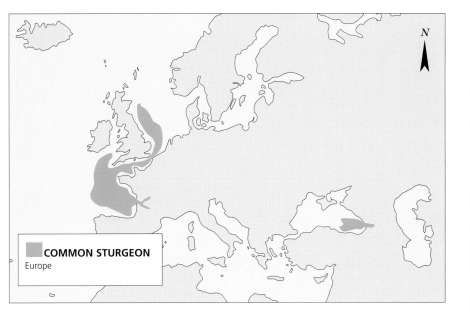

N

COMMON STURGEON
Europe

Common Sturgeon
(Acipenser sturio)

IUCN: Critically endangered

Length: 48 in. (120 cm)
Reproduction: Egg layer
Habitat: Rivers, estuaries, and coastal seas
Range: Gironde-Garonne-Dordogne Basin in France and Rioni Basin in Georgia, Black Sea

the only spawning river that has not yet been altered by humans. This is not enough to sustain the world population and it is believed that natural reproduction of the Beluga sturgeon is in grave danger.

Another threat to the Beluga sturgeon is industrial waste from factories along the rivers. A mass death of sturgeons occurred in the Sea of Azov in 1990, when 55,000 sturgeons of several species were killed as a result of poison in the water. There is also evidence to suggest that industrial chemicals are affecting the normal development of eggs, further reducing the number of juvenile fish being produced. Sturgeon may also be threatened by oil exploration in the Caspian Basin, which will further disturb their habitat and bring the risk of oil pollution.

The outlook for a naturally occurring recovery looks bleak. However, the Beluga sturgeon has been farmed in hatcheries for many years. Adult fish are taken from the wild and the eggs are hatched under controlled conditions in which the juvenile fish

have a much better chance of survival than they do in the wild. Hatcheries have released millions of juveniles into the Caspian Sea and the Volga River. This has proven critical to the survival of the sturgeon, where all the Beluga sturgeon now caught in the Caspian region were originally raised in hatcheries. However, the hatchery program has been much reduced due to economic pressures, and even when operating, the hatcheries are having increasing difficulty finding wild mature fish from which eggs can be taken.

Regulation
Global concern for the future of the Beluga sturgeon and other species led to agreement on the need to regulate the international trade in sturgeon products. This led to all sturgeon being listed on the Convention on International Trade in Endangered Species of Wild Fauna and Flora (CITES). The Beluga sturgeon will only have a future if illegal fishing is halted and countries work together to sustainably manage this species.

DURING THE early part of the 20th century, the larger rivers of Portugal and Spain that flow into the Atlantic Ocean and the Mediterranean Sea used to hold many thousands of common sturgeon. This European relative of the various sturgeon species from North America and Asia could be found in abundance, with some fish reaching a large size and a ripe old age.

Downfall
Unfortunately, as with threatened and endangered sturgeons in other parts of the world, thinking that the supply of fish was endless and that pollution from domestic and industrial sources could be continued at little or no cost, eventually led to the downfall of this magnificent species. The construction of dams was also a significant factor in the severe decline of the common sturgeon.

Sport fishing
As the effectiveness of fishing gear improved, common sturgeon were being caught as they

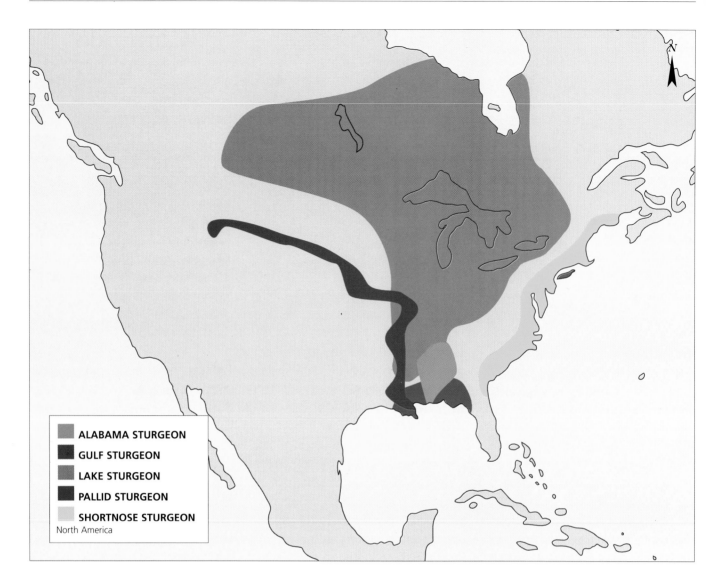

ALABAMA STURGEON
GULF STURGEON
LAKE STURGEON
PALLID STURGEON
SHORTNOSE STURGEON
North America

moved through the large river systems and estuaries of Europe's western Iberian Peninsula. This fish was particularly vulnerable to fishermen during its spring spawning season. At one time the Duoro, Mondego, Tagus (Tejo), Sado, Guadiana, and Guadalquivir Rivers held large populations. During this same period, more and more factories began spewing industrial waste and other pollution into these rivers by the ton. Then came the influx of rural residents seeking good jobs and a better way of life in the burgeoning cities.

Not surprisingly, the discharge of domestic sewage increased quite dramatically.

Eventually, the combination of fishing pressure and pollution threatened the common sturgeon, creating a situation in which the species was incapable of sustaining itself. A final blow came in the forms of hydroelectricity, flood control, and water supply dams that blocked the passage of the sturgeon during its upstream spawning migration and the subsequent return of young to the river estuaries.

Population decline

The construction of no less than four dams during the 1970s and early 1980s on the Duoro River in northern Portugal has been particularly destructive in

this regard. Today, no common sturgeon remain in their one-time stronghold, the Tagus River, and other streams hold only remnant populations.

Assessment

In the 1990s the fish was thought to be extirpated from the Iberian Peninsula. An assessment in 1988 found only a few thousand individuals in the Gironde River. There are no estimates for the Rioni population.

In the late 1990s the main threats to this species were fishing and habitat destruction. The common sturgeon is now banned from international commercial trade under CITES.

Sturgeon characteristics

This fish has all the qualities of its relatives in the sturgeon family, including the armorlike scutes or bony plates; the long, flat head and snout; the barbels, or whiskers, used for trying to discover food; and the forked tail fin. The common sturgeon is also a bottom feeder and consumes primarily aquatic invertebrates that live in river sediments.

Problem recovery

Despite efforts to clean up the rivers through the use of modern waste treatment technology, and despite the restriction of fishing, these measures may be too late to help the common sturgeon. Recovery will be difficult and will take time.

All sturgeons are long-lived and reach sexual maturity at a much older age than most other fish (the common sturgeon requires up to ten years to reach sexual maturity). Males mature in 8–12 years and females mature in 13–16 years. In addition, female common sturgeon do not spawn on a yearly cycle and need three to six years to regain their spawning condition.

Gulf Sturgeon

(Acipenser oxyrhynchus desotoi)

ESA: Threatened

IUCN: Vulnerable

Length: 80 in. (200 cm)
Reproduction: Egg layer
Habitat: Coastal rivers and estuaries
Range: Northeastern Gulf of Mexico coast

THE GULF sturgeon is a goliath of the aquatic world. Despite its size, or more correctly because of it, this placid fish is moving closer to the brink of extinction.

Overfishing produced a disaster in the early 1900s when the gulf sturgeon's total numbers declined sharply. Since that time, numbers have stabilized somewhat but at much lower levels. This fish, as well as other sturgeon, depend heavily on the quality and fitness of the rivers and coastal environments that they inhabit for their well-being. Compounding the problems created by overfishing in the past

were the construction of dams on rivers that the gulf sturgeon uses for spawning, physical alteration of river habitats, and pollution of the waterways from municipal and industrial sources.

A gargantuan fish

As a fully grown adult, the gulf sturgeon is truly an awesome fish. Its long and tubular body can reach a maximum length of 7 feet (2 meters) and weigh more than 200 pounds (91 kilograms). At this size, the typical armorlike scutes or bony plates look impressive. Like other sturgeons, the head and snout are long and flat. The back and sides are uniformly colored dark gray, while the belly is a much lighter cream or white. The gulf sturgeon's dorsal fin is triangular and close to the tail. In all other respects, this sturgeon is much like its relatives.

Gulf sturgeon begin spawning in February after moving upstream from coastal estuaries or the lower reaches of rivers. The female lays sticky eggs over gravel and rubble that quickly adhere to the water bottom and nearby vegetation. The gulf sturgeon is able to lay as many as 2.5 million eggs. Egg incubation depends on the prevailing temperature, but most eggs hatch after about one week.

The gulf sturgeon requires an unusually long period of time to reach sexual maturity, in some cases as long as 25 years. Once it reaches maturity, the reproductive cycle is variable and

The gulf sturgeon is a subspecies of the Atlantic sturgeon and can be found in coastal rivers and estuaries of the northeastern Gulf of Mexico, hence its common name.

spawning does not take place every year. As many as five years can pass in a spawning cycle. When this fish does spawn, it is quite vulnerable to being captured by fishers using gill nets and efficient gear. Clearly the combination of overfishing, the species' own reproductive traits, barriers to successful spawning, and degradation of habitat have dealt this fish a blow that will be difficult to overcome. Fisheries biologists believe that overfishing is the most serious threat to this species.

Hopefully, meaningful limits on catch can be put in place and the trend toward extinction can be reversed. A recovery plan was initiated in 1994 to prevent further decline of the Gulf sturgeon. This species is now fully protected from fishing.

Lake Sturgeon

(Acipenser fulvescens)

> **IUCN:** Vulnerable
>
> **Length:** 60 in. (150 cm)
> **Reproduction:** Egg layer
> **Habitat:** Bottom of lakes and large rivers
> **Range:** Mississippi River Basin and southern Canada

THROUGHOUT ITS large natural range, the lake sturgeon is threatened by a multitude of human activities, the most destructive being overfishing. This primitive species occupies lakes and rivers within the Mississippi River Basin of the United States and southern Canada, and has long been the prize of fishers in search of food, profit, and sport. Despite the enormity of this fish's historic and current territory, threats by humans have forced this mild-mannered bottom-dweller onto the list of threatened fish.

While it is hunted less today by the commercial fishing industry, sportfishers still exact a large toll on this fascinating species. Spear fishing is a common practice, and hook-and-line is also used with success. As with other sturgeon, environmental changes wreak havoc, including outright habitat destruction, toxic pollution, and the exclusion by dams of sexually mature lake sturgeon from spawning grounds.

As a fully grown adult, the lake sturgeon is one of the larger freshwater fish. Its long, tubular body can reach a maximum length of 5 feet (1.5 meters) or more and weigh more than 60 pounds (27 kilograms). The lake sturgeon has the familiar bony plates and whiskers of its family. The back and sides are uniformly blue gray or olive red (depending on where it is found), and the belly is a much lighter cream or white. Dark blotches on the back disappear with age.

The lake sturgeon spawns in either rivers or lakes. Those that spawn in lakes do so along the shoreline where wave action moves oxygenated water past the incubating eggs. River spawners reproduce in the main channel over gravel, rocks, and other rubble. The eggs adhere to whatever they touch to prevent their movement downstream or to deeper and quieter zones. Most spawning occurs in mid-to-late spring, when water temperatures reach 55 to 61 degrees Fahrenheit (12 to 16 degrees Centigrade). The newly-hatched fish rely on microscopic plankton as a food source, while juveniles and adults search the bottom of rivers and lakes for insect larvae and other aquatic invertebrates.

Individual importance

The adverse effects of overfishing, habitat destruction, and migration barriers are amplified by the fish's own biology. The lake sturgeon requires well over a decade to reach sexual maturity, and when females do reach maturity they spawn only once every four to seven years. That makes every mature adult—the same specimens most prized by sportfishers—very important to the species as a whole.

There is still time to save this fish, but conservation efforts must emphasize limits on fishing, reclamation of river and lake habitats, and the restoration of access to the traditional spawning grounds.

Pallid Sturgeon

(Scaphirhynchus albus)

> **ESA:** Endangered
>
> **IUCN:** Endangered
>
> **Length:** 36 in. (90 cm)
> **Reproduction:** Egg layer
> **Habitat:** Murky water and strong currents over gravel or sand
> **Range:** Missouri River and lower Mississippi River

DESPITE its far-flung range extending nearly from the headwaters of the Missouri River in Montana to the mouth of the

Mississippi River in Louisiana, the pallid sturgeon is one of the least well-known and least visible fish in the continental United States. This endangered species is a rare catch for commercial fishers, leading fisheries biologists to believe that it may have always existed in relatively low numbers. It moves up and down its rivers fairly freely, or as freely as dams and other barriers will allow, but individuals tend to be grouped at various locations.

The population of pallid sturgeon, which is aging and exists in scattered pockets of small populations, has been estimated at 6,000–21,000 individuals. In the 1960s there were approximately 500 sightings of this fish each year. In 1990, there were only about 50 sightings. In 1993, a recovery plan was initiated.

The pallid sturgeon has a look all its own. The name pallid literally means pale, and indeed this fish is much lighter across its entire body than other sturgeon. The snout and tip of the tail are both very pointed and long, and the tail section is narrow and slender. The pallid sturgeon has the familiar bony plates, located on its back and sides.

It also displays typical sturgeon traits when it comes to its other physical features.

The biology of this fish is poorly researched, but it does spawn from late spring to mid-summer in swift river currents. Adults probably mature slowly, have a long lifespan, and spawn only once every few years. Recent reports indicate that a lifespan of more than 40 years is possible, as is a capability to produce 150,000 eggs or more during each spawning year. Natural reproduction is hampered by the lack of spawning sites. The pallid sturgeon feeds on insects and other aquatic invertebrates and, reportedly, on small fish.

The main threat to the pallid sturgeon is destruction of habitat within the Missouri and Mississippi Rivers. Like its cousin the Alabama sturgeon, this fish is a victim of the U.S. Army Corps of Engineers, who have done a lot of work on the channels of this river system. New dams and the removal of vegetation are just some of the changes that disrupt habitat. When habitats are altered too severely, a species cannot adapt quickly enough, and breeding failure sets in or the loss of an important food item causes the population to dwindle. Even changes in water temperature, salt content, and sediments can have adverse effects on the species population.

The Atlantic sturgeon (top) and the shortnose sturgeon are both members of the genus *Acipenser*.

In addition to direct loss of individuals due to habitat change, biologists believe alterations may be inducing the most destructive change of all: interbreeding with the more numerous shovelnose sturgeon (*Scaphirhynchus platorynchus*). Regardless of improvement to the pallid sturgeon's habitat, if interbreeding continues, this species will be permanently lost.

Shortnose Sturgeon
(Acipenser brevirostrum)

ESA: Endangered

IUCN: Vulnerable

Length: 36 in. (90 cm)
Reproduction: Egg layer
Habitat: Deep river pools over soft, vegetated bottom
Range: Rivers from New Brunswick, Canada, to Georgia

WHILE THE shortnose sturgeon is listed as a threatened species, the circumstances that led to its listing are slightly different than those for other sturgeons listed here. Most threatened and endangered sturgeons have been plagued by overfishing, which deprives the species of the ability to reproduce in adequate numbers to replace losses.

The shortnose sturgeon is banned from international commercial trade under CITES. This fish is deprived of its ability to reproduce as well but, in this case, dams that block migration to upstream spawning grounds and pollution are the main threats.

Found in rivers along the Atlantic Seaboard of southern Canada and most of the United States, this smaller-sized sturgeon is unable to successfully reproduce in large numbers in the face of migration obstacles and pollution that kills the fish directly or stresses the fish to the point that it is unable to ward off disease.

Habitat

This species lives in streams with other sturgeon, specifically the Atlantic sturgeon (*Acipenser oxyrhynchus oxyrhynchus*). The Atlantic sturgeon is considered a sport fish and, while the shortnose sturgeon is smaller and somewhat different in appearance, it is sometimes mistaken for the Atlantic sturgeon. Federal laws prohibit the capture or harassment of the shortnose sturgeon, but not the Atlantic sturgeon. This means that some shortnose sturgeon do not receive the protection they should get because of mistaken identity. It is unfortunate that the differences between these two fish are not more distinct. Given

this problem, it seems reasonable that an effort to save the shortnose sturgeon should include an effort to educate the public about the differences between the shortnose and Atlantic sturgeon. The most effective solution would include methods to successfully move sturgeon up and down streams during their spawning migration.

Appearance

The adult shortnose sturgeon measures only 3 feet (0.9 meters) in length, which is short by the standards of the genus *Acipenser*. Aside from its shorter total length and shorter snout, however, this fish generally resembles other sturgeon. The bony, plate-like scutes, which are the trademark of all sturgeon, line the middle of the back and sides of this bottom-dweller. The body is tubular, with gray, brown, and greenish coloration on the back and sides and a much lighter belly and underside of the head. Four barbels hang down from the underside of the head to form a line just in front of the mouth.

The fins of the shortnose sturgeon are rayed like other, less primitive fish, but are less flexible and fleshy at the base. All fins, with the exception of the pectoral fins just behind the gills, are set well back in the body and swept back for less drag in river currents. The tail fin is lobed, with the upper lobe much larger than the lower one.

Long-lived fish

The shortnose sturgeon reaches sexual maturity between 4 and 16 years, and can live to the age of 60. It spawns in brackish water between the months of April and

June, depending upon the water temperature. Northern populations spawn later in the year than those to the south. Females spawn only once every three years and release as many as 200,000 eggs. The shortnose sturgeon consumes mollusks like snails and clams, crustaceans such as small shrimp, other aquatic invertebrates, and some plant material.

William E. Manci

Dabry's Sturgeon (Yangtze Sturgeon)

(Acipenser dabryanus)

IUCN: Critically endangered

Length: 4⅓ ft. (1.3 meters)
Weight: About 35 lb. (16kg)
Reproduction: Egg layer
Habitat: Large rivers
Range: Yangtze River, China

DABRY'S STURGEON IS one of only two sturgeon species to be found in the Yangtze River. The other is the Chinese sturgeon (*Acipenser sinensis*). Dabry's sturgeon is a freshwater species restricted to the Yangtze River and its major tributaries.

Dabry's sturgeon is very similar in appearance to other sturgeon, and it can grow to more than 4⅓ feet (1.3 meters) and weigh more than 35 pounds (16 kilograms).

Even at this size, it is one of the smallest members of the sturgeon family.

History

Sturgeons are described in Chinese texts dating back thousands of years. However, the two Yangtze species were not scientifically differentiated until the late 19th century, Dabry's sturgeon being named after the collector. By the end of the 20th century very little was known about the ecology of this sturgeon. Spawning occurs in the spring, although the precise location of the spawning grounds is still a mystery. They are presumed to be in the upper reaches of the river, above the town of Yibin in Sichuan Province.

The fish move upstream individually to spawn, and after spawning they meander slowly back down the river to the feeding grounds. Male sturgeons mature in four to six years and the females in six to eight, the female producing as many as 100,000 eggs in one spawning. The eggs are sticky and adhere to the gravel on the bed of the river. The males can spawn each year, while the females require more than a year to develop their eggs. It is not known how many Dabry's sturgeon there are in the Yangtze River, but the fish is considered rare. The sturgeon is generally found on sandy shoals, in water less than 30 feet (10 meters) deep, where the water flow is not very fast and there is an abundance of food. Dabry's sturgeon is omnivorous, feeding on invertebrates, small fish, and aquatic plants.

River flow

The Yangtze is the world's fourth longest river and flows for 3,400 miles (5,500 kilometers) through

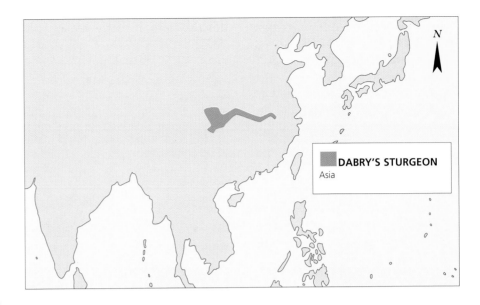

DABRY'S STURGEON
Asia

the most populated country in the world. Until the middle of this century, the river was still in its natural state and Dabry's sturgeon was widely distributed in the upper and middle sections. It now rarely occurs in the middle sections of the river.

In recent decades, considerable human and industrial development has occurred along the densely populated Yangtze River valley. The river regularly floods, depositing nutrient-rich silt on the valley lands. This enriches the soil and is vital for the health of the intensively cultivated cropland. The flooding is occasionally severe, resulting in agricultural land and urban settlements being totally swamped by the flood waters, with a considerable loss of life and livelihood. In recent decades, extensive deforestation of the

watersheds has made the situation worse, as there are fewer barriers to act as natural sponges to reduce the impact of the rains and curtail the worst of the flooding.

Dam threat

Dams have been built to control the floodwater, aid navigation on the river, and provide hydroelectric power to supply growing industrial needs. The Gezhouba Dam was completed in 1981 at Yichang in Hubei Province. The dam blocked the downstream movement of Dabry's sturgeon, restricting it to the upper reaches of the river. All fish below the dam are cut off from the presumed upper river spawning grounds. In 1997, work

Sturgeon are some of the most ancient and primitive fish on the earth.

was begun on the Three Gorges dam just 30 miles (47 kilometers) upstream of the Gezhouba dam; this will partition the population still further. The construction of the dam will affect the flow of the river and the habitats in it, though it is not known how this will affect sturgeons. There are plans for further dam developments in the upper river basin that will change the river's character, with unknown effects on the fish fauna.

Fishing problem

Dabry's sturgeon was an important commercial fish in the upper reaches of the river. Since the 1970s, the number of fish harvested has declined. The fishery mostly caught immature fish, taking them out of the reproductive stock. Fishing was also very intensive in some tributaries, with many boats working around the clock. Commercial fishing was banned in the 1980s, though fish are still caught accidentally.

The sturgeon is also under threat from the pollution produced by the factories and cities that line the banks of the Yangtze, which discharge untreated waste into the water, and the agricultural chemicals that are washed into the river from nearby fields. These contaminants affect the sturgeon either directly because of their toxicity or via the organisms that they eat.

The deforestation of the upper Yangtze valley has considerably added to the silt in the river, muddying the water and changing the habitat for the fish and their food organisms.

Conservation

Recently, Dabry's sturgeon has been artificially cultured, and supplementary stocking to enhance dwindling wild populations could be a possibility. More research is needed into the biology of this sturgeon.

If the species is to be successfully conserved and protected, it is crucial to determine the exact location of the fishes spawning grounds. After that the next step is to construct a program designed to adequately safeguard their welfare.

Megan Cartin

SUCKERS

Class: Actinopterygii

Order: Cypriniformes

Family: Catostomidae

Aptly named for their large lips and toothless mouths that are positioned low on the head, suckers occupy the vast majority of North America. There is also one species in eastern Siberia and one in China. North America appears to be the origin of this family (Catostomidae), with 57 total species. However, some fisheries biologists believe the opposite. They think the fish originated in Asia and then colonized North America.

Regardless of their origin, suckers are without a doubt an important group of fish and contribute to the ecological health of our freshwater aquatic systems. For example, juvenile suckers are used as food by many other fish. Despite their widespread distribution and ecological importance, most people today do not appreciate and understand suckers and view them as "trash fish" because of their bottom-feeding behavior. The disdain for these fish rivals that reserved for the common carp (*Cyprinus carpio*) and catfish (*Ictalurus* spp.). This reputation, however, is undeserved. Historically, suckers and other bottom-dwelling fish were once relied on by early settlers, trappers, and hunters as a high-quality food source. This legacy lives on in certain areas of North America, where smoked, pickled, and fresh suckers are considered to be delicacies.

In general, suckers are hardy fish that can tolerate a fairly broad range of environmental conditions. They are, however, vulnerable during their reproductive and juvenile stages, when they rely on appropriate physical and chemical conditions in flowing streams for their continued survival. The destruction of habitat in streams through artificial flood control, soil erosion and sedimentation, dam construction that alters the flow and chemistry of the water, and pollution have all affected the ability of several sucker species to survive and thrive.

All suckers have some other common traits. The head is short and broad and lacks scales. The jaws have no teeth, but there is a single row of pharyngeal teeth located in the throat for eating. These fish are excellent swimmers in stream currents because they have a body that is very long and cylindrical (or slightly compressed from side to side for low drag), and the tail fin is forked for power and maneuverability. In addition to their fairly obvious physical and behavioral similarities, the males tend to change color during the breeding season to a bright bronze red in preparation for spawning.

June Sucker

(Chasmistes liorus mictus)

ESA: Endangered

Length: 24 in. (60 cm)
Reproduction: Egg layer
Habitat: Shallow and protected areas of the lake
Range: Utah Lake, Utah

ONCE AN IMPORTANT food item of Utah's early Mormon settlers, the June sucker is today on the verge of extinction. Named for its yearly June migration up the Provo River, this fish is a relative of another endangered sucker, the cui-ui.

Popular catch

During the last half of the 1800s and the early 1900s, the June sucker was fished heavily by commercial fishers and sold to those who appreciated its tasty, high-protein meat. June suckers and other fish were plentiful, with a seemingly endless supply.

Water resources were in demand during this time as well as fish, and diversion of water from the Provo River to irrigate crops and feed growing towns often left little water for the fish to spawn in during late spring and early summer. Many sexually mature fish died without an opportunity to reproduce. During particularly dry years when little water was left to flow into Utah Lake, well over 1,000 tons (907 tonnes) of June suckers would die in an attempt to move upriver to spawn.

This unassuming creature reaches a respectable 2 feet (0.6 meters) in total length. Its appearance is typical for the genus, with a relatively long head tipped by a blunt snout, a large mouth positioned low on the face, and a long and torpedolike body that carries large scales. The square dorsal fin is centered on the back and the tail fin is deeply forked, with pointed lobes for powerful swimming in river currents. The pectoral fins just behind the gills and the pelvic fins on the belly are rounded at the tips. The anal fin is quite deep and rounded.

Mating

During the breeding season, males develop a red stripe on each side. Each female is accompanied by several males as it moves up the Provo River, where it spawns in shallow water over sand and gravel. Eggs hatch after four days, and the juveniles remain in the river for many months if adequate water is available. This fish is an opportunistic feeder, consuming whatever is close at hand, including algae, insects, and microscopic planktonic animals.

Population concern

Today, while the situation for the June sucker has improved as a result of protection from the Utah Division of Wildlife Resources, numbers have failed reach anywhere near to their former levels.

This fish is continually plagued by an ongoing scarcity of water in the Provo River, the Tanner Race diversion that blocks its migration up the river, and the deteriorating water quality of Utah Lake. These multiple threats mean that the future of this fish is very uncertain.

Lost River Sucker

(Deltistes luxatus)

ESA: Endangered

IUCN: Endangered

Length: 25 in. (63 cm)
Reproduction: Egg layer
Habitat: Lakes and reservoirs in open water and streams
Range: Klamath River Basin of Oregon and California

THE ENDANGERED Lost River sucker shares its range with another endangered relative, the shortnose sucker (*Chasmistes brevirostris*). Both are native to the Klamath River Basin in southwestern Oregon and northern California. They spend the majority of their time in Upper Klamath Lake, a large reservoir in Oregon's Cascade Range. Dramatic modifications have been made in the river basin's character through the building of dams and reservoirs, particularly the Sprague River Dam, which blocked 95 percent of the fish's spawning range. This gives the Lost River sucker major problems. Water diversion, stream channelization, and the destruction of associated marshes have also had a severe impact on the ability of the Lost River sucker to survive and to thrive.

Many Lost River suckers are interbreeding with the shortnose sucker and other fish within Upper Klamath Lake because of lack of access to their historic spawning grounds. Because hybridization over time can harm the genetic health of a species,

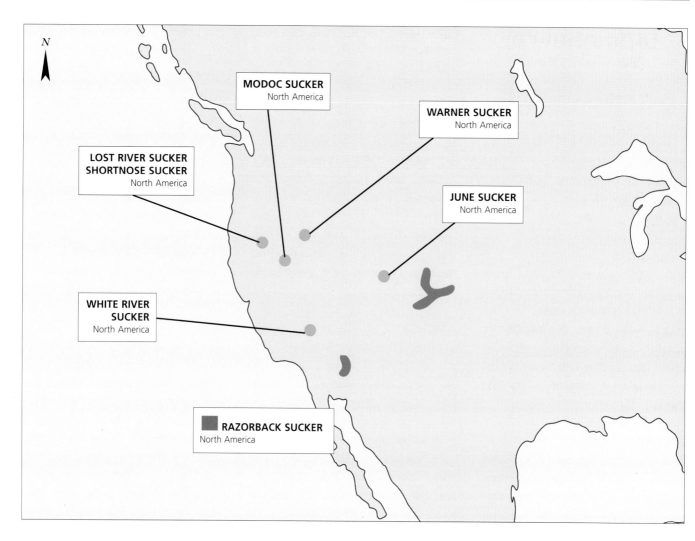

interbreeding may be the last straw for this sucker. Heavy fishing pressure also has played a part in its decline.

Some attempts have been made to save this valuable species. For example, fish ladders were installed at the Sprague River Dam to aid the fish in its move upstream to spawn. (A fish ladder is 'a series of small waterfalls, which resemble a water staircase that the fish can leap over.) Despite the Lost River sucker's strong swimming ability, sexually mature adults were unable to swim up the rungs of the ladder.

The Lost River sucker is a relatively large fish that can weigh up to ten pounds (4.5 kilograms). This fish looks much like

the shortnose sucker, but can easily be identified by the prominent ridge or hump on its snout. Based on the triangular shape of its gill rakers (structures on the gills that filter food from the water and direct it into the stomach) the Lost River sucker was recently moved from the genus *Chasmistes* and given the designation *Deltistes* (delta or triangle). In other aspects, this fish is very similar to other suckers and has a torpedolike body and swept-back fins for low drag. The top of the head, back, and sides are dark, while the belly and underside of the head are cream or white.

Spawning takes place early in spring within rivers or along the shore line of the Upper Klamath Lake, where wave action and

water movement reach the bottom. Females can produce well over 100,000 eggs per year. After the eggs hatch, juvenile fish consume plankton. When they are mature they eat plant material and decaying organic material.

The situation for the Lost River sucker is grave. A cannery once operated on this river to process the large catch. Few adults have spawned successfully (that is, in large numbers) since the construction of the Sprague River Dam in 1970, and most remaining fish are over 20 years old. The life span of the species is as high as 45 years, but unless a new spawning range is opened, surviving individuals will die without producing large numbers of offspring.

Modoc Sucker
(Catostomus microps)

ESA: Endangered

IUCN: Endangered

Length: 7 in. (18 cm)
Reproduction: Egg layer
Habitat: Cool streams and muddy-bottomed pools
Range: Pit River, Modoc Plateau, California

THREATENED BY both the loss of genetic variety and loss of habitat, the Modoc sucker is currently listed as an endangered species. This fish is located only on the Modoc Plateau in northeastern California in the Pit River Basin. The origins of this fish are unclear; other suckers occupy the nearby Klamath River Basin and Sacramento River Basin, but there are surprisingly few similarities.

The water in the Pit River and its tributaries is shallow and slow-moving and, at times, there is no flowing water. The Modoc sucker has evolved a strategy to deal with these conditions that includes small adult size, early sexual maturity, large numbers of eggs per spawn, a short life span, and a natural affinity for these water conditions. Predictably, humans have upset the delicate balance between the local streams and this fish. As a means to control flood waters during rainy periods of the year, much of the Pit River and its offshoots have been channeled by the removal of bank vegetation, bank undercuts, and debris that historically blocked the passage of fish from the Sacramento River into the Pit River. Cattle that use the streams have also severely eroded the banks and promoted siltation. The resulting river has no shade, and water funnels only down its center during low flow. Not only has the preferred stream habitat of the Modoc sucker been destroyed, but non-native fish such as the Sacramento sucker (*Catostomus occidentalis*) have migrated up the Pit River and interbred with the Modoc sucker. Of the eight streams that hold the Modoc sucker, only two hold genetically pure populations.

The Modoc sucker has a long, square dorsal fin on its back, a short, scaleless head, and a low-slung mouth. The tail fin is forked for swimming in currents, but the other fins are triangular and rounded.

This species spawns in April and May during the same time as the Sacramento sucker. Adults reach sexual maturity after the first year of life, and females lay from 6,400 to 12,600 eggs each year. At night the Modoc sucker makes feeding forays into shallow and quiet stream areas in search of its favorite food: algae and decaying organic matter.

The future of this fish is uncertain. However, steps are being taken by government officials and private landowners to prevent the loss of this species. Fences have been erected to exclude cattle, and fish barriers discourage the upstream migration of the Sacramento sucker into the Pit River Basin.

Razorback Sucker
(Xyrauchen texanus)

ESA: Endangered

IUCN: Endangered

Length: 30 in. (76 cm)
Reproduction: Egg layer
Habitat: Warm flowing streams or pools over sand or gravel
Range: Colorado River Basin

RIVALING THE endangered humpback chub (*Gila cypha*) for unconventional looks, the razorback sucker historically occupied many of the same habitats within the Colorado River Basin. Some of the first specimens were sent to a biologist in Texas for

At a maximum length of only 7 inches (18 centimeters), the Modoc sucker is small by sucker standards. The skin is a uniform gray to green brown on the back and sides, while the belly is lighter.

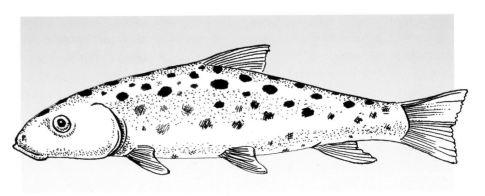

The razorback sucker makes its home in the Colorado River Basin in the states of Colorado, Utah, and Arizona.

identification. The species' name *texanus* was given to this fish by the biologist, who mistakenly thought that it came from the smaller Rio Colorado in Texas.

Today both the humpback chub and the razorback sucker face extinction primarily because of the construction of high dams on the main stem of the Colorado River and its large tributaries. The razorback sucker prefers warm, flowing water and is well adapted to the murky conditions that once dominated most of the river's segments. Projects such as the Hoover Dam and Glen Canyon Dam on the Colorado River, and Flaming Gorge Dam on the Green River, flooded many miles of river upstream from their sites and dramatically altered water flows and chemistry downstream. This is in addition to blocking the migration of fish past the dam sites. Water released from dams is clear and cold, characteristics that are unfamiliar and dangerous for most Colorado River fish.

Dams and their reservoirs not only change the makeup of the water, but its flow patterns as well. Fish rely partially on the seasonal fluctuations in water flow to signal the onset of spawning, as well as other critical processes.

Razorback suckers are not completely intolerant of reservoirs; some have been discovered in reservoirs of the lower Colorado River basin. These populations, however, are not large, and it is feared that as the older fish die, there will be few or no new fish to replace them.

Life in a large river has meant unusual adaptations for this sucker. The most obvious modification is the prominent dorsal keel on the back between the head and dorsal fin (the scientific name *Xyrauchen* means razor nape). This keel is formed by extensions of the vertebrae and provides directional stability in strong, fast-moving water. The razorback sucker also has a low and flat forehead that tends to force the mouth to the bottom as the fish feeds. The swept-back body fins and deeply forked tail

are ideal for the conditions in rivers, and the body is well scaled to prevent abrasion of the skin in the murky water. This is an enormous sucker that can grow to 3 feet (0.9 meters) in length. The upper half of the body is gray-green, while the lower sides and belly are rusty orange and cream, respectively.

In addition to the effects of dams, predation, and competition by introduced non-native fish, interbreeding with other suckers also threatens this species' continued survival. Biologists feel the razorback sucker has a dismal future. However, a recovery team has begun to implement a plan to stabilize razorback sucker populations. Captive breeding is a major component of the plan, and national fish hatcheries in Arizona and New Mexico have had success in propagating this species under artificial conditions. While these steps are encouraging, only major changes and restoration of habitat will put this fish on the road to recovery, but those changes are unlikely in the foreseeable future.

Shortnose Sucker

(Chasmistes brevirostris)

ESA: Endangered

IUCN: Endangered

Length: 24 in. (60 cm)
Reproduction: Egg layer
Habitat: Reservoirs and free-flowing streams
Range: Klamath River Basin, Oregon and California

DURING THE late 1980s, the shortnose sucker experienced a devastating loss in numbers and was listed as an endangered species. This fish claims the Klamath River Basin in southwestern Oregon and northern California as its home and, until 1987, was actively sought as a sport fish. The plight of this fish closely resembles that of another sucker that occupies a nearly identical range: the Lost River sucker. Dramatic modifications of the river basin's character, including damming and reservoir creation, did much of the damage (the Sprague River Dam blocked 85 percent of the fish's spawning range). Water diversion and the destruction of associated marshes have not helped this species either. Other forces, such as heavy fishing and interbreeding, have also contributed to its decline.

The building of fish ladders at the Sprague River Dam to aid the fish's uphill spawning runs did not pay off; not even sexually mature adults were able to swim up the rungs of the ladder.

The shortnose sucker is uniformly dark on the back and sides, lightening to white on the belly. It has the usual blunt snout, low mouth, and a strong body. Spawning begins in April as adults move from lakes and reservoirs to their upstream spawning grounds. Eggs are laid over gravel and rubble, and as many as 70,000 can be deposited by one female. Plankton is an important component of the shortnose sucker's diet, but it will consume whatever is appropriate and available.

The shortnose sucker is in deep trouble. This species has apparently not spawned in large numbers since 1970, and most of the remaining fish are old.

Unless a new spawning range is opened for this fish, surviving individuals will die without reproducing.

Warner Sucker

(Catostomus warnerensis)

ESA: Threatened

IUCN: Vulnerable

Length: 12 in. (30 cm)
Reproduction: Egg layer
Habitat: Lake bottom and adjacent streams
Range: Warner Valley Basin, Oregon

AFTER THE GEOLOGIC period when glaciers advanced and receded from the area known today as Oregon and the Great Basin of the western United States, several large lakes dominated the region. One of those lakes was Warner Lake. In the warmer and drier climate that made the glaciers melt, these water bodies began to evaporate, reducing their size. Warner Lake once filled the Warner Valley, but today only three small lakes remain: Crump, Hart, and Pelican Lakes. These lakes are quite isolated and have survived only by virtue of the runoff they receive from incoming streams. Ancestors of the endangered Warner sucker roamed freely in Warner Lake, but as the lake contracted, so did the range of fish it held. Crump Lake, Hart Lake, and Pelican Lake are the last strongholds of the fish we now call the Warner sucker.

During the late 1800s, the Warner Valley was developed for

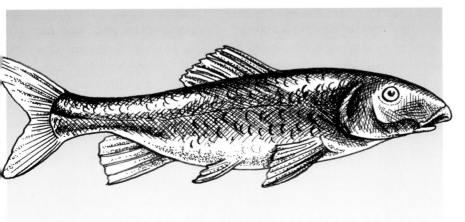

The population of the shortnose sucker is mainly made up of older individuals, who often die without reproducing. The fish has had little success spawning in the last three decades.

1421

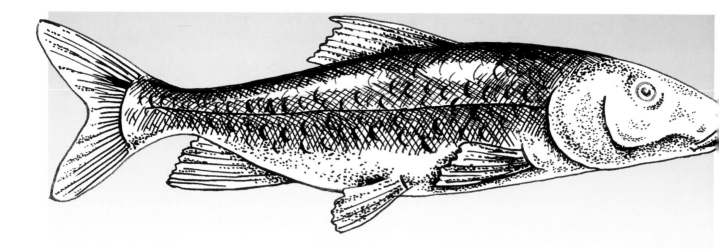

The Warner sucker is typical of most suckers in terms of size, shape, and appearance.

farming and cattle ranching. Water in this high desert region is a precious commodity, and the streams that feed the Warner Valley lakes provided farmers and ranchers with an opportunity to expand and grow.

A complex array of diversion dams and canals was constructed to meet this new demand for water. Unfortunately for fish such as the Warner sucker, these dams and barriers pose such a threat to reproduction that today this species is listed as threatened by the IUCN.

Appearance

This medium-sized fish has a robust and streamlined body with fairly uniform coloration from head to tail. The back and sides are a darker greenish gray, while the head and underside of the belly are cream. The head, with its small eyes, is short, with the sucker mouth on its underside to enable the fish to taste and then remove food from the bottom. The swept-back fins follow the coloration of the body, and the tail is forked.

During the spring breeding season, the male turns bright red across the body and both sexes develop nodulelike breeding tubercles on several surfaces. Tubercles increase the sensitivity of the skin and promote the release of eggs and sperm during spawning. The Warner sucker seeks insect larvae and bottom-dwelling crustaceans during its feeding excursions.

In the spring, the Warner sucker attempts to move up the feeder streams to spawn on gravel bottoms. Water flowing over the eggs provides oxygen and carries away waste products. After eggs hatch, the stream provides food for juveniles until they move to the lakes. Diversion dams pose a double threat to the Warner sucker. Many sexually mature adults are unable to bypass the dams to spawn in streams. Those that do manage to move upstream spawn successfully, but their offspring may be drawn into diversion canals before they reach the lakes, to be stranded in the canals, or they are pumped onto fields with the irrigation water. The problem is so bad that canals, as inadequate as they are, offer the best habitat for this species.

Adding insult to injury, the Warner sucker faces more development within the valley by those interested in tapping its geothermal energy resources. Water temperatures within the streams could be severely affected. Introduced non-native catfish pose problems as well. Juvenile suckers are easy prey for adult catfish, and their numbers are probably reduced substantially by the time they reach the relative safety of the lakes.

White River Sucker

(Catostomus clarki intermedius)

Length: 12 in. (30 cm)
Reproduction: Egg layer
Habitat: Stream pools and rapids
Range: White River, Nevada

THE WHITE RIVER sucker is a subspecies of the desert sucker, a fish that is found from extreme northern Mexico, throughout Arizona, and into central Nevada. As the common name implies, this subspecies is found only in Nevada's White River.

This area of Nevada is, in general, quite dry, and water is a valuable commodity here. As a result, the White River sucker has been subjected to human disturbance and activity for years. Some of these activities include water diversions for agricultural purposes, destruction of instream habitat by cattle, streambed modification, and an overall deterioration in water quality. Adults of this subspecies prefer fast waters, and as water flows lessen, the number of acceptable areas within the river decreases. The bottom line for the White River sucker is shrinking habitat and a real possibility that this subspecies will be lost to extinction.

The foot-long White River sucker has a mildly bulbous belly and a tail section that is narrower than the rest of the body. It displays an overall silvery cast with a brown-green back, top of the head, and upper sides. The lower sides are more yellowish, as are the belly and underside of the head.

Scales on the body are large, but the head is nude. All fins follow the coloration of the body. The dorsal fin on the back is square, and the pectoral fins behind the gills, the pelvic fins on the belly, and the anal fin are rounded. The tail fin is moderately forked, with pointed lobes.

This fish first spawns at about age three during the early spring. Sexually mature males and females move to stream riffles and deposit eggs and sperm over gravel, sand, and rubble. After hatching, the active young move to quiet areas where they consume tiny and microscopic food items until they are stronger swimmers. The adult White River sucker feeds mainly on algae that it scrapes from rocks and other hard surfaces in the river. The fish may need to maneuver onto its back to remove algae from the underside of rocks.

Saving the White River sucker will require an effort to restore instream habitat. Because this activity involves political difficulties, relocation to a much more secure region may be a reasonable alternative.

This fish was previously listed by IUCN as endangered, but was not evaluated by the time the red list was compiled. Until more data is available, the species is included with other endangered taxa, because it may still be at risk.

William Manci

SUNBIRDS

Class: Aves

Order: Passeriformes

Family: Nectariniidae

Sunbirds rival the barbets and parrots for gaudy plumage. Some of them wear ordinary hues of yellow, green, and brown, but many of them sport dazzling colors that glitter in the sun. They range from brilliant greens to shiny metallic purples, with many species decked out in oranges, reds, yellows, and greens together. Sunbirds are never very large. Some are petite at just 3½ inches (9 centimeters). Many of those that reach 8 inches (20 centimeters) owe half their length to extravagant tails. Tubular tongues equip them for taking nectar from flowers. Their small size, marvelous colors, and nectar-feeding habits tempt many casual observers to falsely assume that sunbirds must be related to hummingbirds.

Sunbirds and hummingbirds are considered to be very different. They are separated not only by their anatomy, but also by their distribution. Hummingbirds live only in North and South America, and sunbirds live only in the eastern hemisphere, excluding Australia. More than half of the 116 sunbird species live in Africa. The remaining species are distributed across southern Asia from the Middle East through India into Myanmar (formerly Burma), and southward through Malaysia into Australia. Despite their differences, sunbirds and hummingbirds share a taste for nectar.

Several bird families have at least a few species that eat nectar as a major part of their diet; but, like the hummingbirds, the sunbirds specialize in nectar. Sunbirds hover in front of flowers in order to feed, just like hummingbirds. Because they live in similar ways, the two groups have come to resemble each other. Called *convergent evolution*, this phenomenon occurs in many unrelated groups of animals. The sunbirds do not exactly match the hummingbirds. They lack the ability to hover for as long a time, and they do not enjoy the hummingbirds' unequalled maneuverability.

Most sunbirds live in tropical or subtropical climates where dependable sun keeps flowers in bloom throughout the year. Consequently, sunbirds do not migrate. They do wander widely, however, to find adequate nectar supplies. Their habitat needs often reflect this dependency on flowers. If their habitat is divided up into areas that are too small, they cannot survive.

Apricot-breasted Sunbird

(Nectarinia buettikoferi)

IUCN: Lower risk

Length: 4–4½ in. (10.2–11.4 cm)
Clutch size: Probably 2 eggs
Incubation: Probably 14–17 days
Diet: Insects and nectar
Habitat: Forest
Range: Sumba Island, Indonesia

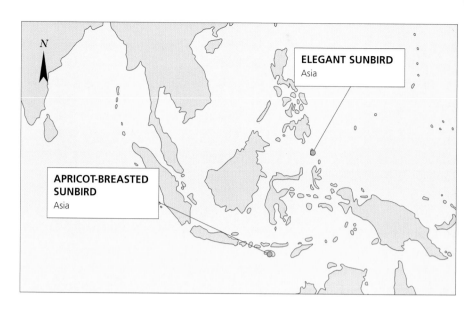

THE APRICOT-BREASTED sunbird lives in a land that blends the unique life forms of Asia with the unique life forms of Australia. This land allows some creatures to pass through, but holds back just as many or more.

The great mass of land that bulges out into the sea in this region is Southeast Asia. This land extends even further south in a strip known as the Malay Peninsula. To the south and east lies a string of islands that form an arc reaching into the waters north of Australia. Sumatra and Java are the first two large islands, making up part of the Greater Sunda Islands. East of Java the islands suddenly shrink dramatically in size and form; this chain is known as the Lesser Sunda Islands. The Sundas form a natural highway for wildlife from Asia to wander south, but the many gaps and climate changes also form a barrier to this same wildlife group.

Unique characteristics

Birds can easily move between the islands once known as the East Indies. However, food supplies, nesting cover, predators, and other factors work against birds that would pioneer into new territories. So even though many birds wander about, many more get stopped and cannot go any further. Left undisturbed and unchallenged by competing species for a long enough period, many island birds develop unique traits that isolate them from relatives on neighboring islands. Some become fully distinct from their parent species that still exist on the mainland. It is this process that probably affected the apricot-breasted sunbird.

Development

Thousands of years ago, a group of sunbirds probably wandered southward from Asia into the Sundas. A few of them flew no farther than Sumba Island, where they survived and prospered. In time and with isolation, they developed into the apricot-breasted sunbird, a unique species to be found nowhere else. A small bird, the apricot-breasted sunbird wears a neutral gray-green on its upperparts. An orange breast patch colors the yellow underparts. This unique little sunbird lived throughout Sumba before people came along and eroded its habitat.

Exploration

The first Asian people probably wandered into the Sundas about 2000 B.C.E. They were the first humans to settle on the islands. During the exploratory era of the 1600s and 1700s, European peoples, including the Dutch, Portuguese, French, English, Germans, and Spanish found the East Indies. Originally, the East Indies, including the Lesser Sundas, were used to channel wealth into the European countries. The 19th and 20th centuries brought independence. The new nations, seeking wealth of their own, continued the agricultural and economic practices of their former mother countries.

Clearing and planting

Sumba has been a victim of human's hunger for wealth. The island's native plant communities have been destroyed so that plantation agriculture could be developed in the coastal lowlands and lower mountain slopes. Plantations produce enormous quantities of valuable commodities such as fruit, lumber, rubber, spices, and coffee. In large quantities, these products can be sold to the foreign market. Unfortunately, unique species such as the apricot-breasted sunbird suffer from change. The bird lives nowhere else in the world except on Sumba, and on Sumba the bird lives only in primary forest. Those forests have been cut for what products they can yield, especially sandalwood (*Santalum* sp.). Lowland areas are then replanted into more valuable crops. The higher slopes are left to recover on their own.

Survival

The human population growth in Indonesia almost defies imagination. Even harder to imagine would be returning the island to native forest conditions. If the apricot-breasted sunbird is to survive, it must cling to the small patches of primary forest that remain intact. At only 4,306 square miles (11,196 square kilometers), the island is not large to begin with, so the habitat for this sunbird was never very expansive.

Threat

The apricot-breasted sunbird cannot survive in larger numbers as long as more habitat remains unavailable. The continued clearing of forest on Sumba for firewood, sandalwood, and agriculture threatens the bird further.

The majority of the sunbird species lives in Africa; other birds are found in Asia, the Middle East, and Australia.

Elegant Sunbird
(Aethopyga duyvenbodei)

IUCN: Endangered

Length: 4–4½ in. (10.2–11.4 cm)
Clutch size: Probably 2 eggs
Incubation: Probably 14–17 days
Diet: Insects and nectar
Habitat: Forest and forest edges
Range: Sangihe and Siau Islands of Indonesia

THE ELEGANT sunbird is one of many species threatened by a world appetite for foods most economically grown in tropical climates, including tea and bananas.

The elegant sunbird is like a rainbow. The yellow-green back fades to a yellow rump, but the small feathers that cover the base of the tail are a shiny purplish blue. The underparts are bright yellow with orangish sides. The crown is a shiny, glittering green, but the cheek and nape are brilliant red and the lore is yellow. Such brightly colored sunbirds typically inhabit open woodlands and shrub lands, but the elegant sunbird seems to be a bird of forests and forest edges. As these habitats have declined on Sangihe and Siau, the sunbird has faded.

Many Indonesian islands have been completely cleared so they could be converted to agricultural production. Bananas, coconuts, rubber, sugarcane, tea, coffee, rice, and other crops can be more profitably grown in large quantities. Plantations can easily cover entire islands. If the plants and animals that live on those islands also live elsewhere, the impact of the plantations and crops is not so dramatic. When a species only lives on one or two small islands, however, the impact of large-scale agriculture can be devastating. The elegant sunbird only lives on two islands, and those islands have a history of habitat loss.

The Sangihe Islands form a line between the northeastern arm of Sulawesi (formerly

Celebes) and Mindanao, the southernmost island of the Philippines. The island chain separates the Celebes Sea from the Molucca Sea, and Sangihe lies almost exactly in the middle. Halfway between Sangihe and Sulawesi lies Siau. The elegant sunbird inhabits only these two islands. The islands have only so much space for people, crops, and sunbirds. Sangihe, the largest of the group, covers only 314 square miles (816 square kilometers). It is a volcanic island tormented by natural and human activities. A volcano, Gunung Awu, built and still dominates the island. It erupted in 1856 and again in 1982. As volcanoes always do, Gunung Awu damaged much natural habitat. It tempered the effect with a spray of ash bearing elements and minerals vital to healthy plant growth. The tropical climate of Sangihe encouraged quick recovery from the volcanoes.

The island has not recovered from problems created by humans. Dutch merchants established themselves in Sangihe in 1677. They milked the island for its fruit, spices, fibers, and other wealth. When the natural forests had yielded all they could, they were replaced. Bananas, coconuts, rubber, and tea became the standard crop of wealth in the East Indies.

After centuries of volcanoes and plantation agriculture, Sangihe's primary forests have withered to only a few small patches. In the closing years of the 20th century, and at the beginning of the 21st century, Sangihe was dominated as much by coconuts, hemp, and nutmeg as by Gunung Awu. The coconuts are processed into copra, the hemp into fiber for ropes, and the nutmeg into spice. Sangihe produces nothing that is not grown elsewhere; but the pressure to produce even more is relentless: people need jobs and food, and plantations provide jobs, while the protection of sunbirds does not.

Population figures for the elegant sunbird are not available. However, the bird has shown no willingness to accept altered habitat, even those areas returning to native forest. Some element in the primary forest provides for the elegant sunbird's needs, but ornithologists know so little about the bird that answers about its survival needs remain unknown.

Recovery plan

The dwindling availability of habitat and the bird's refusal to use secondary forest or other habitats paint a picture of a bird in trouble. With no detailed studies of the bird's natural history and no estimates of its surviving population, it is difficult to recommend a specific recovery plan, and none has been enacted.

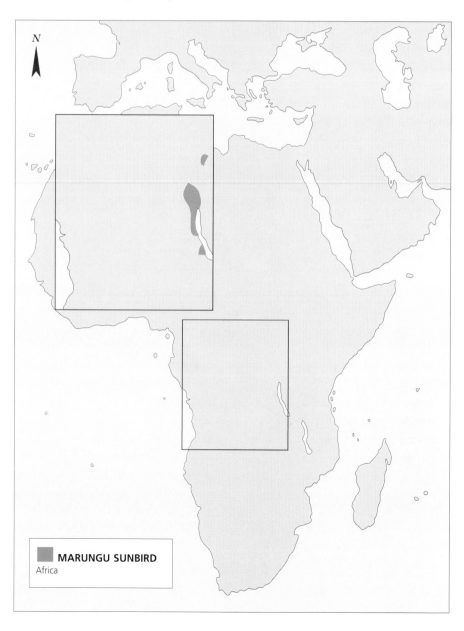

MARUNGU SUNBIRD
Africa

Marungu Sunbird

(Nectarinia prigoginei)

ESA: Endangered

Length: 4–4½ in. (10.2–11.4 cm)
Clutch size: Probably 2 eggs
Incubation: Probably 14–17 days
Diet: Insects and nectar
Habitat: Riparian forest
Range: Marungu Highlands of southeastern Democratic Republic of Congo

WHERE THE equator slices across the African continent, a great variety of wonderfully strange plants and animals live. For centuries it was a land isolated by its own character. Its thick forests, heavy rains, high temperatures, malaria-carrying mosquitoes, and other features made it largely inhospitable to humans. Yet in this very environment, certain creatures thrived. Among them were many songbirds, including the Marungu sunbird.

The Democratic Republic of Congo is one of the equatorial countries of Central Africa. Its eastern limits are marked by valleys, lakes, and ridges that can isolate small animals that do not move great distances. The Marungu Highlands is just such a place. The highland streams isolate the Marungu sunbird, which lives in the forests that adjoin the water. These are prized for their big trees and the lumber they produce. Riparian areas also provide rich soil that is good for agriculture, so both humans and the Marungu sunbird are drawn to these native forests, but the needs of the sunbird clash with the those of humans.

The Marungu sunbird occurs only in a small portion of the Democratic Republic of Congo. No historic estimates of population size are available, and no recent estimates of present population numbers have been published. Unless some riparian forest in the Marungu Highlands is preserved, the sunbird that lives there will disappear.

Wider effects

There are other consequences to these highlands should the Marungu sunbird disappear. Sunbirds pollinate flowers in their search for nectar, and many pollinators are specialized for certain flowers. The flowers, in turn, may be dependent upon that pollinator. An incomplete knowledge of the Marungu sunbird leaves doubts about other creatures and plants that may be affected by the extinction of the Marungu sunbird. Creatures yet unknown may suffer.

Kevin Cook

Spring Pygmy Sunfish

(Elassoma sp.)

Class: Actinopterygii
Order: Perciformes
Family: Centrarchidae
Length: ¾ in. (2 cm)
Reproduction: Egg layer
Habitat: Limestone springs and their outflows in vegetation
Range: Beaverdam-Moss Springs complex, Alabama

MANY PEOPLE are familiar with the fish of the family Centrarchidae. They include popular sport fish such as the largemouth bass (*Micropterus salmoides*), the bluegill (*Lepomis macrochirus*), the black crappie (*Pomoxis nigromaculatus*), and other sunfish. However, few people have ever heard of the spring pygmy sunfish. This fish can be found only in remote northern Alabama where underground limestone rock formations have been dissolved and eroded by thousands of years of water movement. Groundwater has forced its way to the surface, creating the Beaverdam-Moss Springs complex.

First discovered in 1937, the spring pygmy sunfish was found in a system called Cave Springs. Unfortunately, this system was flooded when the construction of a dam by the Tennessee Valley Authority created Pickwick Lake. Its population of spring pygmy sunfish was lost.

A second spring system, Pryor Spring, also held this species. A

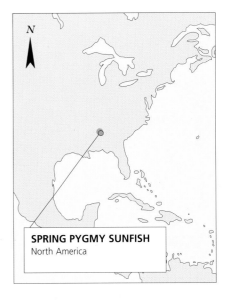

SPRING PYGMY SUNFISH
North America

Like the spring pygmy sunfish, the Everglades pygmy sunfish seeks the protection of dense vegetation.

non-native plant called parrots feather was introduced into this system, choking the spring and impeding water flow. It also dammed the outflow and created a small pond. Mosquitoes flourished in the new pond, and people decided to eliminate this pest's new breeding ground. In 1945, herbicides were used to kill the vegetation, and the outflow was improved to assist the flow of water away from the area. The exact reasons are unclear, but since 1941 no spring pygmy sunfish have been collected from Pryor Springs.

All hopes of finding a third population were dim until 1973, when this fish was located in the Beaverdam-Moss Springs complex. This complex includes Beaverdam Spring and Moss Springs and their outflows, Beaverdam Swamp, and Lowe's Ditch, an artificial waterway used

to divert irrigation water. Despite problems with sedimentation during heavy rain, the complex is fairly secure from domestic and industrial pollution. The fish population has responded positively by producing relatively large numbers of fish. However, there is the potential for a catastrophic loss of fish if agricultural pesticides are applied to nearby fields immediately before a strong rainstorm. Toxic runoff would have serious consequences for the spring pygmy sunfish.

As with many other fish, the coloration pattern of males and females differs in this species. The male has a dark brown background that is highlighted by gold vertical bars on the sides. The fins are dark brown, except for a clear window spot in the dorsal and anal fins. The color of the female is highly variable; background color ranges from light to dark brown, and the vertical bars may be present.

With the benefit of underground water that supplies

near-constant water temperatures, it is likely that the spring pygmy sunfish spawns throughout the year. A female produces few eggs; only 60 to 65 per spawn. Offspring live only for a year. Given their short lifespan, reproductive success is a must. This fish consumes small insects and other aquatic invertebrates during its year-long stay in the spring complex.

As insurance against a catastrophe at the Beaverdam-Moss Springs complex, officials hope to reclaim habitats such as Pryor Springs by eliminating non-native vegetation and reintroducing the spring pygmy sunfish into part of its historic range. This would improve the long-term survival of this species.

This fish was previously listed by IUCN as threatened, but was not evaluated by the time the red list was compiled. Until more data is available, the species is included here, because it may still be at risk.

William E. Manci

SUNFLOWERS

Class: Magnoliopsida
Order: Asterales
Family: Asteraceae

The genus *Helianthus* contains 40 species, distributed throughout North America. Helianthus are in the family Compositae (Asteraceae), which is one of the largest families of flowering plants. In this family, inflorescences are made up of many small disk and ray flowers. The genus *Helianthus* can be recognized by a *pappus* that is a pair of scales attached to the ovary; a flat receptacle that holds the flowers; and the presence of chaff (bracts) between flowers.

Eggert's Sunflower

(Helianthus eggertii)

ESA: Threatened

IUCN: Vulnerable

Height: 3–6 ft. (1–2 m)
Leaves: Lanceolate, up to 6 in. (15 cm) long, 1 in. (3 cm) wide
Flowering season: Early August to mid-September
Habitat: Barrens, edges of woods, and roadsides
Range: Tennessee, Kentucky, one site in Alabama

EGGERT'S SUNFLOWER is a perennial that has roots which branch in all directions. Its stems rise from elongated rhizomes. The stems are purple and hairless and are covered with whitish blooms. Stems have 7 to 15 pairs of opposite, or occasionally whorled, leaves. The leaves are hairless and waxy and the whole plant has a bluish white cast which makes it conspicuous from a distance.

Structure

The leaves are tapered, single veined or faintly triple-veined, and are held on a short stalk of less than ¼ inch (0.5 centimeter). A few flower heads are produced, held on elongated stalks 4 to 6 inches (10 to 15 centimeters) long.

The leaves at the flower base are spear-shaped with hairy edges, and are about the same length as the flower head.

The chaff separating the flowers has smooth edges with three blunt points. The center of the flower is yellow and ½ to ¾ inch (1.2 to 2 centimeters) wide.

The ray flowers are also yellow, and can be up to ¾ inch (2 centimeters) long. The whole bloom can have a diameter of 3 inches (8 centimeters) across the rays. The seeds of Eggert's

The Eggert's sunflower brightens up the sides of this country road in the Great Smoky Mountains.

sunflower are blackish, or gray mottled, and 5–6 millimeters long. The seeds are topped by a pappus of two or three scales.

This species may have arisen from a cross between *Helianthus laevigatus*, which is a species found in the shale barrens of the Allegheny Mountains, and *Helianthus decapetalus*, which is widespread in the eastern United States. Eggert's sunflower will hybridize with other hexaploid sunflower species.

Close relation

Eggert's sunflower appears to be closely related to *Helianthus laevigatus*, with which it shares many chemical compounds, but also resembles *Helianthus strumosus* in its colonial growth habit and smooth stems. In the past, researchers considered *Helianthus eggertii* to be a variant of

Helianthus strumosus, though the two species share very few chemical compounds, and *Helianthus strumosus* differs morphologically from Eggert's sunflower by having a longer leafstem, and distinctly three-veined leaves, with no waxy blue coating.

EGGERT'S SUNFLOWER
North America

Habitat

Eggert's sunflower prefers the habitat of roadsides or edges of woods, rocky hills, barrens, or open upland woods. The three centers of distribution of this plant have similar conditions. Sites from the highland rim in Tennessee range from 755 to 1,100 feet (230 to 335 meters) in elevation. Cumberland Plateau sites in Marion County Tennessee are 1,200 feet (370 meters) and the single Blount County site in Alabama is 655 feet (200 meters) high. The Shawnee Hills sites in Kentucky range from 690 to 855 feet (210 to 260 meters).

Soils and rock

All of these sites are associated with limestone or sandstone rocks, which are covered in shallow, well-drained silt loams or clays. These soils have moderate to high acidity and low levels of organic matter. Most of these sites are covered in oak forest, made up of white oak (*Quercus alba*), black oak (*Quercus velutina*) and southern red oak (*Quercus falcata*), and can also include hickories and pines. Openings in these forests are known as barrens, and are dominated by grasses and herbs. Eggert's sunflower is usually found in open places such as barrens, along woodland edges, or on roadsides. It seems to prefer full sun or part shade, and moist places, though it is occasionally also found in dry situations.

There are 26 known populations of Eggert's sunflower. Of these, 18 populations occur at sites in 8 counties in Tennessee, seven sites in Lincoln, Jackson, and Edmonson Counties in Kentucky, and one site in Blount county, Alabama. Less than half of these 26 populations occurred on natural barrens habitats, and there are many barren habitats that do not support this species. Half of these sites have fewer than 200 stems, and at 4 sites there were fewer than 50 stems counted.

Breeding system

Eggert's sunflower flowers from early August to the middle of September. This species is reliant on insect pollination. Many different types of insects have been observed visiting the flower heads, though bees and bumblebees were the most frequent visitors. The seeds are relatively large and do not have a particularly efficient dispersal mechanism, so most are probably dropped near the parent plant.

When long-distance dispersal occurs, it is most likely to be due to large birds swallowing some uncracked seeds, or to human transport of soil for road building or other activities.

Reproduction

Eggert's sunflower can reproduce vegetatively, and sometimes one individual can form very large colonies of hundreds of stems. This colonial growth habit makes it difficult to evaluate the exact number of individuals that are present at a site, and this has implications for the health of the species, since the plant is dependent on pollen being transferred between different individuals for the seeds to set. A site could appear to have a large thriving population, but if this population is made up of only one root-connected individual plant, chances for cross-pollination are slim and the population will not be able to reproduce.

Threats

Eggert's sunflower is threatened by the disappearance of barrens in Tennessee and Kentucky. This plant, along with many other barren plants, is being shaded out by weedy competitors and forest succession. Like many fire-dependent plants, *Helianthus eggertii* has moved into human-made habitats such as roadsides and rights of way, and as the barrens disappear, these habitats are more important for their survival. This species is also threatened by the use of herbicides and by the widening of roadways.

Larval threat

The flower heads of Eggert's sunflower are sometimes infected with 5-millimeter long whitish insect larva, which eat the embryos of the fruit. At some sites nearly all the seeds have been destroyed.

Schweinitz's Sunflower

(Helianthus schweinitzii)

ESA: Endangered

IUCN: Vulnerable

Height: 3–6 ft. (1–2 m)
Flowers: Yellow, raylike
Flowering season: September to October
Habitat: Open places, and the edges of woods
Range: North Carolina, South Carolina, and Alabama

SCHWEINITZ'S sunflower is a perennial plant that forms a solitary partially underground stem, or rhizome, from a cluster of tuberous roots. The stems are often deep red or purple and are thinly covered in stiff hairs. Secondary branches form only from

nodes on the upper half of the stem. Leaves are arranged opposite each other on the lower part of the exposed stem, and alternate above. The upper surface of the leaves is dotted with resin and rough in texture, with a rolled under edge. The underside of the leaves is covered in soft white hairs. The leaves are spear-shaped and may have a few serrations. They grow up to 7 inches (18 centimeters) long and 1 inch (2.5 centimeters) wide. The lower stem leaves are usually the largest, with subsequent leaves becoming smaller up the stem. They are held on a petiole ½ inch (1.5 centimeters) long.

The plants produce several heads of flowers. The central part of the flower, or disk, is yellow and ¼ to ½ inch (1 to 1.5 centimeters) across. Each head has 15 or fewer yellow ray flowers, which are about ¾ inch (2 centimeters) long. The bract leaves

just beneath the flower are slender and shorter than the disk. The chaff between the flowers on the disk has three teeth, and the middle tooth is pointed and hairy. The smooth seeds are 3–4 millimeters long and have rounded tips. This plant begins flowering in September and continues until there is frost.

Distribution

Schweinitz's sunflower is endemic to the Piedmont Plateau of North and South Carolina. This plant currently grows in 10 populations in Union, Stanley, Cabarrus, Mecklenverg and Rowan Counties in North Carolina, and 6 populations in South Carolina. Two thirds of these populations occur on road-

Each head of the Schweinitz's sunflower has 15 or fewer yellow ray flowers around ½ inch (2 centimeters) long.

sides, or utility rights of way, where they are susceptible to chance destruction. This species occurs in clearings on the edges of woods, in clay, clay-limes, or sandy clay-loam which often have a high gravel content.

The underlying rock types generally have high weather-ability, with little resistant material such as granite, and produce fine-textured soils. The open habitats where Schweinitz's sunflower grows are not typical of the landscape of the Piedmont plateau.

Often species associated with this plant will be more typical of glade and prairie habitats of the Midwest, or fire-dependent long-leaf pine sandhills and savannas of the Atlantic Coastal Plain. The rarity of Schweinitz's sunflower may be due to recent habitat changes caused by human disturbance and changes in the fire patterns in the area.

Schweinitz's sunflower is threatened by the degradation of its habitat due to fire and native herbivores, as well as by habitat loss due to residential and industrial development. Other threats include mining and competition from exotic vegetation. Since many of the remaining populations of Schweinitz's sunflower occur on roadsides and utility rights of way, they could be affected by the use of herbicides for vegetation control, and populations could be destroyed by highway construction such as the proposed widening of state highway 16 near Charlotte, where the species occurs.

Conservation

Fortunately, considerable effort is being made to conserve this species in North and South Carolina. Both North Carolina and South Carolina have received grants for monitoring and man-

aging populations of this species. Agreements have been made with the Duke Power Company and Carolina Power and Light Company to protect and manage populations that grow on utility rights of way, by discontinuing the use of herbicides and mowing only after the reproductive season of the plants is over.

Site protection

Also, the Natural Heritage program initiated a cooperative effort with the North Carolina Department of Transportation to prevent grading or mowing of roadsides supporting Schweinitz's sunflower populations during their reproductive period. Initial attempts were unsuccessful, but efforts have doubled and signs have been posted at the boundaries of all roadside population. The Nature Conservancy has purchased one site and part of a second where this species occurs, and has negotiated a management agree-ment with the landowners for a third. In 1992, the Nature Conservancy began cutting woody vegetation on the sites it owns, and in 1993 it began a program of controlled burns.

Seed collection

The North Carolina Botanic Garden is also collecting seeds from all remaining populations, and Winthrop College in South Carolina is propagating the species for potential reintroduction or population augmentation. Botanists at the University of North Carolina are also involved in the monitoring and management of Schweinitz's sunflower.

Christina Oliver

N

SCHWEINITZ'S SUNFLOWER
North America

SWIFTLETS

Class: Aves

Order: Apodiformes

Family: Apodidae

Subfamily: Apodinae

Swiftlets construct their nests of sticky, gluelike saliva. Some Asian people collect their nests for the popular recipe known as bird's nest soup. Such nest collecting has endangered several swiftlets in the genus *Collocalia*.

The swiftlets' order name—Apodiformes—translates roughly as "without feet." Swifts spend far more time airborne than any other birds: they bathe and drink in flight; they catch all their food in flight; they pick up nesting material in flight; they mate when they are in flight; they even sleep in flight. Because, centuries ago, observers never found the swiftlets landing on twigs or the ground or water, they presumed that the birds had no feet. In fact, swiftlets do have short legs, tiny feet, and small toes.

Mariana Gray Swiftlet

(Aerodramus vanikorensis bartschi)

ESA: Endangered

Length: 4 in. (10.2 cm)

Weight: 0.2–0.3 oz. (6–8.5 g)

Clutch size: 1 egg

Incubation: 12–14 days

Diet: Insects

Habitat: Aerial nests in caves

Range: Marianas Islands in western Pacific Ocean

GLIDING OVER the treetops, the gray swiftlet flies through the skies over India, Southeast Asia, and the islands of the southern Pacific Ocean. Its long, narrow wings seem to flutter rather than flap and its body is long and narrow, starting with only the tiniest nub of a beak and ending with a modestly forked tail. It appears all black above, has a dark face, and is gray or grayish brown from chin to undertail. Once common almost everywhere within its range, the gray swiftlet has severely declined in some places.

Particularly drastic has been its disappearance from the Marianas Islands.

Separating the Philippine Sea from the Pacific Ocean, the Marianas Islands stretch 513 miles (820 kilometers) from Guam in the south to Farallon de Pajaros in the north. Guam covers 209 square miles (543 square kilometers), making it the largest of the islands. A patchwork of forest, woodland, savanna, shrub land, and coastal mangrove swamp once covered the island. The gray swiftlet's vital need was caves where it could build its nest on the vertical rock walls. Most of the cave openings were protected by the dense vegetation of island forests. The caves remain, but the gray swiftlet has declined. It no longer occurs on Rota and is rare on Agiguan, Saipan, and Tinian. The Guam population is also imperiled.

No single cause has been proved to be the culprit in the gray swiftlet's decline. Whatever the cause or causes, they must have affected the species on all the Marianas Islands at the same time. Excessive use of pesticides,

habitat destruction, and exotic species are all possibilities. Almost without doubt, together these factors account for the problems of the gray swiftlet and other birds in the Marianas.

After the United States took control of Guam in World War II, the pesticide DDT was heavily used for controlling mosquitoes and agricultural pests. What was unknown at the time is that DDT interferes with a female bird's ability to deposit calcium in her eggs, making the shells too thin. Thin eggs break easily and reduce breeding success. This problem radically affects birds that are exposed for many years because the effects build up over time. Ornithologists first began noting a severe bird decline in the 1960s, about 20 years after DDT was first used.

The 1960s also marked about 20 years into the invasion of Guam by the brown tree snake (*Boiga irregularis*). Native to Southeast Asia, the brown tree snake was probably introduced to Guam shortly after World War II. This snake prefers small birds as food, and it stalks them at night. It takes adult birds, nestlings, and eggs. Without any serious competition or threat from predators, the brown tree snake enjoyed an unrestrained population explosion. Snakes were welcomed for their ability to control rat populations, so by the time people realized what a serious pest the snake was, its population was nearly beyond control.

While it is known to eat many small birds, the brown tree snake has not proved to be a major threat to the gray swiftlet. This is because the bird nests in caves where tree snakes may not be able to reach them. The bird has also vanished from islands where the brown tree snake does not occur, so the snake is not the only reason for its decline.

Destruction

After World War II, Guam entered an era of dramatic development. Much bird habitat was lost to agriculture, housing, road building, city growth, and other developments. Habitat loss alone cannot explain the bird's decline because some completely uninhabited patches of suitable habitat survived into the 1980s. The answer to this puzzle may involve all three problems. Habitat destruction initially reduced the bird populations. Heavy use of pesticides such as DDT reduced breeding success, and the available food supply. Smaller bird populations in smaller habitat patches are far more vulnerable to exotic predators such as brown tree snakes. On smaller islands, the predators could also be rats (*Rattus* sp.).

Predator control

Researchers have studied brown tree snakes since the 1980s. They hope to find a way to suppress the snake on Guam, if not eradicate it altogether. The use of DDT for general insect control was outlawed in the early 1970s. Other predators, particularly rats, need to be controlled, remaining native habitat must be preserved, and damaged habitat must be restored. The potential of exotic bird diseases must be carefully examined as well. Such measures will help all the endangered and threatened native birds of Guam.

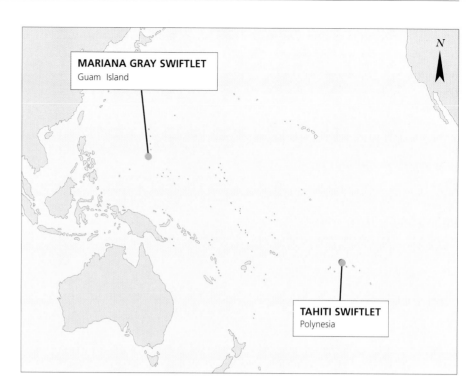

Tahiti Swiftlet

(Aerodramus leucophaeus)

IUCN: Threatened

Length: 4 in. (10.2 cm)
Diet: Insects
Habitat: Aerial
Range: Tahiti and Moorea of Society Islands in southern and western Pacific Ocean

THERE IS A PLAIN, gray little bird that inhabits the colorful island of Tahiti. Because people have seldom, if ever, considered this bird, the Tahiti swiftlet now faces a grim future. Fewer than 500 individuals survive.

The Tahiti swiftlet has dull, sooty black plumage above and gray-black plumage below. Its plain appearance and characteristic swift physique distinguish it from other small island birds.

The swiftlet may once have ranged over much of Tahiti, but it now haunts only the forested valleys high in the mountains. This swiftlet once flew over Huahine, Bora Bora, and Moorea, but it has now completely gone from all of these other islands. A few were spotted on Moorea in 1973, but have never been verified since.

Island exploration

British explorer James Cook reached Tahiti and its people in 1773. France ultimately gained control of Tahiti and a dozen other small islands and atolls that form an archipelago known as the Society Islands. The largest of the group, Tahiti only covers 402 square miles (1,045 square kilometers). Much of the island's coastal lowlands have been developed as tourist resorts or for agriculture. At higher elevations, Tahiti's forests have also been cut down, in part if not completely.

The threats

The cause of the Tahiti swiftlet's decline has not been completely explained. Reduced forest cover on the island and a growing use of agricultural pesticides may have worked together to reduce the aerial insects on which the swiftlets feed.

Exotic rats (*Rattus* sp.) may also be a problem because they rob nests of eggs and young. Neither of these problems has been proved to be linked to the swiftlet's decline, but both probably play a part in some unknown way. Introduced bird diseases may also be a factor, but they have not been studied on Tahiti.

Recovery

The Tahiti swiftlet counts as one of only 12 land birds native to Tahiti. The other eight species have all been introduced by people. The role that the Tahiti swiftlet plays in insect populations, and the way those insects affect plant pollination or other natural processes remain entirely unknown.

No recovery plan for the Tahiti swiftlet has yet been proposed. If the small, plain bird is lost, however, its absence will have a profound effect.

Kevin Cook

Arabian Tahr

(Hemitragus jayakari)

ESA: Endangered

IUCN: Endangered

Nilgiri Tahr

(Hemitragus hylocrius)

IUCN: Endangered

Class: Mammalia
Order: Artiodactyla
Family: Bovidae
Subfamily: Caprinae
Weight: 110–220 lb. (50–100 kg)
Shoulder height: 24–43 in. (60–110 cm)
Diet: Leaves, shoots, grass, and fruits
Gestation period: 150–179 days
Longevity: 10–18 years
Habitat: Mountain grasslands up to 6,000 ft. (1,830 m)
Range: Arabian tahr is found in Oman; U.A.E.; Nilgiri tahr inhabits southwest India

TAHRS ARE MEMBERS of the same family as goats, sheep, muskox, and even buffalo. They are bovines, which are hooved animals with horns. Bovines are generally territorial, living in small social groups. There are three species of tahr in the Old World. Two live in Asia, the Himalayan and Nilgiri tahrs. The Arabian tahr lives in Oman.

The Arabian tahr is the smallest of the three tahr species, with a shoulder height of barely 2 feet (0.6 meter). Its coat, or pelage, is a gray to tawny brown. An old ram's coat can become quite spectacular, sporting long, heavy hair over the shoulders and neck, so the animal appears to have a mane. Tahrs do not have the beards typical of true male goats.

The environment of the Arabian tahr is extremely harsh. The Arabian peninsula is an arid place. The Arabian tahr lives amid the dry slopes of Oman and the neighboring United Arab Emirates at the southeastern tip of the peninsula. There, sparse vegetation and an annual rainfall of only 4 to 8 inches (10 to 20 centimeters) leaves this a desolate place. Because of this harsh environment, the tahr population density is extremely low.

The tahr is a shy and retiring animal, difficult to see in the wild because its coat keeps it camouflaged. There have been few studies of the Arabian species, so little is known about its habits. The reproductive cycle appears to be similar to that of the Nilgiri and the Himalayan tahr; that is, baby tahrs are born singly or in pairs, usually during January and February.

Arabian tahrs are endangered because of uncontrolled hunting and competition with domestic goats that require the same type of vegetation (and receive protection from their owners). There are barely 1,000 Arabian tahrs left in the wild. Currently there is probably a very small captive population, and few animals have ever been kept outside their home range.

The tahr of India

The Nilgiri tahr lives in the Nilgiri Hills of southern India. In contrast to its Arabian cousin, the Nilgiri tahr is found in an extremely moist climate. The weather in this region is unusually wet, with up to 13 feet (4 meters) of rainfall per year. The Nilgiri Hills have plateaus that rise up to 6,400 feet (1,925 meters), and they are covered with a damp evergreen forest that is interspersed with rolling grasslands. This, along with areas of rock outcroppings, is the typical habitat of the Nilgiri tahr. All species of tahr are excellent climbers, able to maintain their balance and agility even on the roughest, toughest slopes littered with loose rock.

Breeding

The Nilgiri tahr is commonly found in sizable groups of 20 to as many as 150 animals. The rut or breeding period of the Nilgiri tahr occurs during July and August, which happens to coincide with the middle of the monsoon season. This annual weather acts like a biological cue and promotes breeding activity, so that the young will be born in January and February, when the weather is cooler and drier.

Competition

There is considerable battling among male tahrs for dominance and, by rights, access to mates. Their method of combat is to stand side by side and rake backward at their opponents with their short, heavy, curved horns. Unlike other bovine males, who send their rivals off to so-called

The Nilgiri tahr has become an endangered species due to destruction of its habitat and uncontrolled hunting.

bachelor herds, the losers in a tahr battle for dominance are not chased from their herd.

Limited population

There is a small population of Nilgiri tahrs in captivity. Less than 30 live in North America, and as many as 20 reside in Asian collections. The North American specimens stem from just a few individuals, which means that these particular individuals have a narrow genetic base. This is not a healthy situation for this threatened species.

It is estimated that only 2,500 Nilgiri tahr are left in the wild, isolated in more than a dozen separate populations.

Warren D. Thomas

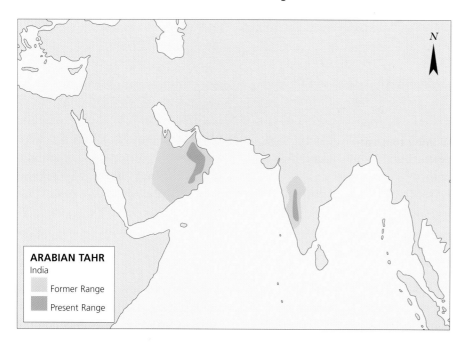

ARABIAN TAHR
India

Former Range

Present Range

GLOSSARY

actinopterygii: the scientific name for bony fish

apically: relating to, or situated at the apex

arboreal: living in or adapted for living in trees; arboreal animals seldom, if ever, descend to the ground (see terrestrial)

aves: the Latin scientific name for birds

awns: slender bristles on the bracts at the base of a spikelet

barbels: a slender growth on the mouths or nostrils of certain fishes, used as a sensory organ for touch

bipedal: any organism that walks on two feet

bract: a leaf at the base of a flower stalk in plants

buff: in bird species, a yellow-white color used to describe the plumage

calyx: the green outer whorl of a flower made up of sepals

captive breeding: any method of bringing several animals of the same species into a zoo or other closed environment for the purpose of mating; if successful, these methods can increase the population of that species

carnivore: any flesh-eating animal

carrion: the decaying flesh of a dead organism

clutch, clutch size: the number of eggs laid during one nesting cycle

corolla: the separate petals, or the fused petals of a flower

cotyledon: the first leaf developed by the embryo of a seed plant

cymose: type of inflorescence where each floral axis ends in a single flower

decurved: curving downward; a bird's beak is decurved if it points toward the ground

defoliate: to strip trees and bushes of their leaves

deforestation: the process of removing trees from a particular area

diurnal: active during the day; some animals are diurnal, while others are active at night (see nocturnal)

dominance: the ability to overpower the behavior of other individuals; an animal is dominant if it affects others of its own species in a way that benefits itself; also, the trait of abundance that determines the character of a plant community: grasses dominate a prairie, and trees dominate a forest

dorsal: pertaining to or situated on the back of an organism; a dorsal fin is on the back of a fish

ecology: the study of the interrelationship between a living organism and its environment

ecosystem: a community of animals, plants, and bacteria and its interrelated physical and chemical environment

endemic: native to a particular geographic region

estrous: the time period when female mammals can become pregnant

exotic species: a plant or animal species that is not native to its habitat

feral: a wild animal that is descended from tame or domesticated species

fishery, fisheries: any system, body of water, or portion of a body of water that supports finfish or shellfish; can also be used as an adjective describing a person or thing (for example, a fisheries biologist)

forest: a plant community in which trees grow closely enough together that their crowns interlock to form a continuous overhead canopy

fry: young fish

gene pool: the total hereditary traits available within a group; when isolated from other members of their species, individual organisms may produce healthy offspring if there is enough variety in the genes available through mating

gestation: the period of active embryonic growth inside a mammal's body between the time the embryo attaches to the uterus and the time of birth; some mammals carry dormant embryos for several weeks or months before the embryo attaches to the uterus and begins to develop actively, and this dormancy period is not part of the gestation period; gestation period is the time length of a pregnancy

granivore: any seed-feeding animal

granivorous: seed feeding

guano: manure, especially of sea birds and bats

habitat: the environment where a species is normally found; habitat degradation is the decline in quality of a species' home until it can no longer survive there

herbivore: any plant-eating animal

herbivorous: plant eating

hibernate: to spend the winter season in a dormant or inactive state; some species hibernate to save energy during months when food is scarce

hierarchy: the relationships among individuals of the same species or among species that determine in what order animals may have access to food, water, mates, nesting or denning sites, and other vital resources

home range: the area normally traveled by an individual species during its lifespan

hybrid: the offspring of two different species who mate; see interbreed

hybridization: the gradual

decline of a species through continued breeding with another species; see interbreed

immature(s): a young bird that has not yet reached breeding maturity; it usually has plumage differing from an adult bird of the same species

in captivity: a species that exists in zoos, captive breeding programs, or in private collections, perhaps because the species can no longer be found in the wild

incubation: the period when an egg is kept warm until the embryo develops and hatches

indigenous species: any species native to its habitat

inflorescence: a group of flowers that grow from one point

insular species: a species isolated on an island or islands

interbreed: when two separate species mate and produce offspring; see hybrid

invertebrate(s): any organism without a backbone (spinal column)

juvenal: a bird with an intermediate set of feathers after its young downy plumage molts and before growing adult feathers

juvenile(s): an immature young bird or other animal

litter: the animals born to a species that normally pro-

duces several young at birth

lore(s): the irregularly shaped facial area of a bird between the eye and the base of the beak

mammalia: the Latin scientific name for mammals

migrate, migratory: to move from one range to another, particularly with the change of seasons; many species are migratory

mollusca: the Latin scientific name for mussels, clams, and snails

montane forest: a forest found in mountainous regions

nocturnal: active at night; some animals are nocturnal, while others are active by day (see diurnal)

nomadic species: a species with no permanent range or territory; nomadic species wander for food and water

old growth forest: forest that has not experienced extensive deforestation

omnivore: any species that eats both plants and animals

ornithologist(s): a scientist who studies birds

pelage: the hairy covering of a mammal

pelagic: related to the oceans or open sea; pelagic birds rarely roost on land

perennial: persisting for several years

plumage: the feathers that cover a bird

predation: the act of one species hunting another

predator: a species that preys upon other species

primary forest: a forest of native trees that results from natural processes, often called virgin forest

primate(s): a biological ranking of species in the same order, including gorillas, chimpanzees, monkeys, and human beings (Homo sapiens)

range: the geographic area where a species roams

recovery plan(s): any document that outlines a public or private program for assisting an endangered or threatened species

reptilia: the Latin scientific name for reptiles

riffle(s): a shallow rapid stretch of water caused by a rocky outcropping or obstruction in a stream

rufous: in bird species, plumage that is orange-brown and pink

secondary forest: a forest that has grown back after cutting, forest fire, or other deforestation; secondary forests may or may not contain exotic tree species, but they almost always differ in character from primary forests

sedentary species: one that does not migrate

territory: the area occupied more or less exclusively by an organism or group, usually defended by aggressive displays and physical combat

veld: a grassland region with some scattered bushes and virtually no trees; other terms are *steppe*, *pampas*, and *prairie*

ventral: on or near the belly; the ventral fin is located on the underside of a fish and corresponds with the hind limbs of other vertebrates

vertebrates: any organism that has a backbone (spinal column)

INDEX

The scientific name of a plant or animal is entered in *italics*; its common name is in roman type. Page numbers in *italics* refer to picture captions.